LEAVES FROM A RUSSIAN DIARY

Leaves from
A RUSSIAN DIARY
— and Thirty Years After

PITIRIM A. SOROKIN

Enlarged Edition

Boston · THE BEACON PRESS · 1950

CONTENTS

FOREWORD TO THE EDITION OF 1950 . . . vii

PART I : 1917

PRELUDE 1
   I. FIRST DAY 5
  II. NEXT DAY 14
 III. "SINCE FREEDOM EVERYTHING IS PER-
     MITTED" 25
 IV. LIGHT AND SHADOWS . . . 40
  V. AGONY 47
 VI. THE EXPLOSION 61
VII. NEW CRISES 76
VIII. THE ABYSS 98

PART II : 1918

  IX. IN THE BASTILLE OF PETROGRAD . . 117
   X. THE CAT AND THE MICE . . . 133
  XI. WANDERING 154
 XII. IN THE BOSOM OF NATURE . . . 165
XIII. "LASCIATE OGNI SPERANZA VOI CH'
     ENTRATE" 174
XIV. THE RED MASS 181
 XV. RESURRECTION 202
XVI. FIRST STEPS IN THE COMMUNISTIC PARA-
     DISE 208

PART III : 1919-1920

XVII. IN THE BOSOM OF COMMUNISTIC CUL-
TURE 217
XVIII. "MEMENTO MORI" 229
XIX. IN THE HOME OF THE CZARS . . . 235
XX. RED "SCHOLARSHIP" 243

PART IV : 1921-1922

XXI. THE AVENGERS 253
XXII. EXPIATION 261
XXIII. NEW BUTCHERY 270
XXIV. S. O. S.. 282
XXV. NEW PLAYS 292
XXVI. BANISHMENT 298

PART V : THIRTY YEARS AFTER

XXVII. THE RUSSIAN REVOLUTION AS A GIGAN-
TIC SUCCESS AND A COLOSSAL FAILURE 313

FOREWORD
TO THE EDITION OF 1950

At the time of the first publication of this book in 1924, several Don Quixotes of the Revolution accused the author of distorting the beautiful Dulcinea of the Revolution into a bloody slut of Toboso. At present there are few, if any, such naive Don Quixotes, except, of course, the Communists. Being panders of the Revolution, it is their *métier* to glorify it. The events have proved my "close-up" of the Revolution to be correct. Millions of victims of the Revolution, its unsatiable bloodthirstiness, its overcrowded prisons and concentration or labor camps — all this has become too obvious during the past thirty years not to dispel all quixotic illusions about the Revolution's beauty, humaneness, virtue, and generosity.

If anything, public opinion in the West suffers now from the opposite one-sidedness, ascribing to the Revolution many sins it does not have and denying some of its actual virtues. This opinion suffers also from two other errors: it views the Russian Revolution as a self-sufficient phenomenon, dangerous to an otherwise sound Western culture; and it regards it as an especially vicious type of revolution, quite different from other revolutions, of which the reactionary posterity of our own revolutionary forefathers — the Sons and Daughters of This or That Revolution — are proud. The naked truth is that the horrors of the Russian Revolution are not peculiar to it, but are typical of practically all violent

revolutions, regardless of time, place, race, creed, or
nationality. Likewise, the Russian Revolution is not
an isolated disease, miraculously produced by the
evil genius of Lenin, but is one of the four clearest
manifestations of the disintegration of our Western
sensate socio-cultural order, the others being the
two World Wars and the Fascist-Nazi revolutions.
It is not the Russian Revolution that produced the
endless calamities of humanity after 1914, but it is
this basic process of decay of our sensate order that
produced the First World War, the Russian Revolution, the Fascist-Nazi revolutions, the Second World
War, and the numerous revolts and anarchy in the
Orient and the Occident. As long as this disintegration of the Western sensate order continues, all attempts to prevent revolutionary and war processes
are bound to fail.

It is futile to try to stop these processes by building a *cordon sanitaire* around the Soviet bloc: since
the germs of the disintegration are as virulent and
numerous in the West as in the East, a *cordon sanitaire* will not eliminate them. An even greater folly
is to attempt to cure the disease by mutual aggressiveness, toughness, "cold war," and preparations
for an apocalyptic new war. All such policies are but
twin brothers of the Revolution — of its destructive-
ness, its bloodiness, its tyranny, its totalitarianism.
All such crusades, no matter how conservative their
names and how highfalutin their mottoes, merely
reinforce, multiply, and spread the germs of the disease. Only a basic reintegration of our culture can
stop the diffusion and growth of these destructive

processes. This reintegration can be achieved neither by the methods of the Revolution nor by the essentially similar techniques of the vociferous Crusaders against the Revolution. The techniques of love instead of hate, of creative construction rather than destruction, of reverence for life in place of serving death, of real freedom instead of coercion and pseudo-freedom — such are the techniques needed for rebuilding the house of humanity. The essay, "Thirty Years After," somewhat substantiates the main propositions of this foreword — the propositions distasteful equally to the proponents and to the opponents of the Russian Revolution. The only excuse I have for being disagreeable to both parties is the old maxim: *Amico Plato sed veritas amicissima.*

Winchester, Mass., 1950.

PART I

1917

LEAVES FROM A RUSSIAN DIARY

PRELUDE

January-February, 1917—

KEEPING a diary is a childish habit, but this childish habit may now be worth while even to a serious man. It is clear that we are now entering the storm of the Revolution. The authority of the Czar, the Czarina, and all of Government has terribly broken down. Defeat of Russian arms, poverty and wide discontent of the people inevitably call forth anew revolutionary clamor. The speeches of Shulgin, Milyukoff, and Kerensky in the Duma, and especially Milyukoff's denunciation of the "stupidity and treason" of the Government, have awakened a dangerous echo throughout the country.

At a meeting yesterday of deputies, politicians, scholars, and writers at the house of Shubin-Posdeef, even the most conservative men talked about the coming Revolution as a certainty. ₁ Counts and barons, landlords and business men all applauded scathing criticisms of the Government and acclaimed the approaching Revolution. These men, weary, effeminized, accustomed to lives of comfort, calling for revolution, presented a curious spectacle. Like heedless children, they manifested a curiosity and a joy in meeting such an "interesting" development. I had a vision of the French ruling classes before

1

the eighteenth-century Revolution. Like these Russians, their emasculated aristocracy, too, greeted the storm with laughter, not reflecting that it might rob them of their property and even of their lives.

In my lecture rooms it was the same. Those parts of my lectures in which I scored the defects of aristocratic societies were met by the students with ardent applause. University life tends to become more and more disorderly. On the walls of lavatories one reads such sentences as: "Down with the Czar!" "Death to the Czarina of Rasputin!" "Long life to the Revolution!" These have been erased by the police, but immediately they reappear. The newspapers have become audacious in attacking the Government.

"Do you think that the guillotine will be necessary for us also in the near future?" asked one of my students in the Workers' University of the Viborg district of Petrograd.

"I do not know," I replied. "But I am certain that if you contemplate the guillotine for your enemies, the same guillotine will cut off your head a little later. The guillotine always kills first the well-fed, but later on it gets the poor also. Do not forget this. It may be useful to you if revolution really comes."

Prices are rising frightfully. Bread lines before the shops are longer and longer. Bitter complaints from poor people waiting hours in these lines, or as they are called, *"khwosts"* ("queues"), becomes more and more rebellious. Today I met three soldiers, friends of mine, just returned from the front. One of them spoke with such hatred against the Government, the expressions of the others of indignation and discontent in the army were so extreme that they shocked me. The army then may precipitate the Revolution. I should prefer not to have it so. . . . But perhaps I am wrong.

Street demonstrations by poor women and children demanding "Bread and herrings," eternal voice of all revolutions, have previously led to the looting of one or two shops, and today the demonstration became larger and noisier. The rioters today stopped tram cars, turning over some of them, plundering a good many shops, and even attacking policemen. Many workmen have joined the women and a general strike and great excitement resulted. After the wrecking of the trams, something more important may next be overthrown,—the Czar's throne, for instance. Things are drifting that way.

If future historians look for the group that began the Russian Revolution, let him not create any involved theory. The Russian Revolution was begun by hungry women and children demanding bread and herrings. They started by wrecking tram cars and looting a few small shops. Only later did they, together with workmen and politicians, become ambitious to wreck that mighty edifice the Russian Autocracy.

It goes steadily on. Yesterday three men and one woman were killed. Today more. The orderly routine of life is broken. Shops and offices are closed. In the University, instead of lectures political meetings are held. Newspapers appear irregularly. Revolution has pushed one foot over the threshold of my country.

Today the same. Crowds on the Nevsky Prospekt are larger. The police are idle and irresolute. One hears that even the Cossacks have refused to disperse the crowds. This means that the Government is helpless and their machine broken. Rioters have begun to kill policemen.

The Pavlovsky Regiment is in revolt. We are told that Protopopoff, Minister of the Interior, is recruiting special squads of police and is equipping them with machine guns to be placed on rooftops for merciless suppression of demonstrations. This half-mad paralytic can do nothing much however. The end is very near . . . or is it only the beginning?

CHAPTER I

It has come at last. At two o'clock in the morning, just now returned from the Duma, I hasten to set down the stirring events of this day. In the morning being not quite well, and lectures at the University being virtually stopped, I decided to stay at home and read the new work of V. Pareto, *Tratatto di Sociologia Generale*. From time to time I was interrupted by telephone, friends asking me for news and in turn giving their own to me.

"Crowds on the Nevsky are bigger than ever today."

"Workmen of the Putylovsky factory and of the Viborg side have gone out into the streets."

"Heavy firing is heard from different quarters of the town."

"They say that the Duma has been dissolved."

At noon telephone service was discontinued, and undisturbed I resumed my studies until about three o'clock when one of my students rushed in with the news that two regiments, armed and carrying red flags, had left their barrack and were marching on the Duma, there to unite with workmen.

"Is this true?" I exclaimed incredulously.

"I saw them myself."

Hastily leaving the house, we hurried to the Troizky Bridge. Here we found a large but orderly crowd listening to the firing and greedily drinking in every bit of news. Nobody knew anything positively. Cavalry police kept the crowds in check and allowed nobody to cross the Neva.

Boom! Rat-a-tat, tat-tat-tat-tat. . . .

"Who's firing? On whom?"

"Let's go to the central part of town," I suggested. "We may learn something there."

"But the bridges are ripped to pieces."

"We have the ice of the Neva," I urged.

"Well, I'm game."

Not without difficulty did we cross the river and reach the Economic Committee of the Union of Cities and Zemstvos (County Councils) where I hoped to get authentic information, but here they knew no more than we. Somehow or other we had to find out what was happening. Also it occurred to me that if the regiments did reach the Duma they would probably have to be fed. So I said to my friends—the members of Committee: "You try to get some food together, and at a message from me send it to the Duma." An old acquaintance, Mr. Kusmin, at this moment joined us and we started. Nevsky Prospekt near the Ekaterina Canal was still quiet, but as we turned into the Liteiny the crowd grew larger and much louder grew the sound of the guns. The frantic efforts of the police to disperse the crowds were utterly without effect.

"Ah-h! Pharaohs! Your end is coming!" howled the mob.

From where we stood we could see the red glow of a fire near the Nicolaevsky Station. "At last!

At last!" cried a man pointing to the ominous reflection.

"What is burning?"

"The police station," he exulted.

"But there is a fire station in the same building."

"That won't help. We are going to destroy all Government offices, burn, smash, kill all police, all tyrants, all despots!" he cried in frenzy.

Advancing cautiously along the Liteiny, we came upon fresh bloodstains and saw on the pavement two dead bodies. Before our horrified eyes a man, trying to cross the street, fell mortally wounded by a flying bullet. Skillfully manoeuvering, we finally reached the Tauride Palace, finding around the building vast crowds of people, soldiers and workmen. No attempt had yet been made to enter the Russian Parliament, but cannon and machine guns were everywhere in evidence.

"Revolutionists are prepared to defend their Duma," said my friend Kusmin [1] with approval.

"On the contrary," I replied. "A crazy mob is forcing the Duma into a revolution which it does not want. You will soon behold the real object of this demonstration."

The hall of the Duma presented a striking contrast to the tumult without. Here was comfort, dignity, order. Only here and there in corners could be seen small groups of deputies discussing the situation. At the door I met the Social Democrat Skobeleff.

[1] Many names I cannot mention here, because to give these names might mean persecution by the Soviet Government.

"Hurrah! It has come at last," he greeted us with out-stretched hand.

"Have the soldiers had any food?" I asked.

"Little enough. Can you do anything about this?"

"I am going to try to do something," I assured him.

The Duma, the deputy Rjevsky told me, had actually been dissolved, but an executive committee had been appointed as a temporary Government.

"Does this mean that you have allied yourself with the Revolution?" I asked.

"No. . . . However, perhaps I have," he replied nervously.

This same confusion and uncertainty I observed in utterances of other deputies. The captains who were steering the Ship of State into the teeth of hurricane were not sure of their own course. "A bad symptom," I thought to myself. "But perhaps I do them injustice."

I next made an attempt to call various friends by telephone, but the service by this time was impossible, so I went back to the court of the Duma and explained to a group of soldiers that I was trying to get provisions brought for them. They found an automobile, with a red flag flying from it, and we drove off through the crowd.

"This is enough to hang us all in case the Revolution is put down," I said to my guards jestingly.

"Don't worry. All will be right," they answered.

Near the Duma lived the lawyer Grusenberg. His telephone was working and I got in touch with friends who promised that food for the troops would soon be forthcoming. Returning to the Duma I found the crowds massed closer than ever. In the courtyard and in all adjacent streets were excited groups surrounding orators, members of the Duma, soldiers, and workmen, all holding forth on the significance of the day's events, hailing the Revolution and the fall of Czarist despotism. All exalted the rising power of the people and called on all citizens to support the Revolution. These incendiary speeches aroused immense enthusiasm. At the doors of the Palace the crowd were calling for one and another of the more popular deputies, and compelled to appear, they all mounted the rostrum and spoke.

"These feather-headed politicians are enjoying themselves now," said a skeptical friend who stood at my side. "Let us see what they will think about things a few days from now."

But I myself, having caught some of the spirit of the hour, exclaimed confidently: "Ah, pessimist! You do not know the people. Today they are satisfied with speeches from their leaders. Tomorrow they will demand action."

"To the devil with it all," he retorted. "Let us go in."

Hall and corridors of the Duma were packed with people. Soldiers behind rifles and machine guns were there. But still order prevailed. The street had not yet broken in.

"Ah, comrade Sorokin, at last, Revolution! At last the day of glory has arrived!" cried one of the workers—my student; others with him approaching me joyfully. In their faces was the light of hope and exaltation.

"What are you doing here, boys?" I asked.

"We were told to come here to help organize the Soviet of Workmen, as in the Revolution of 1905," they chorused.

"Why is a soviet necessary?"

"To defend the Revolution and the interests of the workers, to control the Government, and to proclaim our dictatorship," they replied. "You'll join us, won't you?"

"I haven't been elected, thank you," I returned dryly.

"Neither have we been elected, but that doesn't matter. In such times such formalities are needless."

"I don't agree with you," I said, and I added: "It may be, for the defense of the Revolution, a workmen's committee will have to be formed, but be careful about any dictatorship."

Entering a committee room I found several Social Democratic deputies and about twelve workmen, the nucleus of the future Soviet. From them I received an urgent invitation to become a member, but I felt no call just then to join a soviet, so I left them for a meeting of writers who were organizing an official press committee of the Revolution. Among these men were Stekloff-Nakhamkes, Sukhanoff-Gimmer, Ermansky, and two or three other Social Democrats discussing the situation and wrangling over positions in the committee.

"Who elected these men as representatives of the press?" again I asked myself. Here they were, self-appointed censors, assuming power to suppress whatever in their judgment seemed undesirable newspapers, preparing to stifle liberty of speech and the press. Suddenly there came into my mind the words of Flaubert: "In every revolutionist is hidden a gendarme." But I told myself that it was not fair to generalize from the actions of a few hot-heads. Meanwhile the rooms and corridors of the Duma became more densely thronged.

"What's the latest?" I asked of a deputy shouldering his way through the mass.

"Rodzianko is trying to get into communication by telegraph with the Czar. The Executive Committee is discussing the organization of a new Ministry responsible jointly to the Czar and to the Duma."

"Is anybody in control and regulation of this Revolution?"

"Nobody. It is developing spontaneously."

"How about the monarchy and the Czar?"

"I know absolutely nothing."

"Too bad if even you don't know about these things," I remarked sarcastically.

Food was being brought in, a buffet was set up, and girl students began to feed the soldiers. This produced a sudden lull. But outside, I learned, things were going badly. Fires continued to break out. The people were growing hysterical with excitement, and as for the police they had retreated. Again I sought the courtyard of the Palace. The

fever of liberty had by this time fairly intoxicated
the multitude. Wild speeches and shrieks of applause filled the air. Excited in spite of myself I
too listened and applauded, and it was midnight
before I could tear myself from the place.

As no trams or cabs were to be had, I walked to
the Petrogradksaia, a long distance from the Duma.
It was very dark and no street lamps burned. Incessant firing reached my ears, and sometimes the
firing seemed so near that all pedestrians stopped,
looking around for shelter. Groups of citizens
huddled against the walls of houses to avoid flying
bullets. On the Liteiny blazed a very fierce fire, the
magnificent building of the Okroujny Soud (the
High Court) being in flames.

"Who started that fire?" someone exclaimed. "Is
it not necessary to have a court building for New
Russia?" The question went unanswered. We
could see that other Government buildings were also
burning, among them police stations, and that no
efforts were being made to extinguish the fires. On
the faces of many spectators of this destruction
were expressions of intense satisfaction. Their
countenances, in the red blaze, looked demoniac as
they shouted, laughed, and danced. Here and there
were heaped wooden carvings of the Russian double
eagle, and these emblems of Empire, torn from shops
and from Government buildings were being thrown
on the fires, to the cheers of the crowd. The old
régime was disappearing in ashes and no one regretted them. No one cared even when the fires
spread to private houses. "Let them go," one man
said defiantly. "When wood is chopped chips fly."

Twice I came on groups of soldiers and street loafers looting wine-shops with no one to stop them. But the farther we went from the Duma the more nearly normal things appeared. Here a few policemen remained at their posts. The firing was fainter. But when we crossed the Neva there came such a burst of rifle firing that everybody dropped flat on the ice until it ceased. As we reached the opposite shore we saw corpses lying on the snow.

At two o'clock I reached home and sat down to write these hurried notes. Am I glad or am I sorry? I can hardly tell, but certainly in my mind are persistent apprehensions. Tonight only a part of the city is in the hands of Revolutionists, but what will happen tomorrow? How long will this disorder continue? How many lives will be taken? Will these events weaken, or perhaps even destroy the army? Is it possible that they may result in the invasion of Russia by the Germans? It seems a terribly dangerous time to launch a revolution. But perhaps my premonitions are foolish. So many rejoicing and patriotic people cannot be wrong. Who was it said: "Individuals may be mistaken, but a whole nation never"? Very well, long live the Revolution! The Autocracy had to be destroyed some time. Therefore, away with doubts and premonitions.

I looked at my books and manuscripts. I suppose they will have to be put aside for a time, I reflected. This is no time for study. Action is the thing. Good-bye, beloved friends.

The firing begins again. . . .

CHAPTER II

February 28, 1917—

THIS morning, with two friends, I started on foot for the Duma. The streets were full of excited people. All shops were closed, all business suspended. The sound of firing was heard from several directions. Motor cars full of soldiers and young men with rifles and machine guns rushed up and down. They were searching for police and counter-revolutionaries said to be concealed in private houses ready to sally forth and suppress the revolt. From time to time men and soldiers surrounded a house firing into the windows. Dangerous as they were, they made me think of nothing so much as a gang of boys in a spirit of malicious mischief bent on destruction. I saw no hidden police taken by them, but I did see many dwellers in these unhappy houses, some of them wounded. I also perceived that incendiary fires were more numerous than they had been the night before.

On the corner of Barmalieva Street and the Bolshoy Prospekt we came upon a group of men pitilessly beating a policeman with butts of revolvers and with heavy boot heels. Almost dead the wretched victim lay bloody and senseless on the pavement while blows rained on his head and body.

"Stop that, you brutes!" cried my companion.

"Arrest the man if you like, but don't kill him."

"Who are you to hinder us from killing a Pharaoh?" they yelled. "Are you also a counter-revolutionary?"

With the assistance of passers-by we forced these hooligans to release their victim and to leave the street.

"This is promising," said my friend indignantly.

"Alas, it may be only a presage of what is to follow," I answered, all my doubts returning.

As we passed on the most disquieting rumors reached our ears. Many military regiments in Petrograd and the suburbs were in a state of mutiny. However, the Petropavlovskaia Fortress (Peter and Paul), the Admiralty and the headquarters of the Governor of Petrograd were still in the hands of the Czarist Government and only a portion of the city was dominated by the mob. What was going on outside Petrograd, in the army, in Moscow and the country, no one seemed to know. But no one doubted that the whole Empire would join the Revolution.

Everywhere speeding motor cars. Everywhere hustling crowds mad with excitement. Everywhere the smell of burning buildings and the spectacle of soldiers and workmen searching out police and counter-revolutionists. Before a house on the Neva, not far from the Winter Palace, a more than usually turbulent crowd had gathered.

"What's happening here?"

"They're searching the house of a reactionary general," voices screamed at us. At the moment a window on the fourth floor of the house smashed outward and a man, hurled forth by the hands of soldiers, fell to the street below, his piercing shriek of agony almost drowned in the exultant cries of the crowd. As the body crashed on the stones men rushed forward stamping on it, lashing it with whatever they held in their hands. Deathly sick with the hideousness of the sight I ran on, my companion following. The nearer we approached the Duma the denser the crowds became, the more numerous red posters and red flags, hailing the Revolution. Suddenly two desperate hands grasped my arm.

"Sorokin! I know you are generous. Save me! In the name of God, save me!"

In this man I recognized a spy of the secret service who, two years before, had denounced and had me arrested.

"Go home quickly," I said. "Destroy your uniform, and then if you can, change your lodgings. If anything happens let me know." That was all I could do for him.

"Here they come! Here they come! They are led! They are led!" And following the pointing hands of the crowd I saw one of the Ministers of the Czar, accompanied by a squad of soldiers and preceded by Kerensky's slight figure.

"At last! At last! Long life to the Revolution, and death to all enemies of the people!" A hundred bloodthirsty hands were flung out to seize the unhappy official.

"In the name of the Revolution I forbid you to touch this man," cried Kerensky. "It is not for you to judge him. He and all the others will be tried, and I swear to you that they will receive justice." These words alone saved the Minister from being torn limb from limb.

"Long live Kerensky!" cried the fickle mob.

It was true, as he had told them, Ministers and officials of the Court were being arrested and hurried to the Duma. Nothing short of this arrest and segregation would have saved any of them that day.

Today the Hall of the Duma presented quite a different picture from yesterday. Soldiers, workmen, students, citizens, men and women, young and old crowded the place. Order, cleanliness, and restraint were conspicuous by their absence. His Majesty, the people, was master of the scene. In every room and corner were extemporaneous meetings and much loud oratory. "Down with the Czar!" "Death to all enemies of the people!" "Long life to Revolution and the democratic Republic!" One grew tired of their endless repetition. Today the existence of two centers of power was apparent. One center was the Executive Committee of the Duma with Rodzianko as its leader, the other was the Soviet of Workmen and Soldiers, sitting at the opposite end of the Russian Parliament, with the Social Democrat Chkeidze as chairman and Kerensky as vice-chairman. Kerensky served as a connecting link between the two centers. With a group of my workmen students I entered the Soviet room. Instead of the original twelve there were now present three or four hundred men. It seems that anyone who aspires can become a member of

this body. A very informal "election" indeed. In
the over-crowded room, full of tobacco smoke, wild
harangues were being delivered, more than one at
a time. In vain the chairman, Chkeidze, rang his
bell, trying at the top of his voice to call the "delegates" to order. No one paid the slightest attention. Speakers interrupted each other, scores of
independent motions were made. The dominant
question which was being discussed as we came in
was whether or not Rodzianko, president of the
Duma, should be arrested as a counter-revolutionary.

I was astounded. Had these people overnight
lost their minds? I asked for a chance to speak and
was recognized by the chairman. In spite of this
fact I found it impossible to make myself heard,
partly because, at this moment, an intense firing
broke out almost at the doors of the Duma. "The
Czarist Army is attacking the Duma!" ran through
the room, and instantly this belligerent assembly
became a prey to wildest panic. The delegates took
to their heels, jostling each other roughly in the mad
desire to escape. In the rush they jammed and
almost completely blocked the doorways. Throughout the building the panic spread, and for a few
minutes the pandemonium was indescribable.

Almost abruptly the firing ceased, and voices
rose: "No attack! No Czarist army! Misunderstanding!" Whereat the deputies bravely began to
return to the Soviet room.

"You foolish men," I addressed them, "while
not even all Petrograd is in the hands of the Revolution this panic reveals its weakness and your own.

The Revolution is only beginning, and if it is to succeed we must have complete union and accord of all anti-Czarist forces. There must be no anarchy. In this hour of peril you, a small group of men, debating such a question as the arrest of Rodzianko, are simply wasting time. Can't you see that you yourselves are the Revolution? If you persist in following this petty political program, you will inevitably bring disaster on Russia, the Russian people, and on your own selves. I demand that these minor considerations be dropped at once.''

Maxim Gorky followed me, speaking in the same strain, and for the moment the question of Rodzianko's arrest was put aside. However, it was only too plain that mob mind was beginning to show itself and that not only the beast but the fool in man was striving to get the upper hand.

Meanwhile further news reached us. Rodzianko was advocating a new Government responsible to the Czar and to the Duma. The Czar, we heard, was returning to Petrograd. At the same time we heard that the revolutionary movement had broken out with violence in Moscow. General Ivanoff was on his way to the capital with Cossacks to restore order. Guchkoff, Shulgin, and other deputies were demanding the abdication of Nicholas in favor of the Czarevitch, and railroad workers had refused to allow the Czar's train to return to Petrograd. On the way to the room where the Executive Committee of the Duma was sitting I met one of its members, Mr. Efremoff, and learned from him that the struggle between the Committee and the Soviet had begun in earnest, and that a dual power was now contending for control of the Revolution. Mr. Efremoff, greatly agitated, feared that the efforts of the Duma to reach an agreement with the Soviet were hopeless. He foresaw the substitution of responsible government by the mob. "But what can we do?" he asked despairingly.

"Who is acting in the name of the Soviet?"

"Sukhanoff, Nakhamkes, Chkeidze and a few others," he answered.

"Is it not possible to order soldiers to arrest these men and to disperse the Soviet?" I asked, at the same time knowing the proposition to be a rash one.

"Such aggression and conflict cannot take place in the first days of the Revolution," was the reply.

"Then get ready for your own dismissal very soon," I warned him. "Were I a member of your Committee I would act immediately. The Duma is still the highest authority in Russia."

At this moment Professor Gronsky joined us. "Can you write the proclamation of the future Government?" he asked me.

"Why should I do it? Nabokoff is a specialist in such matters. Go to him." In the midst of our conversation an officer burst into the room demanding to be conducted to the Committee of the Duma. "What has happened?" we asked.

"All the officers of the Baltic Fleet are being murdered by soldiers and sailors," he cried, his face pallid with excitement. "The Committee must interfere."

My heart turned to ice. It was madness to expect a revolution without some bloodshed, yet as the officer hurried on to the Committee, which would doubtless do its best to save the human life, what would its best amount to? Mastering my fears, I made two speeches to the crowds outside, praising Liberty and the Revolution. After that I returned to the Duma. Participating in a conference of the Committee of Supplies, of which I was a member, I learned that markets were being plundered wholesale by the people. Very late at night I reached home. No joy was in my soul, yet I bade myself hope. Tomorrow things might be better.

Tomorrow things were not better. In the streets the same unruly crowds, the same motor cars with men firing wildly, the same man-hunt of policemen and counter-revolutionaries. In the Duma we received definite news that the Czar was to abdicate in favor of the Czarevitch Alexis.

Today was issued the first copy of a new newspaper, *Isvestia*.

The Soviet has grown to four or five hundred members. The Committee of the Duma and the Soviet are organizing the Provisional Government, Kerensky acting as a mediator and a liaison between the two bodies. He is vice-president of the Soviet and Minister of Justice. I met him. He was exhausted.

"Please write and send a telegram to the governors of prisons throughout Russia to liberate all political prisoners."

"If you think best," I assented.

The telegram written he signed it, "Minister of Justice, Citizen Kerensky." This "citizen" is new, a little theatrical, but perhaps appropriate. I am not sure how strong will prove Kerensky's mediating powers, and I fear that this dual rule of the Provisional (or Visionary) Government and the extremists of the Soviet cannot last long. One will certainly swallow the other. Which? Certainly the Soviet, representatives of the people, is too weak, its members shrink in fear from any coercion or violence. Well, perhaps they are right. . . .

Among others in the Duma I heard Milyukoff speak, proposing a constitutional monarchy with Grand Duke Michael as Czar. The mob heard the proposal coldly. Monarchy has fallen. The mind of the people has become solidly republican. Even a simple bourgeois republic is not radical enough for many. Socialism is demanded. I fear these extremists. I fear mob mind.

Frightful news! The massacre of officers increases. In Kronstadt Admiral Wiren and many other officers of the Fleet have been killed. They say that officers are being murdered according to lists prepared by the Germans. I do not know if this is true, but the murder of many of our best officers is a fact. What will happen if this horror continues? It may lead to the complete demoralization of our forces and the invasion of the country by the Germans.

What I observe now in the soldiers in Petrograd,

their manners, the expression of their faces, does not please me. Something distinctly menacing is reflected in their behavior.

I have just read "Order No. 1," issued by the Soviet and in essence authorizing disobedience of soldiers to the orders of their officers. What madman wrote and published this thing?

In the library of the Duma I met, among others, Mr. Nabokoff who showed me his draft of the Proclamation of the Provisional Government. All liberties, all guarantees are promised, not only to citizens but to soldiers. Russia is to be one of the most democratic countries and the freest in all the world.

"What do you think of it?" he asked proudly.

"It's an admirable document, but—"

"But what?"

"I fear it is a little too inclusive in time of Revolution, in the midst of a world war," I was forced to admit.

"I have some apprehensions too," he said, "but I hope it will be all right."

"I can only echo your hope."

"Now I am about to write a declaration of the abolition of capital punishment," said Nabokoff.

"What! Even in the army, in wartime?"

"Yes."

"But this is madness!" cried one man present. "Only lunatics would think of such a thing in this hour, when officers are daily butchered like sheep. I hate Czarism as much as any man, but I am sorry that at this precise time it had to fall. In its way it knew how to govern better than all these visionary fools."

In spite of myself I felt he was right. The old régime has undoubtedly perished. In both Petrograd and Moscow the populace is as joyful as at Easter. Everyone acclaims the new régime and the Republic. "Liberty! Holy Liberty!" is everywhere shouted and sung. "Wonderful Revolution! Revolution without blood, pure as the robes of sinless angels!" I have heard this last from crowds of students parading the streets.

It is all quite true, of course. Bloodshed has not been very terrible. If there are no further victims of the fanatics our Revolution may yet go down to history as the Bloodless Revolution.

Long live the Bloodless Revolution!

CHAPTER III

March-April, 1917—

THE old régime has fallen throughout Russia and very few regret it. The whole country rejoices. The Czar has abdicated for himself and for his son. Grand Duke Michael has refused the throne. A Provisional Government has been elected, and its manifesto is one of the most liberal and democratic documents which has ever been issued. All Czarist officers from Ministers to policemen have been dismissed and replaced by men devoted to the Republic—for no one doubts that we shall have a Republic. The majority of people are hopeful, and expect the war to be carried on more successfully. Everybody, soldiers, statesmen, students, citizens, and peasants, displays immense activity. Peasants are bringing corn to the towns and to the army, sometimes even free of charge. Military regiments and workmen groups display standards: "Long life to the Revolution!" "The Peasants to the Plow, the Workers to the Looms and Presses, the Soldiers to the Trenches!" "We, the Free People of Russia, will Defend the Country and the Revolution!"

"See how splendid the people are!" exulted a friend of mine, pointing to one of these demonstrations.

"It certainly seems to be all right," I answered

But trying to convince myself that it was all right I cannot shut my eyes to certain realities. While the workers bear aloft their banners: "The Workers to the Looms and Presses," they have ceased to work and spend almost all their time at political meetings. They begin to demand an eight-hour, and even a six-hour working day. How can we allow such a reduction of working hours when war and revolution call for increased effort, increased production? The soldiers are apparently ready to fight, but yesterday when one of the regiments was ordered to the front the men refused to go, under the pretext that they were needed in Petrograd to defend the Revolution. In these days we have also received information that peasants are seizing private estates, sacking and burning them. In the streets I have observed many intoxicated men, bawling obscenities, and crying: "Long Life to Freedom! Since we have freedom, everything is permitted."

Passing a house near the Bestuzhevsky Women's University I saw a crowd of men laughing and gesticulating crazily. In the shadow of the gate, in plain sight, were a man and a woman behaving in the most indecent manner. "Ha, ha!" laughed the crowd, "Since freedom, everything is permitted!" Today on the Basseynaia Street a group of scoundrels began to loot the Cherepeynikoff wine-shop. "Now we have freedom, therefore don't interfere with us," they protested to citizens who tried to restrain them. This kind of thing, and the inci-

dents are very numerous, means something dangerous. But patience. Perhaps my apprehensions are
premature.

Today has been full of sensations. In the morning
two of my friends who are examining the archives
and the record office of the Czarist Ohkranka (State
Department for the Persecution of Political and
Revolutionary Activity), told me that some of the
trusted leaders of the Social Revolutionary Party
and of the Social Democratic Bolshevist Party have
also been agents and spies of the Ohkranka. Among
these were the editor-in-chief of the Bolshevist newspaper *Pravda*, Mr. Chermonasoff, an intimate friend
of Lenin, and one of our own workers, a man regarded as a most sincere Social Revolutionary. At
the very time when these men and their kind had
been working for the Revolution they had been denouncing for something like twenty-five to fifty
roubles a month their own comrades, causing them
to be arrested, imprisoned, and exiled.

What villains! Now we understand why, during
all these years, revolutionary organizations were so
easily discovered by the Czar's Government, why
so many men of our secret councils were arrested
in 1913. Betrayed by their own comrades! How
many times it has happened during the last few
years, beginning with the Azev case. All this time,
it appears, among revolutionary and socialistic
parties have existed *provocateurs,* creatures posing
as revolutionists, pretending to be ready any day

to assassinate the Czar and his Ministers, yet really plotting to deliver their associates to the hangman. What a revelation of human depravity!

Last night we held the first meeting of old members of the Social Revolutionary Party, twenty or thirty tried and trusted leaders. Among these impudently appeared this worker-*provocateur*, who had not yet learned of his unmasking. The object of our meeting was to define our relation to the Provisional Government and to complete the legal organization of the party. Listening to the discussion I discovered that the talk was becoming more and more radical, some of the men, and especially this *provocateur*, insisting upon a negative attitude towards the Provisional Government, an immediate ending of war, according to the Kyntal and Zimmerwald resolution of 1916, and finally upon the organization of a purely socialistic Government. As soon as he finished his tirade, a friend and I called the man aside and said to him: "Your connection with the Ohkranka is known to us. Tomorrow it will be universally known. Unless you immediately leave this meeting we shall denounce you here and now."

"You are insulting me," blustered he, turning very pale nevertheless.

"We are really saving your worthless life," we replied. "Unless you clear out this minute we shall stand up and tell what we know."

The man grabbed his overcoat and fled. After his departure I challenged the proposals of the extremists and finally forced through a resolution to support the Government. This resolution was accepted by the majority, with a characteristic reservation: "Provided the Government adheres to its program." This meeting showed me that the even balance of mind in the members of old and reliable men of the Party had begun to waver. If it is so even with these men what will happen in the mob? Truly we have entered a critical period, more critical than I had feared.

Today there was another meeting of Social Revolutionary leaders to found a newspaper and to appoint its editors. The discussion was heated and disclosed clearly the existence within the party of two different elements, social patriots and internationalists. The first are more moderate. They are ready to support the Provisional Government, and are opposed to rushing the country into Socialism. While they agree to the policy of "no annexations or contributions," they are, at the same time, partisans of a defensive war for the protection of Russia and the Revolution. They want the war to end as soon as possible, but they oppose a separate peace as being treachery to the Allies. The extreme element, on the other hand, want to substitute for a defensive war the class struggle. They demand immediate termination of the War even by a separate peace with Germany. They call for immediate socialization of the land and the factories, the dictatorship of workmen and peasants, and the substitution of the present bourgeois government by a socialistic state. After a long and tedious debate the five editors of the newspaper, to be called the *Delo Naroda* (the "Affair of the People"), were elected. They are Russanoff, Ivanoff-Razumnik, Mstislavsky, Gukovsky, and myself. I can't quite see how we are to agree on the policies of the paper, Gukovsky and I being very moderate social patriots, the others internationalists.

Alas! At the very first meeting of the editors to arrange for the paper's initial appearance five hours were wasted in vain dispute. Articles submitted by the internationalists were rejected by us, and all our articles were denounced by them. Three times we started to leave the room, but each time returned. At last we all began to reread the leading editorials, pitilessly blue penciling the most telling passages of each. As a result both moderate and radical articles were shorn of value without losing any of their contradictions. An auspicious beginning! *Delo Naroda,* as issued, proved a newspaper in which one article appeared denouncing another on the same page. This sort of thing cannot go on, and we all admit it. We agreed to continue publication in this form only up to the next conference of the Petrograd branch of the Party, but how the quarrel will be decided is easy enough to foretell. The mind of the people is drifting towards extreme radicalism. Newspapers, even the reactionary *Novoe Vremya* vie with each other in radical utterances. All monarchist newspapers have been suppressed and their printing establishments confiscated. The Socialists agree that this is perfectly proper, but how does this square with the liberty of the press once so ardently advocated by them? As soon as "ambition's debt is paid" it seems that radicals become even more despotic than the reactionaries. Power incites tyranny.

Speaking at meetings of workmen I hear oftener and oftener demands to finish the War. More and more I hear the "capitalists" denounced and even menaced. The workers have it obstinately in their heads that all their misfortunes were deliberately caused by the bourgeois. That the Government must be purely socialistic, and that a general massacre of all "exploiters" must take place is rapidly spreading among the people. Every attempt of engineers and managers to maintain dicipline in works and factories, to keep up the scale of production, or to discharge slackers is considered counter-revolution. Among the soldiers the situation is no better. Obedience and discipline have almost disappeared. The soldiers are becoming loafers, doing nothing and respecting nobody, calling themselves heroes who have a right to do what they like and appropriate whatever they desire. On the front conditions are a little more encouraging. But a thousand agitators and propagandists have been allowed to go to the army to "reinforce" it, and I think they will soon succeed in demoralizing it.

As for the *muzhiks* (the peasants), even they begin to grow restless and may soon join themselves to the Soviets. My God! These adventurers, self-elected deputies of soldiers and workmen, these destitute intellectuals, play-acting the drama of revolution, assuming the characters of French Revolutionaries. Talking, talking, talking endlessly, all their energies devoted to the destruction of the Provisional Government and to preparations for the "dictatorship of the proletariat," which fears its own Soviet. The Soviet interferes in everything, and whatever constructive ideas any of its members may possess, their acts lead only to disorganization of government and unleashing the wild beast instincts of the mob.

The Government? It may be better to say nothing about these men. High-minded and idealistic, they do not know the A B C of the science of government. They do not appear to know what they themselves want done, and even if they did know they could accomplish nothing. Strangely perhaps, I sometimes long for some powerful force to appear and put a tight bridle on all these rabid and uncertain groups. I think it would be better for us than this general unrest and division which threatens I know not what misfortunes for my country.

Today was held the funeral of the victims who died for the Revolution. What a moving spectacle. Hundreds of thousands of people moving behind thousands of red and black banners with the words: "Glory to Those Who Perished for Liberty." Marvelous music, voices, and bands joining in the funeral hymn. Perfect order and discipline as for hours the endless procession wound through the streets. The faces of the marchers were solemn and uplifted. Such a crowd thrills me. It is so human.[1]

Tonight it was my turn to act as editor-in-chief of *Delo Naroda*. The paper went to press at about three o'clock in the morning and, as usual, I went home on foot. The night streets are not so crowded and it is easier to observe changes which have taken place in Petrograd during this month of Revolution. The picture is not very pleasant. The streets are littered with papers, dust, dung, and sunflower seeds (Russian equivalent of peanut shells). Windows of many houses, bullet-shattered, are stopped with paper. In fire-swept rooms marks of bullets can plainly be traced on the walls. In the parks trees and shrubs have ruthlessly been damaged, and every blank wall is patched over with placards, notices, and political proclamations. Soldiers and prostitutes in every by-street behave with revolting indecency.

"Comrade! Let the proletarians of all countries unite. Come home with me," a painted creature accosted me. A most original application of the revolutionary slogan!

Everywhere are seen couples embracing and kissing as they walk along or sit on the roofs of houses. Some dance madly in the streets. From time to time firing is heard. Laughter and weeping of women breaks into the general chorus of "Freedom now! No pharaoh has the right to touch us. Long live the Revolution!"

[1] As a matter of fact, many of these heroes of the Revolution were victims of the mob who murdered them as suspected counter-revolutionaries.

All political prisoners have been released and are flocking home from Siberia and from abroad. They are met triumphally by Government committees, by soldiers, workmen, and the public generally. Bands, flags, and speeches greet each new group of arrivals. The returned exiles bear themselves like conquering heroes who deserve to be worshiped by the people as liberators and benefactors. There is an amusing aspect of the case, for a large number of these people never were political offenders, but common convicts, thieves, murderers, and ordinary swindlers. All, however, are treated alike, as victims of Czarism. It appears that among other forms of vanity there is a revolutionary vanity which claims everything for itself. This form is ridiculous, but it may easily be dangerous also.

Many returned politicals show evidences of disturbed minds and unbalanced emotions. Full of ambition for revenge they naturally ally themselves with the extremists, trying to carry revolution to its utmost limits. Their arrival means the increase of forces of social disintegration. There is grave danger that these people, as in revolutions before this one, will be given power. Having spent years in prison and exile, at hard and degrading labor, they inevitably begin to introduce into society the methods and cruelties they themselves have lived under. Hatred, cruelty and contempt of human life and suffering, such are the invariable manifestations of their minds.

"For the success of the Revolution it is necessary to destroy or to imprison all capitalists, all rich

people, and aristocrats," said one of these returned
exiles, who immediately after his arrival began to
incite peasants to burn estates and murder landlords.

"I think your program a little ferocious," I ex-
postulated him. "Not a bit of it," he retorted
fiercely, "it's the only thorough and efficient program possible."

The Soviet, packed with these heroes, loses more
and more sense of reality. It directs its energy to
obstructing the Government, preaching Socialism,
and doing nothing at all towards the re-education
and reorganization of Russian society. Its proclamations are addressed "To All, All, All," or "to
the Whole World." The speeches and demeanor of
the leaders are absurdedly pompous. They seem
to possess no sense of humor, and are unable to see
how comic is their pose. Stekloff-Nakhamkes, who
two years ago petitioned the Czar to be allowed to
preface his somewhat plebian surname Nakhamkes
with the more aristocratic Stekloff, now plays the
part of an old revolutionist. It is disgusting. He
is a dirty person, dirty both physically and mentally,
and it is certain that he will change his opinions according to the situation. Gimmer, a mixture of Jew
and German, an obscure journalist, now imitates
first Robespierre, then Talleyrand. As Robespierre
he appears with a red rose in his buttonhole, de-
livering himself of long and tedious speeches without a whole idea in any of them. Chkeidze, chairman
of the Soviet, is a rather simple-minded, sympa-
thetic Georgian, possessed of a strong voice and all

the catchword patter of Marxianism. Liber is a very emotional Jew, a good speaker, delirious with revolutionary ardor, but on occasions capable of reason. Tseretelly, also a Georgian, is one of the best and cleverest men in the Soviet. I hope in time he may become a normal and even a creative statesman. Skobeleff is merely a rather stupid son of a merchant family. His is the characteristic face of a Russian shop-clerk who admires himself and thinks all servant girls in love with him. He has neither brains, will power, nor oratorical ability. Gotz, a good Jew, clever and talented, is spoiled by long imprisonment and fixed ideas on Socialism. Dan, a Jewish surgeon who knows his specialty about as well as I know the simple principles of medicine, is convinced that he is one of the cleverest of politicians. If you mix together all average Marxians, under-sized, fat-minded, and deficient in clear thought, and add to the mixture the whole collection of Socialist mottoes and slogans, you will have Dan. Mstislavsky is a man who is not a soldier, who opposes the war, and yet who dresses in uniform and up to the very outbreak of Revolution, was a contributor to official Czarist newspapers. A perfect Tartuffe. As for other leaders, they are hangers-on from nowhere in particular. And it is these people who tell the army that the war was made by capitalists for their own selfish purposes! They are not even consistent in this declaration. At one time they say to the soldiers: "Your officers are all reactionaries. Disobey them when you see fit, and end the war as soon as possible." At another time they exclaim: "Soldiers, obey your officers, fight, defend the Revolution!" What but utter confusion and chaos can result from such contradictions?

As for the Government, it is equally chaotic and impotent. Division of authority is now complete and the Government loses ground every day.

"What the devil are they doing? Whom are they sending to the army, and for what purpose?" a young officer, newly from the front, asked in my office recently. He had listened to speeches of agitators sent down by the Soviet and had returned to Petrograd full of indignation. "If we are to carry on the War," he said, "we must stop this propaganda which is simply demoralizing the whole army. If we are to withdraw from the War, then let the Government and the Soviet announce it at once. Then they can preach their Socialism as much as they please. As it is now, the Government and the Soviet order us to defend the country, and all the time they are sending their agitators to tell the soldiers that the War is being fought only for capitalists, that it is time to stop it, and that officers who order them to maintain discipline are only counter-revolutionists. What madness!"

I sympathized with this officer, a former student who had fought bravely during all the campaigns, but all I could do was to refer him to my colleague, Mr. Mstislavsky, who was one of these demoralizers of the army. An hour later the officer came out of Mstislavsky's office, red and excited. I asked him what he had learned, and he replied hotly: "I have learned what we must do immediately if Russia is to live. That is to march the army back to Petrograd, arrest all these traitors, and send them to Germany. If we don't, our country is ruined, the War is lost, and the Revolution is defeated."

In my heart I feared that this man spoke the truth.

Mr. Flekkel, secretary of the Petrograd branch of the Social Revolutionary Party, told me today that "things are going on well," that hundreds of thousands of people, students, peasants, and workmen, were joining our party. "Is it not wonderful?" he said.

"It is indeed wonderful that in one month millions suddenly become Socialists who, a month ago, had not the remotest idea of what Socialism means," I replied sarcastically. "But I would be better satisfied if the Party, instead of taking in all these people, could agree on a policy among the leaders."

"What do you propose then for the success of the Revolution?"

"I want a little more intelligence and judgment, fewer promises, less obstruction, and above all, discouragement of the beast impulses of the mob. In this sudden success of Socialistic parties I see only the disappearance of normal common sense and caution, only loosening of the animal in man."

Angrily the secretary turned away.

Today in two principal book-shops (the Wolf and

Karbasnikoff shops) they told me that books about revolution, particularly the French Revolution, were selling rapidly. On the tables of many politicians also I have seen these books. It is understandable now why, in speech and manners, so many of them recall French leaders and *sans coulottes!*

CHAPTER IV

LIGHT AND SHADOWS

TODAY, April 22, was held a conference of the Social Revolutionary Party of Petrograd. The frame of mind of the new "March" socialist-revolutionaries is radical in the extreme. Many old leaders of the party, Zenzinoff, Gotz, and others, tried to reconcile the irreconcilables, but succeeded only in reinforcing the left wing. The conference was attended by "Babushka" Breshkovskaia, the venerable "Grandmother of the Revolution" and also by Kerensky, "The Minister of Justice, Citizen Kerensky" dressed in a simple jacket suit. Breshkovskaia also was simply dressed, as always. In vain these two supported our efforts to persuade the conference to moderate measures. It was all quite useless. The extremists simply insinuated that Kerensky was not a real revolutionist at all, but merely a Minister of a bourgeois government. *Sic transit gloria mundi!* New "revolutionists" today are treating the oldest leaders as their servants. The new ones had a majority in the conference and passed a resolution that the War be brought to an immediate end, and that a Socialist Government be established. I declared that I could not accept this program, walked out of the conference and resigned my position as editor of *Delo Naroda*. Many old members followed me, most of

the right wing abandoning the conference. Sooner
or later this had to happen, so it was better to let
it happen now.

Gukovsky and I are organizing a right wing So-
cialist-Revolutionary newspaper, *The Will of the
People.* "Grandmother" Breshkovskaia, Mirolyu-
boff, Stalinsky, and Argunoff will be our co-editors.
To hope for success at this time is impossible; still
we have to do our duty. *Delo Naroda,* after our departure, became even more radical than before.
Now it is in the hands of the middle and left sec-
tions of the Party.

The political immigrants continue to return. Of
our Party leaders these have appeared: Chernoff,
Avksentieff, Bunakoff, Stalinsky, Argunoff, Lebedeff and others. In a few days are expected the
Bolshevist leaders, Lenin, Trotzky, Zinovieff and
others. They are returning through Germany with
the assistance of the German Government, which
has loaned them a special *"plombiert"* wagon.
Some of our people are indignant with the Provisional Government which permitted these persons to
return. The rumor is spreading that Lenin and his
companions (about forty men) were hired by the
German staff to incite civil war in Russia and still
further to demoralize the Russian Army. I know
not if this is true, but if it is, what can the Government do to prevent it? By the inflamed masses any
attempt on the Government's part would be regarded as counter-revolution.

Along with the organization of our new paper
we are organizing the right wing members into a
group called "The Will of the People." The fanaticism of the working classes and the intellectual
proletarians of the town increases every day. These
minorities are determined to rule Russia without
consulting the peasants, who, as everyone knows,
are the majority. Without the participation of the
peasants it will be impossible to decide the future
destiny of Russia. I am convinced of the necessity
of summoning an All-Russian Peasants' Conference
or Soviet, to counterbalance the Soviet of idle
workers and soldiers of the town.

Night. . . . Wearied by speeches, meetings, and
a hundred depressing incidents, I have returned
home feeling like a man who tries to stop with his
bare hands a great movement of ice from the mountains. A hopeless task. It might be better to step
aside and let the ice crash down demolishing the
village and all its population. Yet of course I
cannot.

With my friends we began the organization of
the All-Russian Peasants' Conference.

I started yesterday from Petrograd to Veliky
Ustyug, summoned there by the peasants and other
inhabitants of the district. What a relief to leave
the capital with its constantly moving crowds, its
disorder, dirt, and hysteria, and to be again in the
tranquil places I love. The steamer is gliding swiftly
along the Sukhona. Above me is the blue sky, under
and around me the gleaming river and the beautiful

scenery. How perfect is the calm of it all. How pure and still the air, as if no Revolution exists. Only the constant chatter of the passengers recalls its presence. On the steamer a former friend, Mr. Vetoshkin, is traveling. Alas, this man, three months ago patriot, now has become a Bolshevik and is going to Veliky Ustyug to spread Bolshevist propaganda. On seeing me he was at first a little abashed, but later he began to expound to me his new faith. I made no comment, and my silence appeared to irritate him more than objections might have done. I have reasons to think the motives of his change of doctrine are mercenary, and that he has hopes of profiteering. Perhaps he suspected my opinion of him.

At my beloved Veliky Ustyug a group of friends met me. From the steamer I was driven to the market-place where thousands of people were assembled. My speech evoked great patriotic enthusiasm. Hundreds pressed forward to subscribe to the State Loan of Freedom issued by the Government for the economic improvement of the State. Many peasants who had come to town to sell their corn gave it to the army without charge. I had a similar triumph at a meeting of teachers and among the simple people of three neighboring villages.

At the teachers' conference Mr. Vetoshkin tried to speak, but the audience refused to listen to him. Thank God, the state of mind here is saner than in Petrograd.

To return to the unhealthy atmosphere, the disorder, and unrestraint of the capital was frightful.

Lenin and his companions have arrived. Their first speeches at the Bolshevist Conference embarrassed even members of the extreme left. Lenin and his group are now very rich men, and as a consequence the number of Bolshevist newspapers, pamphlets, proclamations, etc., have greatly increased. Trotzky has taken a very expensive apartment. Where did all this money come from? That is the question.

"Socialization" has begun. The Bolsheviki have forcibly taken possession of the villa of the dancer Kshessinsky, the anarchists have seized the villa of Durnovo and other houses, the proprietors being summarily expelled. Although the owners have appealed to the courts and to the Government, nothing has been done to restore their property.

April 21, 1917—

TODAY we have had a real taste of mob revolt. The Foreign Office note to the Allies, stating that the Provisional Government would be faithful to all treaties and obligations undertaken by Russia, was furiously attacked by the Soviets and by the Bolsheviki, who saw in it a declaration in favor of "annexations and contributions," and of old imperialistic aspirations. To any reasoning mind it was absurd to speak of "annexations" by a Russia already half-dead. Of course the real object of the attack was destruction of the "bourgeois" Government. Hundreds of propagandist speakers fill the town, protesting and raising demonstrations. Hun-

dreds of thousands of proclamations calling for
revolt, demanding the dismissal of Milyukoff and
other "capitalistic" Ministers, are displayed in
factories, barracks, offices, and on the streets.
Everywhere are open-air as well as indoor meetings.
Side by side with Bolshevist speakers stand others
defending the policies of the Government. Violent
speeches are often followed by fights. About noon
today came a rumor that two regiments, fully armed,
had left their barrack to support the rioters. Firing began. Sacking of shops by criminals became
general. The situation resembled the first days of
anti-Czarist revolt, but in those days citizens were
able to control the masses. Late last night the
rioters were momentarily dispersed, but they had
already achieved their purpose. The Government
has announced that Milyukoff is to be dismissed.

This means that the Government has fallen, for
this first concession to the mob and to the Bolsheviki is the beginning of the end of the Provisional
Government. We are all living on the edge of a
volcano, and at any moment an eruption may burst
forth. Not a pleasant situation, but step by step we
manage to adapt ourselves to it. At any rate it is
all interesting enough.

Today we published the first copy of *The Will of
the People*. The paper met with an instant success,
almost all old Social Revolutionaries buying it, and
sending us letters, questions, and greetings. I am
not too optimistic, yet I think we may be able to

make an impression. The organization of the All-Russian Peasants' Conference is proceeding successfully and is approaching achievement.

Vandervelde and De Brouker, leaders of the Belgian Socialists, paid a visit to our office today. "You are the first Russian Socialists who do not denounce our patriotism and our 'bourgeois' opinions," said Vandervelde in shaking hands with me. It is true. These distinguished men, leaders of international Socialism, as well as Henderson, Albert Thomas, and representatives of the English, Belgian, and French working classes have been treated with great discourtesy by the Soviet and by many who, two or three months ago, were moderate Socialist Party members. I am bitterly ashamed of this, but Vandervelde seems to understand the abnormal conditions in which we struggle.

This evening we gave a dinner to Albert Thomas. He, like Vandervelde, regards the situation rather pessimistically, but he treated the rudeness of the Soviet with good humor. "They are like irresponsible children," he said.

My manner of living has become regular in its irregularity. I have no definite time for dinner, for sleeping, rising, or working. Day after day I tire myself out in agitation, excitement, and in carrying on a multitude of business. I sometimes feel like a homeless dog.

CHAPTER V

AGONY

May-June, 1917—

THE Peasants' Conference has opened with about one thousand representatives of real peasants and loyal soldiers from the front. As far as it is possible to judge, the peasants' frame of mind is incomparably more sane and balanced than that of the workmen or of the city soldiery. Patriotism, a real desire to suppress disorders, and even a willingness to abstain from taking the land until a definite settlement of this question has been reached; perfect readiness to support the Government and to oppose the Bolsheviki; all these sentiments were heartily expressed by the conference.

An interesting episode was the appearance at the conference of Lenin. Mounting the platform he dramatically threw off his overcoat and began to speak. This man's face reminds me of those of congenital criminals in the albums of Lombroso, and at the same time it has something in it which recalls religious fanatics of the *Starover* (old Orthodox Church). He is a dull speaker and his efforts to arouse enthusiasm for Bolshevism fell absolutely flat. His speech was received coldly, his personality excited animosity, and in the end he retired in evident embarrassment. The Bolshevist *Pravda*, and other internationalist newspapers renewed their at-

47

tack on the Peasants' Conference, calling it a "cita-
del of the social patriots and the little bourgeois."
Well, let them attack it. At least, we may be sure
that for some time the mental balance of these representatives will remain secure.

The Peasants' Conference adjourned after voting
to organize a special Peasants' Soviet, electing
deputies, an executive committee, and representatives of its organization in different institutions. I
was elected a member of the executive committee and
a delegate to the "Commission for Elaboration of
the Law for Election of Members of the Constitutional Assembly."

On my way downtown I passed the villa Kshessinsky which was siezed by the Bolsheviki and is being
used by them as a headquarters. Day after day
they deliver orations from the balcony of the palace
to crowds of workmen and soldiers. All efforts of
the Government to expel the intruders from this
place have failed. The Durnovo Palace, taken by
the Anarchists, as well as other villas illegally held
by criminals calling themselves anarchists or communists, are still in their possession. In vain the
courts have ordered the intruders to vacate, and
equally in vain the Minister of Justice has issued his
orders. No results. Either the Government has no
forces at its disposal or it is afraid to act in the
matter. I stopped before the Kshessinsky Palace
to listen to Lenin. Although a poor speaker and a
repellent personality it seems to me that this man
may go far. Why? Because he is ready and de-

termined to encourage all the violence, the criminality, and obscenity which the mob, under these demoralized conditions, is straining to let loose.

"Comrade workers," thus went Lenin's speech, "take the factories from your exploiters! Comrade peasants, take the lands from your enemies, the landlords! Comrade soldiers, stop the War, go home. Make peace with the Germans and declare war on the rich! Poor wretches, you are starving while all around you are plutocrats and bankers. Why do you not seize all this wealth? Steal what has been stolen! Pitilessly destroy this whole capitalistic society! Down with it! Down with the Government! Down with all war! Long life to the social Revolution! Long life to class war! Long life to the dictatorship of the proletariat!"

Such a speech always meets a lively response. Just now it is gospel to all criminals, idlers, robbers, parasites, and all unbalanced minds. Well does Lenin know that the quickest road to his goal lies in rousing the lowest beast-instincts in the unthinking masses. Zinovieff followed Lenin. What a disgusting creature this Zinovieff! In his high womanish voice, his face, his fat figure, there is something hideous and obscene, an extraordinary moral and mental degenerate. A perfect pupil has Lenin found in this man.

Having listened for about an hour I crossed the Troitzky bridge to my office. The day was beautiful. The sun shone brilliantly, and the Neva reflected a cloudless sky. But my soul was full of dark forebodings. These men, I knew, presaged very terrible

things. If I were the Government I would arrest
them without hesitation. If necessary I would
execute them in order to prevent the horrible catastrophe into which they plan to plunge this country.
The army is rapidly becoming demoralized. Discipline and obedience have all but disappeared. Demands for peace are reiterated, and always the
brutal murder of officers goes on unchecked. Poor
Kerensky does his best. He delivers one eloquent
speech after another, but wild beasts cannot be controlled by speeches, however eloquent. In the towns
starvation threatens, for work has practically
ceased. The Bolsheviki, with unlimited money to
spend, manifest furious energy. I must say that
their *Pravda* as a propagandist newspaper is very
ably edited. Especially brilliant are the sarcastic
articles of Trotzky in which he lashes and jeers his
opponents, myself among them. Excellent satire.
In the factories, in the parks and streets are held
incessant Bolshevist meetings with their tireless
slogans of "Down with the bourgeois Government!"
"Down with the War." Even "Down with the
Soviet." We try, with more or less success, to
neutralize the activities of these drunken helots, as
Kerensky calls the revolutionary masses. A fair
designation, though rather different from his previous one, "A high-minded people who make no
mistakes."

Both Kerensky, Dan, Gotz, Liber, and other leaders in the Soviet begin to realize that we are rushing
towards the abyss. From being themselves instiga-
tors of anarchy they are now veering towards

moderation. The fatal weakness of all these men is that much as they fear Bolshevism they fear still more an imaginary counter-revolution. They fear to lose their reputation as revolutionists, which in these days is aristocracy. Therefore, they remain both hopeless and helpless. Many times lately I have talked with Kerensky and with Breshkovskaia. The "Grandmother" seems in good spirits, although she is well aware of the coming catastrophe. Kerensky is plainly worried over the disorganized Soviet, the Bolsheviki, and the army. He hopes much from the next offensive which he believes will check the growing disintegration of the army. Well, there may be a chance, provided the army offensive is coincident with an offensive against anarchy behind the lines.

The Peasants' Soviet is still a bulwark. Most of the *muzhiks,* representatives of the peasant majority, keep their mental balance. The left Social Revolutionaries, Spiridonova, Katz, Natanson, and others try to demoralize them, but in vain. I regret that Spiridonova is such an extremist, for she is a sincere person, though unhappily simple-minded and credulous.

"In order to prevent starvation and make everyone prosperous we have only to seize all the money in the banks," she said to me.

"How much actual money do you think you would find in the banks?" I asked her.

"Oh, billions in gold roubles," she exclaimed.

"Don't you know that the entire national income

of Russia is less than ten billion gold roubles a year?"

"No I don't," she replied. "And I don't believe it."

"It is nevertheless true," I assured her. "If you do seize the banks, you will find stocks, bonds, papers, but very little money. The only thing you would accomplish would be the destruction of credit and economic life."

"Rubbish!" she cried angrily.

A tragic situation when the leaders understand not even the rudiments of economics.

May 26, 1917, was my marriage day. It was a real revolutionary wedding. After the ceremony in the church, to which I came straight from an important meeting, my wife and our friends took only half an hour for luncheon; and then I had to hurry off to another cursed conference. Only in war or revolution could such a thing have happened. In the evening I consigned revolution to the devil and returned home to my beloved. The tornado approaches, but in spite of everything I bless this day as the happiest in my whole life.

Today Professor Masaryk of Prague visited me in my office. It was a great pleasure to talk with this man, rational, intelligent, serious, and broad-minded. We discussed the Czech problem, of which I have written. Surely with such leaders as Masaryk the Czech nation will regain its independence. In *The Will of the People* we support their cause.

Work in the Peasants' Soviet goes on satisfactorily. The principal problems of future Russia, agrarian reform, the constitution, organization of government, defense of the country, and so on, are already tentatively arranged. Meetings of the Executive Committee are held daily, conferences of the Soviet three or four times a week. Local peasants' soviets are being organized all over Russia. Members have enough to do to attend meetings, visit the army at the front, participate in governmental commissions, and settle vexed questions in the provinces. Meetings of the Soviets—the Workmen's and Soldiers' and the Peasants'—are conducted separately. The old Soviet at first tried to dominate, but now it has been obliged to recognize the equal status of the peasant's organization. Yet joint sessions are allowed only when very important problems are under discussion. In the Hall of the Duma the members of our Soviet occupy the right side, while on the extreme left are seated the small group of Bolsheviki, the Internationalists, and the left Social Revolutionaries. At the right of the presidium we see Chkeidze, Tseretelly, Dan, Gotz, Avksentieff; on the left side Trotzky, Lunacharsky, Kameneff, Nogin, and other Bolsheviki. As our men enter these reds meet us with derisive cries: "Here come the little bourgeois!" And we retaliate: "Hear the traitors!" The speeches of the Bolsheviki amuse the Soviet and are generally listened to with jeers.

A very grave crisis has arrived. As the Executive

Committee of the Peasants' Soviet was in session, we were suddenly informed by telephone that the Bolsheviki had organized for the next morning an armed demonstration of soldiers and workmen with the demand: "Down with the Capitalistic Government! Down with the War! All the power to the Soviets!" There was no doubt that such a demonstration would mean the fall of the Government and the final breakdown of the offensive. It would mean bloodshed, death, civil war. At once, in co-operation with the other Soviet we determined to issue an appeal to the soldiers, workmen, and citizens to abstain from this demonstration. We warned the factories and barracks that the Bolsheviki, in calling the demonstration in the name of the Soviets, were grossly deceiving the people. As a counter to their action we voted to take part in an unarmed demonstration to take place the following week. Visiting two regiments and one factory I found the atmosphere rather pro-Bolshevist. Nevertheless, my speeches were well received. Returning home I found that my voice was entirely lost and that I was in for a sleepless night. No matter. We have thwarted the attempted armed demonstration. Next morning *Pravda* announced that the Bolsheviki would join in our peaceful march. This time we won, but I fear that the next victory will be theirs.

The peaceful demonstration was a success, but the influence of the fanatics was everywhere apparent. At least half the banners bore their slogans: "Down with the Capitalistic Ministers!" "All Power to the Soviets!" "Peace to the Huts and War to the

Palaces!'' In the evening were riots and several
street murders. The bloodless skirts of the Revolution become more and more bloodstained. Starvation is increasing.

Our offensive on the front began brilliantly, and
at once the spirit of the people was immensely uplifted. Patriotic demonstrations filled all the streets
and Kerensky's popularity was wildly acclaimed.
The Bolsheviki, for the moment, suffered complete
eclipse. Oh, if this would only last. But I cannot
hope that half-disorganized army can continue victorious. I fear this splendid beginning will end in
inglorious defeat. What then? The catastrophe.
Nothing less.

Yes, the catastrophe has come. Our revolutionary
army is defeated. In mad panic it has broken, fled,
and in its flight it is destroying everything in its
path; murders, violations, looting, devastated fields,
and destroyed villages mark its way. No discipline,
no authority, no mercy for innocent women or civil-
ians. General Korniloff and B. Savinkoff demand
the return of capital punishment for deserters. In
vain! The impotent Government and the Soviets,
even in this frightful emergency, have no will to act.
Again Bolshevism and anarchy prevail.

Today Savinkoff came to our office giving us the
ghastly details of events. To imagine greater horrors is impossible. ''Iron discipline and ruthless
punishment must be restored in the army or else
Russia perishes,'' declared Savinkoff.

"But is it possible any more to find troops to enforce such measures?" we asked despairingly.

"It is possible now," he said. "But very soon it won't be."

In this man is something of an adventurer, but in this crisis he may be useful.

A significant thing has happened. At a meeting to-day, addressed by "Grandmother" Breshkovskaia, Savinkoff, Plekhanoff, Tschaikovsky, and myself, the audience of soldiers and workers suddenly broke out in hisses and denunciations of these oldest friends of the Revolution. Against such martyrs as Breshkovskaia and Tschaikovsky were hurled epithets such as "Traitors!" "Counter-Revolutionaries!" Springing to his feet Savinkoff shouted: "Who are you to treat us in this way? What have you slackers ever done for the Revolution? Nothing at all. What have you ever risked? Nothing. But these men and women here," pointing to us, "have lain in prison, starved, and frozen in Siberia, risked their lives over and over again. It was I and not any of you who threw a bomb at the tyrant Min. It was I and not you who for that deed heard the death penalty pronounced against me by the Czarist Government. How dare you accuse us of being counter-revolutionaries? What are you anyhow but a mob of fools and loafers who are plotting the ruin of Russia, the destruction of the Revolution and of your selves?"

This outburst somewhat awed and impressed the mob. But it is plain that all the great revolution-

aries are facing tragedy. The work and sacrifice of
their lives are forgotten. In comparison with the
March Revolutionists they are now counted as reactionary and out of date.

"Have you ever thought of yourself as a reactionary counter-revolutionist?" I asked the veteran
Plekhanoff.

"If these maniacs are revolutionists, then I am
proud to be called a reactionary," replied the founder of the Social Democratic Party.

"Have a care, Mr. Plekhanoff," I said, "lest you
be arrested as soon as these people, your own pupils,
become dictators."

"Since these people have become even greater
reactionaries than the Czarist Government itself,
what have I to expect but arrest?" he asked bitterly.

I like Plekhanoff. It seems to me that he grasps
the truth of conditions better than do his pupils in
the Soviet who will not even admit him as a member.
All the old revolutionaries and the founders of Russian Socialism now count themselves as moderates,
or in the patter of the Bolsheviki, counter-revolutionists. I see that my "conservatism" is identical
with what in all revolutions and social upheavals
comes to be called by the mob "counter-revolution."
All of us are beginning to see that revolution and
radicalism, in practice are quite different from the
same ideas in theory.

The disintegration of Russia is beginning in earnest. Finland, the Ukraine, and the Caucasus have
declared their independence. Kronstadt, Sclissel-

burg, and many small districts in various parts of
Russia have voted their own independence. Even
the anarchist groups barricaded in the Durnovo
Villa, and the Bolsheviki in the Kshessinsky Palace
have the effrontery to call themselves independent
states. My poor country is breaking to pieces. Yesterday came to me some Ziryane, people of the
north of Russia, proposing that our paper declare
the independence of the Ziryane Republic, and offer-
ing me the presidency of the new state! Madness
possesses all minds.

On the impending catastrophe I published yesterday an article which I called "The Damnation of
the Russian Nation." Today all the other newspapers commented on it; the Bolshevist sheets utter-
ing threats against me. Many citizens, however,
called to thank me for the article. Their sympathy
cannot save the situation, which is now quite hopeless. As for me, I have no personal fears.

The Social Democratic as well as the Social Revolutionary Parties have split into three branches—
right, left, and center. Efforts of our Central Committee to form a coalition of the right and left Social
Revolutionaries have utterly failed. Now all the
committee can do is to act as a balance between the
two wings. The same situation exists with the
Social Democrats. Today, I and my colleagues were
summoned to a meeting of the Central Committee
and were thus admonished by Chernoff, Zenzinoff,
and others: "We feel that we must warn you that
you are leading *The Will of the People* in a too

conservative direction. In the name of the Central Committee we demand that you make your paper less patriotic and more radical, or else that you resign your membership in the Party. In either event your newspaper will lose our motto: 'Through Struggle We Attain Our Rights.' "

"My dear friends," I said with a laugh, "in every issue of your paper, *Delo Naroda,* you publish absolutely contradictory articles. In every decision you make you show the same inconsistency. Your example is not good enough for us to follow. The Party motto we will not relinquish since we have as much right to express Party opinion as you have. You may resign if you like, but you cannot force us to do so. Good-bye."

Life in Petrograd becomes more and more difficult. Riots, murders, starvation, and death are every-day commonplaces. We wait the next eruption, knowing that it will surely come. Yesterday I disputed at a public meeting with Trotzky and Madame Kollontay. As for this woman, it is plain that her revolutionary enthusiasm is nothing but a gratification of her sexual satyriasis. In spite of her numerous "husbands," Kollontay, first the wife of a general, later the mistress of a dozen men, is not yet satiated. She seeks new forms of sexual sadism. I wish she might come under the observation of Freud and other psychiatrists. She would indeed be a rare subject for them.

As for Trotzky, granted favorable conditions, he will certainly rise to the top. This theatrical brigand is a true adventurer. His comrades in the Social Democratic Party (Menshevik) used to say of him: "Trotzky brings to every meeting his own chair. Today he sits with this party, tomorrow he sits with another." For the moment he places his chair in the Communist Party. Well, for an adventurer seeking a career this is not ill-advised. The Bolsheviki will probably give him all he longs for.

CHAPTER VI

July-September, 1917.

July 3-5. The eruption has come. In the afternoon of the 3d when the Peasants' Soviet was in the midst of an afternoon session, we were summoned by telephone to the Tavrichesky Palace for a joint session with the Workmen's Soviet. "Come as soon as possible," we were urged, "a new Bolshevist riot has broken out." Without any delay we started. On Sergievskaia Street all was serene, but as soon as we turned into the Liteiny we saw a number of heavy motor trucks, full of armed soldiers and sailors and fitted with machine guns, being driven furiously in the direction of the Tavrichesky Palace. Private automobiles were being stopped and seized by the rioters. We saw a mutinous regiment crossing the Liteiny Bridge and near at hand we heard the crack of rifles. Revolution was hungry again and was calling for human sacrifice. Near the gates of their houses groups of terrified citizens stood talking in frightened whispers. Streets surrounding the Palace and its large courtyard were full of soldiers and sailors, and standing up in an automobile was Trotzky, haranguing the men from Krondstadt.

"You, comrade sailors, are the pride and glory of the Russian Revolution. You are its best promoters and defenders. By your deeds, by your devotion to

61

communism, by your ruthless hatred and massacres
of all exploiters and enemies of the proletariat you
have written deathless pages in the history of the
Revolution. Now there is before you a new task—
to sweep the Revolution free from all its enemies, to
overthrow the capitalistic Government, to push
revolution to its ultimate limits, to create the kingdom of communism, the dictatorship of the proletariat and to start a world-revolution. The great
drama has begun. Victory and everlasting glory call
us. Let our enemies tremble. No pity, no mercy
for them. Summon all your hatred. Destroy them
once and forever!''

A wild animal roar was the answer to this speech.

With extreme difficulty we forced our way into the
Palace, and in the Hall of the Duma found many
representatives of the Workmen's Soviet and of the
Social Democratic Party. The atmosphere was
tense with excitement. "This is terrible!" "This
is a crime against the Revolution!" cried these leaders of the left.

"Ah, imbeciles!" shouted Chernoff to Kamkoff-
katz and Schreider, leaders of the left wing of the
Social Revolutionary Party—his own pupils; "what
have you done? Do you realize that all the blood
that is now being spilled is on your hands?"

The pupils smiled ironically. "What we have
done," they retorted, "is exactly what you taught
us to do and what you are too cowardly to do yourself.''

And they were right. The Chernoff pupils are
simply consistent in carrying out his theories.

While Chernoff, Chkeidze, Dan, Tseretelly, and Gotz stood pale and terror-stricken, the uproar outside rose higher and more mad, and in the midst of it Trotzky, Lunacharsky, Zinovieff, and other Bolsheviki burst into the Hall with victorious smiles on their lips. "Who has won this time?" their exultant expressions seemed to demand. Thus to the explosion of gun fire and demoniac shrieks from without, the joint meeting of the Soviets, the Soldiers' and Workmen's and the Peasants', was called to order by Chkeidze.

"In the name of the board of the Soviets," said Dan, "I offer the following motion: That at this meeting only those members be seated who will swear to submit themselves to the decisions of the Soviet, who recognize that its authority is supreme, and will not attempt to repudiate, try to overthrow, or even to attack this highest organ of the Russian Revolutionary Democracy. Secondly, all members of the Soviet here present must swear to do everything, even to die, if necessary, in order to suppress this criminal revolt against the Soviet and the Revolution. Those who are unwilling to take this oath shall immediately withdraw."

Deep silence for a moment, and then deafening applause. Around me I saw the pale faces of the deputies. I heard fervent murmurs: "Yes, we are ready to die." Something tragical and heroic took possession of us all. Surrounded by the unbridled mob, amid roars of cannon and rattle of machine guns, defended only by two soldiers guarding the door of the Hall, the members of the Soviet for the

first time rose to a height of grandeur and nobility
when man is indeed ready to vanquish or die.

The next moment groups of Bolsheviki, internationalists, and left Social Revolutionaries, led by
Trotzky, Lunacharsky, Gimmer, and Kamkoff,
pressed forward. "We protest this motion," they
shouted in unison. "Behold the sea of workers and
soldiers surrounding this building. In their name
we demand that the Soviet declare the Provisional
Government dismissed. We demand that all power
be taken over by the Soviets. We demand that the
War be ended at once. We demand a Dictatorship
of the Proletariat. We demand that the capitalistic
system be abolished and a communistic state be
established in its stead. If you don't accept this
willingly, we will force it down your throats. The
time of hesitation is past. What the revolutionary
proletariat commands you must obey."

Such was the essence of their speeches. The Bolsheviki, feeling themselves victorious, no longer appealed to the Soviet; they issued orders. Trying to
control their indignation and anger, the Soviet attended calmly.

"What is it that you demand?" asked the chairman. "The dictatorship of the Soviet or your own
dictatorship of the Soviet? If the former, then stop
threatening, sit down, wait for the decision of the
Soviet, and obey it. If, on the contrary, you are
seeking to dictate to the Soviet why are you here?
Do you think us so cowardly as to be terrorized by
your threats, or so lacking in principle as to surrender the sovereignty of the Soviet to you? No-

body in this Hall has any doubts as to what you mean. Not 'All Power to the Soviets,' but all power to yourselves is your object. For this you have inflamed the ignorant and misguided masses. For this you have incited civil war. Very well, we accept your challenge. With scorn we refuse your demands. Go out and do your worst." Such was our reply to the Bolsheviki. After a few minutes of hesitation they blustered out, and the resolution of Dan was unanimously adopted.

One fiery speech succeeded another. From time to time these were interrupted from outside with wild news, rumors which the Board of the Soviet tried to verify by messages dispatched to regiments in Petrograd and at the front. In Petrograd this was difficult enough, and to get in touch with the army at the front seemed for the time utterly impossible. Meanwhile the crowd outside grew into a dense throng. Bolshevist speakers urged the throng to break down the doors of the Palace and to disperse the Soviet. My head bursting with excitement and the close atmosphere of the room, I went out into the yard of the Duma. In the gray twilight of the July night I saw a perfect sea of soldiers, workmen, sailors. . . . Here and there cannon and machine guns pointing at the Palace, and everywhere red banners floating and incessant firing. It was like a madhouse. Here was the mob demanding "All the Power to the Soviets" and at the same time training cannon on the Soviets, threatening it with death and extinction.

As soon as I was recognized a crowd surrounded

me, hot questions, fierce threats being hurled at my head. I tried to tell that crowd that the Soviets could not wield all power because the Bolshevist demands were impossible. I tried to tell them what calamities might result from their excesses. But I spoke not to a crowd but to a monster. Deaf to all reason, crazed with hate and insensate fury, the monster simply howled aloud the idiotic slogans of the Bolsheviki. Never shall I forget the faces of this maddened crowd. The faces had lost all human traits and had become purely bestial. The crowd yelled and shrieked and shook their fists furiously.

"The Soviet members have sold out to the capitalists!"

"Traitor—Judas!" "Enemy of the people!" "Death to him!"

I shouted over this din of voices: "Will my death bring you land or fill your empty stomachs?"

Strangely enough this caused a number of the animals to burst into roars of laughter. So easily is the mob swayed one way or another!

"Now I am going back and see what the Soviets are doing," I shouted.

"Go back," they yelled, "and tell them that we will not leave until the Soviet has all power!"

In the Hall of the Duma speeches, speeches, speeches, were still going on. . . . By the time daylight dawned some of the members lay sleeping the sleep of exhaustion. Others staggered up and down, still talking. Outside remained the mob, reinforced now by several more regiments. One strategic position after another was occupied by mutinous soldiers. Only a few regiments of Cossacks and two or three line regiments remained loyal to the Government, and even among them were many who showed themselves weak and wavering. The last hope of the Soviets and the Government was a message received from the front, which said: "Forces will be sent you."

Incited by Zinovieff and other Bolsheviki, the crowd now began to call for Chernoff and Tseretelly. Only a few days before these two had been popular idols, but now they were objects of bitterest hatred. Pale but courageous Chernoff went out and made an effort to address the crowd. But wild hands tore at him, and but for the intervention of Trotzky himself, the man would have been rent limb from limb. The situation grew hourly more desperate. About noon a crowd of about two hundred men broke into the Hall shouting that they were representatives of the workers and had come to the Soviet as plenipotentiary members. The Soviet refused to recognize them and as a result a chorus of curses, cries, and roars filled the place. Members of the Soviet trying to restore order, a crowd of sailors who had invaded the galleries jeered and howled and actually raised their rifles. A single shot was fired, and at the sound absolute bedlam broke loose.

At the top of his vigorous lungs Chkeidze roared out: "Members of the Soviet! Sit down and be silent! I also will keep my seat and will not leave it. Let these ruffians bawl until they get tired. Let us see which of us can outstay the others."

These words shouted in a Caucasian accent, half-angrily, half-ironically, restored a semblance of order. For a moment there was comparative quiet. "Now," cried Chkeidze, still master of himself, "as soon as you have ceased to be possessed of the devil, I will announce that it is time for luncheon. That is, if there is anything to eat. After you have had a little food you will be able to meet this crisis more calmly. I declare a recess until four o'clock, members, however, to remain in this building and yard." The Soviet members, "plenipotentiaries of the people" and spectators quickly left the Hall. Meanwhile in the Board room new information had been received. Between the Cossacks and the rioters a fight had taken place in the Liteiny, with casualties on both sides. Bolshevist troops with dawning apprehensions of activities from loyal soldiers at the front had begun to entrench themselves in upper stories of buildings. The fact was that a military detachment from the front had started for Petrograd on bicycles to suppress the riot. Moreover, two Cossack regiments and what armored automobiles remained in Petrograd were mobilizing to protect the Soviet.

Within the Hall of the Duma, however, the situation was still very serious. The firing sounded more heavily than during the night, and very frequently bullets struck the walls of the building. Exhausted after a sleepless night, I went out again into the garden of the Duma. Here I saw three armored automobiles. For us or against? Against, of course. Crowding the garden were soldiers and sailors with rifles. Suddenly there came a loud explosion, and all these valiant warriors threw themselves in panic to the ground.

Tat, tat, tat-a-tat, tat, tat, tat. . . . the machine guns began to chatter and spit.

But in a moment they stopped as suddenly as they had begun, and the frightened soldiers and sailors picked themselves up somewhat sheepishly. The panic had been caused by the Bolsheviki themselves. One of their soldiers had dropped a hand grenade, killing several. Thinking their forces attacked by the Government the Bolshevik machine gunners opened fire, killing more people. After this a part of the rioters decided to go home.

At five o'clock the Soviet reconvened, the Bolshevist deputies and their following being present. They knew that the moment had arrived when they must either conquer or be conquered, and in order to conquer they were resolved to apply force to the utmost. But just as one of them was roaring out a speech full of bloodiest threats, the door was flung open and three officers, their uniforms white with dust and caked with mud, marched into the Hall and advanced with rapid steps to Chkeidze's seat on the rostrum. Saluting him formally they turned and the ranking officer addressed the Bolshevik groups with these words:

"While the Russian Army has gathered all its forces to defend the country from the enemy, you soldiers and sailors who have never faced war, you idlers and traitors who spend your time in vicious babblings, you adventurers and turncoats—what have you been doing here? Instead of fighting like

men against an invading enemy you have been murdering peaceful citizens, organizing riots, encouraging the enemy, and meeting us, the soldiers of the
great Russian Army, with machine guns and cannon.
What infamy! But all your treachery is in vain.
I, the commander of the regiment of bicyclists, inform you that my troops have entered Petrograd.
Your rioters are dispersed. Your machine guns
are in my hands. Your fighters, so brave in the
faces of unarmed citizens, confronted with real
soldiers, have fled like the cowards they are. And
I tell you that at the first attempt to continue or to
repeat your uprising you will be shot down like
dogs.''

Turning to the chairman, and once more saluting,
he said: ''I have the honor to declare to the Soviet
that we are at the disposal of the Government and
the Soviet, and that we await their orders.''

The explosion of a bomb could scarcely have produced such an effect. Wild, joyous applause on the
one hand, shrieks, groans, maledictions on the other.
As for Trotzky, Lunacharsky, Gimmer, Katz, and
Zinovieff, as one of my colleagues expressed it, they
''shriveled like the devil before holy water.'' One of
them did make an effort to say something, but was
instantly howled down. ''Out of here! Away!''
shouted the Soviet, and with their partisans at their
heels they left.

Half an hour later military music filled the halls
and corridors of the Palace. Two regiments of
Petrograd with full ammunition had entered the
Duma. The Bolsheviki had been definitely defeated

and once more the forces of order had won. Followed quickly dispersal of the crowds, arrest and disarming of mutinous soldiers. About two o'clock in the morning I reached home, fell on my bed, and was instantly asleep.

July 5-6, 1917.

In today's newspapers were published documents proving that the Bolshevik leaders, before their departure for Russia, received large sums of money from the German Military Staff. The news created universal indignation.

"Traitors! German spies! Murderers!"

"Death to them! Death to the Bolsheviki!"

Thus roared and howled the mob, which yesterday was just as lustful for the blood of Bolshevik enemies. The public mind had veered so completely that now it was necessary to defend the Bolshevist leaders from violence. Stekloff-Nakhamkes, among others, in order to save his life, voluntarily sought arrest. To prevent the lynching of Krondstadt sailors Tschaikovsky and I were obliged to accompany them from Petropavlovskyaia fortress to their ships. Realizing the fate in store for them if they fell into the hands of the fickle mob, the "pride and glory of the Revolution," as Trotzky had called them only a few days ago, now behaved like condemned criminals. Under the hoots and curses of the street crowds they cringed like dogs.

"Are you alive? Is everything all right with you?" This was a telegram from my wife, who was in Samara. Of course I was all right.

Today Trotzky, Kollontay, and others were arrested. Lenin and Zinovieff escaped. Now the question is, what to do. We moderates are not bloodthirsty, yet in order to prevent repetitions of these murderous uprisings we must exercise great firmness. If it is necessary to execute a few thousand ruffians in order to save millions of Russians, then we must be prepared to do it. The Soviet is inclined to leniency, but was not Napoleon right when he said: "When they say a king is good they mean that he is a bad ruler?" I think leniency at this juncture is nothing but weakness.

Riot is put down, but nothing has happened to suppress the orators or to punish the rioters.

Passing by the Fontanka, at the corner of the Nevsky Prospekt, I heard the following speech: "Comrades, I have traveled all over the world, and have seen all countries, and I tell you that if you divide all land equally every man will then have not less than five hundred acres. Shall we not then divide the land?"

"Yes, yes! Divide the land!" cried the crowd.

"I have visited all countries, comrades, I have studied economics, and I tell you that if we divide equally all the world's money, every man will then have no less than ten thousand gold roubles. What do you think of that, comrades?"

"Great! Bravo! Hurray!"

"I have visited all countries and have seen all peoples, but such sheep as you are, believe me, I have never seen. What do you think of that, my stupid comrades?"

Again the crowd laughed and applauded.

Later I witnessed another scene quite as characteristic. The Bolshevik who was speaking wore a soldier's uniform and prominent on his tunic was a military medal. Furiously he denounced the Czar, all aristocrats, all officers, and loudly he called for the abolition of all honors and privileges, all distinctions and insignia.

"Why do you wear that medal on your breast?" someone demanded.

"Oh, this medal is quite a different thing," returned the orator. "It was given me by the Czar himself for my military services."

This time the crowd did laugh, and I laughed with it. Every leveler wants equality only as it abolishes the privileges of others. As soon as himself is affected, then he wants inequality. What a light on the human comedy.

I have been offered three posts under the Provisional Government, that of Assistant Minister of the Interior, Director of the Russian Telegraphic Service, and Secretary to Prime Minister Kerensky. After reflection I decided to accept the secretaryship, although in present circumstances I doubt if I can be of great service to the country. However, as Kerensky's aid, I shall do my utmost. Kerensky is now installed in the Winter Palace, though why he chose the Palace rather than a private house I do not know. I fear his presence there may give rise to unpleasant gossip, but others, Breshkovskaia among them, are also living in the Palace; Bresh-

kovskaia in two modest rooms. Kerensky occupies
three or four. The old servants of the Czar are still
in the Palace. They are polite and kind, and do not
seem to look upon us as noisy intruders and par-
venues. Well, our mode of living is quiet enough.
Perhaps if it were a little less modest it would give
more impression of power and permanence.

The elaboration of the law regarding elections to
the Constitutional Assembly is almost complete. It
is most democratic, allowing for full proportional
representation. Only it seems to me that it is about
as suitable for poor Russia as evening dress would
be for a horse.

A few days before I assumed my responsibilities
as secretary to Kerensky an event occurred which
deeply impressed all sober-minded Russians, even
those who for years had been committed to the Revolution. I refer to the exile of Czar Nicholas II and
his family to Tobolsk in Siberia. This was done
secretly, but several days before my old friend and
collaborator, Mr. Pankratoff, called on me at the
office of *"The Will of the People,"* and told me that
he had been appointed as chief of the Emperor's
guard to escort him into exile. Pankratoff was an
old revolutionist who had spent twenty years of his
life in close confinement in the Fortress of Schlissel-
burg. Notwithstanding this, he was a thoroughly
humane man, having not the slightest animosity to
the Czar or to the old régime. Therefore, I was glad
that he had been chosen and I felt sure that he
would do all in his power to make the Imperial

Family as comfortable as they could be under confinement. The purpose of this banishment was not in any way malicious. On the contrary, I know that it was Kerensky's desire that the family be sent to England. His plan failed simply because the Soviet would not consent to it. The extremists, always imitating the French Revolution, pretended to see in such complete liberation, a danger to the State. It was these same extremists, especially Stekloff, Gimmer, Mstislavsky, Sokoloff, and other left wing deputies, who were guilty of the worst features of the Czar's imprisonment in the Palace at Czarskoe Selo. His position there finally became entirely unsafe, and had the July riots lasted even a few days longer I am positive that he would have been murdered by the Bolsheviki. It was really necessary to send the family somewhere where their lives would be safe, and where at the same time there would be no quarrel with the extremists concerning the safety of the Revolution. At Tobolsk there was little Revolutionary sentiment, and no fanaticism at all, and under the guard commanded by Pankratoff there was no danger of attempts at assassination. Yet, if the Bolsheviki ever gained an upper hand, said Pankratoff, God alone knew what might befall. Pankratoff thought that if worst came to worst it might be possible to send the family abroad through Siberia.

CHAPTER VII

NEW CRISES

Mingled with the telegrams from cities, Semestvo, peasants and workers expressing devotion to the Government are disturbing telegraphic reports of strikes among workmen, riots of soldiers, and anarchistic conditions among the peasants. All these I read, referring all important communications to Kerensky. To little purpose, however, as Kerensky ✓ does almost no constructive work, busying himself instead with the framing of resolutions which get the business of Government nowhere. The wheels of the State are moving in a vacuum. Sometimes I feel sympathy, sometimes rage with Kerensky. As a man he is honest, sincere, and ready to give his life for the country's good. But he is incompetent, weak-willed, and without mental direction. He knows nothing whatever of the art of governing and imagines that he is doing great things when he makes paper plans for the abolishment of capital punishment in time of war and revolution. Force, coercion, and cruelty are abhorent to him, and he believes that it is entirely possible to rule by kind words and lofty sentiments. Above all, he seems to revel in the consciousness of his own purity, humanity, and high idealism. A good man, but a poor leader, in fact a perfect type of the Russian intelligentsia.

I have concluded that I shall be most useful giving most of my time to the newspaper and the Soviet, reserving one or two hours a day to work at the Winter Palace.

Within a few days I found this decision well justified, for another crisis was plainly approaching. Again sleepless nights, fruitless debates, and endless divisions in the Government. In order to establish some kind of stability it was voted to summon in Moscow an All-Russian Conference of all social classes, groups, and organizations. This conference, scarcely might bring serious results, but . . . The Government has pronounced the Bolshevist newspaper, "*Pravda,*" an illegal publication, and has succeeded at last in expelling the anarchists from the villas which were seized by them. At the same time these villas, or some of them, are being reoccupied, and other elements, conservative citizens, capitalists, patriots, military men, and intellectuals, are joining the radicals in ill-concealed contempt for the Government. A new center of social forces to put an end to anarchy is called for. Pray God that it may not come too late.

A few hours ago we left Petrograd for the All-Russian Conference in Moscow. The morning before leaving I had a very interesting conversation with Kerensky. As I left my office in the Winter Palace to go to his study in an adjoining room, I met Professor Kokoshkin, Minister of Social Welfare, just returning from an interview with Keren-

sky. Seeing that he was laboring under great
excitement, I asked: "How are you? What is the
matter?"

With a hopeless sort of a gesture he replied:
"We, the Ministers, members of the Constitutional
Democratic Party, have just tendered our joint
resignations. It is impossible for us longer to endure the present situation."

"But this means a new crisis in the Government,"
I protested.

"It does indeed. Perhaps it means something
even more serious," he muttered, walking on.

Entering the study, I found Kerensky pacing the
room in great agitation. "This is terrible!" he
exclaimed. "To resign the day before the Conference is simply a crime. Have you seen Kokoshkin?"

"Yes, I have just seen him."

"He has handed me his resignation in the name
of all Constitutional Democratic Ministers," blurted
the Prime Minister.

"What reasons did he give?" I asked.

"Reasons! Why those men are demanding immediate militarization of the railroads, ironclad discipline in the army, limitation of Soviet interference
in governmental functions, and even, if necessary,
dispersal of the Soviet. Briefly, they think a dictatorship may be necessary. This might not be so
bad—if it could only be accomplished, but I have
my doubts about that. As a fact, the thing is absolutely impossible. Where are the forces through
which we could execute such a plan? Nowhere.
They accuse me of inefficiency, they think I am

ambitious for power. Fools! If I could only resign, get away from all this and retire to some quiet village, I would be the happiest man in the world. But to whom could I resign my office? Where is the man? I know they are plotting against the Government. Days ago this same scheme was proposed to me by Savinkoff, then by Korniloff, and now Kokoshkin proposes it. God knows, if I could see any possibility of its realization I would welcome it with all my heart. But I know that the first attempt to put it into execution would result in new and more terrible riots."

"Perhaps it would," I said, "but what hope do you see in the present situation? Continuation of this state of things is bound to end in anarchy and chaos."

"I see that clearly," said Kerensky, "but I know that their plan would result in immediate anarchy, whereas time may bring us some solution. At least the Ministers should have waited the results of the Moscow Conference. Ah!" he exclaimed, "if you knew how tired I am with all this hopeless striving, this watching the State drift on and on towards the abyss!"

"It may be," I said, "that if we abandon the War, give the land to the peasants, make all possible concessions to the working classes, we might avoid the final catastrophe."

"All this is impossible, too," was the despairing reply. "A separate peace would be shameful. No, no. Better perish with honor than with infamy."

Deeply moved, I left Kerensky alone in his study.

More than ever I realized that the head of the State did not know in what direction he was driving. Nothing but ruin could result from such irresolution. Moscow might help the situation temporarily. With all my soul I hoped so.

I am writing these notes while the train is rushing through the night to Moscow. I am deeply depressed. My poor country, where are you drifting? Who can save you from annihilation? I see nobody, nobody at all.

Moscow. The marvel of the Kremlin, old churches, old palaces, old monuments. From my window I look out on centuries of Russian history. What a terrible epoch in Russian history we are living through today, when all traditions, all national ideals have been flung to the winds. Great and terrible events have happened in Moscow. In my mind's eye I see it, first a little ancient town, then a city under the Tartar yoke. I see Russia slowly developing into a nation, throwing off her eastern tyrants, creating a strong and independent State, a national culture. Then comes the anarchy of the seventeenth century, attended, as now, with bloodshed, riots, foreign invasion, famine, cannibalism, death. But when all hope seemed lost, Russia arose with new strength, new life, new nationalistic spirit. How far removed is this epoch, yet how like it is to the present. Here in these streets, in these very buildings, were enacted the bloodiest scenes in our whole history. Here once reigned as Czar a

Russian adventurer. Here was he killed. Here plotted and raged the anarchists and extremists of his time, the blind and besotted mob. Here flocked foreigners and adventurers of all countries. But here also, after crushing the mob and rescuing Moscow from the adventurers, Minin and Pozharsky restored order and unity. From their great and imposing monument they seem to say to us, as of old: "If it is necessary, in order to save the country we will even sell our wives and children." They did have to sell them, but they saved Russia. Where are Russia's saviors now? Do they exist, or must we again, as in the dark seventeenth century, live through years of terror and suffering?

I find no answer to my sad musings. I see no strong leader. In my heart I know that Russia will not remain forever the devil's plaything, no, not after her thousand years of existence. We are not destined for destruction. Let anarchy do its worst. Through superhuman suffering, if need be, my country will live, and as in the seventeenth century, it will at last find the mental and moral strength to rise again. Great leaders will spring up. . . . The booming of the Kremlin bells breaks in on my tortured thoughts. . . . "How Glorious is Our God. . . ."

My soul inundated with faith that fears no calamity, I left my window and went almost hopefully to the opening session of the Conference. The Great Theater in Moscow, where the Conference was held, was completely filled with people. The right side of the hall was occupied by representatives of

the "capitalistic" groups and with higher officers
of the army. On the left sat members of the Soviet,
peasants, and workmen. The Bolsheviki sent no
representatives to the Conference.

Kerensky opened the session in a speech almost
hysterical in intensity. He harangued the left as
well as the right plotters, threatening to crush them
pitilessly, but behind his threats no one felt any
force. "Hamlet wavering to and fro," such was
the impression Kerensky created. Many representatives spoke, and an appearance of harmony was
at least affected. As a leader of the left wing Tseretelly and Bublikoff, prominent representative of the
bourgeois side, solemnly embraced, indicating an
alliance between the two parties. Many sentimental-
ists seemed profoundly touched. Other sensational
scenes were staged, other episodes, tragic as well as
comic, were enacted, but definite results were nil.

The most serious result of the Moscow Conference was the stormy debate and final split between
Kerensky and General Korniloff. General Korniloff's arrival in Moscow was the signal for a tremendous ovation, and when he appeared in the
Conference the entire right side of the house sprang
to its feet and greeted him with deafening applause.
The left, on the other hand, remained seated, and
some delegates even hissed the Commander-in-Chief
of the Russian Army. This was in deference to
Kerensky's wishes, if not according to his direct
orders. He was undoubtedly jealous of Korniloff
and his jealousy led to the disastrous division of
the Conference, which no demonstrative embraces

of delegates could heal. Korniloff, in a long and well-reasoned address, gave a plain statement of the disorganized condition of the army, and pleaded for power to restore discipline and to order capital punishment for all deserters and mutineers. This Kerensky tacitly agreed to, but his sentimental speech in which he expressed horror and remorse for his "weakness" in countenancing the death penalty, even for deserters in the face of battle, did much to nullify the effect of Korniloff's appeal. Anybody could see that this antagonism between Kerensky and Korniloff, the one Prime Minister, and the other head of the army, was bound to bring the greatest misfortune to the State. Enthusiasm died out of the Conference, friction between the right and left became as sharp as before. As for the working classes in Moscow, they showed their morale by calling a general strike while the Conference was still sitting. The whole thing ended in a resolution to call a Democratic Conference in Petrograd. Another conference! Madness!

From Moscow I traveled to Vologda to organize the electoral campaign for the Constitutional Assembly. Peasants' conventions in three districts of Vologda Government unanimously nominated me as deputy, and the Social Revolutionary Party in Vologda did the same.

At the railway station in Moscow I found it difficult either to buy a ticket or to get a seat in the train, and again I had opportunity to observe the destructive tendency of the people's mind.

"What a pity all the railway workers did not

strike," I heard one man say. "If they had, it would have prevented these bourgeois Soviet and Conference delegates from leaving Moscow."

In Vologda the state of mind was decidedly better. Even here Bolshevism had made some progress, but the majority of the population, and especially the peasantry, were anti-Bolshevist. I made a number of speeches, attended local conferences of the peasants, and having given all necessary directions, I left for home, going by way of Saratoff, where lived the parents of my wife. Before leaving Vologda I talked with Mr. Eliava, who had suddenly embraced Bolshevism. I asked him his reasons, whereat he became so embarrassed, so confused and illogical in speech that I said: "Do not try to invent motives. You believe that the Bolsheviki are in the ascendant and you want to ensure your life as well as your career. Is that not the case?"

"Perhaps it is," he admitted.

The train to Saratoff was over-crowded with the same disorderly, mannerless, and unclean set of travelers. Obscenities and vile language seemed their only expression. In spite of myself I could not avoid hearing their conversation.

"Eh! Let the officers do the fighting themselves," said a slovenly soldier. "I don't care who wins the War. It's only for a lot of capitalists anyhow."

"But how about Russia? Who will defend it from invasion?" asked an old peasant.

"Oh, my house is far from the front," replied this patriot. "The Germans will never get to my village. Let those fight who want to. I don't, and that's all there is to it."

"But in old times our soldiers thought another way," persisted the peasant. "I am an ignorant old man. I do not understand all this Revolution, but it seems to me," and he waved his hand, "that this will end badly. Badly, badly," he repeated, as though to himself.

Traveling in these days was exceedingly uncomfortable. Crowded in a corner of the compartment, my neighbors and I could neither move nor get out into the corridor. With nothing to do, we remained in the same cramped posture until we reached Moscow. There I changed trains. In the confusion someone stole my small portmanteau, but such a thing, in the general state of chaos in which we live, seemed an insignificant matter. Early in the morning I reached the home of our relatives in Saratoff. What happiness to forget for two or three days the Revolution, to live peacefully as normal people live, without political meetings, riots, mobs, or murders. Of course there was a local Soviet in Saratoff, but very moderate and reasonable. Strolling with my wife beside the calm river, under a blue sky and in wonderful autumn weather, all this refreshed me very much and renewed me body and mind.

Again Petrograd, still dirty, still demoralized, still starving. The political situation has become worse, and the moment for crushing anarchism, I fear, has definitely passed. The German Army is advancing, and our own army is on the brink of collapse. Soldiers' deputies clamor at the doors of the Soviets: "Give us peace, even a shameful peace. We can endure no more. If you don't declare peace we will make it ourselves." The Bolsheviki with intense energy spread anti-war propaganda under the camouflage of demands for "Bread, Peace, and Liberty!" In desperation all patriotic elements of the country have organized, not only against the Bolsheviki, but against the Soviet and the shadowy Government. The Government, as a matter of fact, has practically ceased to function. A new calamity is on the way.

It happened at last, the catastrophe, the titanic cataclysm. On August 26, Korniloff began it by marching an army on Petrograd with the intention of overthrowing the Soviet, and the Government, and making himself dictator. This, at least, was Kerensky's version of events. But to me Korniloff appeared less culpable.

"There must be a misunderstanding," I told Kerensky. "Was it not you, yourself, who ordered the military forces to be sent to Petrograd to check the threatened uprising of the Bolsheviki? Surely Korniloff is simply obeying your orders."

"No. Korniloff has sent me his ultimatum by the hand of Lvov."

"This cannot be true," I insisted. "Lvov is confused, he misunderstands."

"There is no misunderstanding," said Kerensky,

"I am trying to affect a peaceful settlement, but at the same time I have denounced General Korniloff as a criminal and I have given orders to mobilize all forces against him, and have called on all democracy to suppress this criminal attempt to crush liberty and the Revolution."

"I entreat you not to act too hastily," I said. But Kerensky's only response was a peremptory order to inform the Soviets of his decision and to demand their help in the suppression of Korniloff's alleged *coup d'etat*. Very much disturbed, I went out, fairly dazed by the desperate crisis we were facing. I knew that the relations between Kerensky and Korniloff had long since reached the breaking point and that Korniloff's group of non-Socialists were absolutely opposed to Kerensky's Government, which they charged with the guilt of Russia's rapidly approaching disintegration. Kerensky, on his side, characterized Korniloff and his following as traitors against the State. New forces had been organizing for defense against the Bolsheviki, but instead of uniting against the common foe, here was an army of patriots divided in three separate camps. Who was responsible? Whose agent was Lvov? I could not decide, but the terrible significance of the division was only too plain to my mind. With the Government and the Soviets at hopeless odds and the Bolsheviki quite united, what chance had Korniloff to reorganize and control the army? And if he was not allowed to reorganize the army, then the Bolsheviki must triumph.

Nothing was done. Proclamations, contradictory and opposing, were issued, and Korniloff's march on Petrograd began. The Bolsheviki, of course, were beside themselves with joy. What better fortune could they have asked for? In the Soviets was feverish activity. A High Committee of twenty-two members "For the Struggle with Counter-Revolution" was elected, I being included in its membership. Characteristically, the Soviets elected a few Bolshevist members, and we found ourselves in the anomalous position of working with Reds for the suppression of Reds. The first thing these committee members demanded was release from prison of their Bolshevist associates, Trotzky, Kollontay, and others, and against my energetic protests this was conceded.

If in other respects the Soviet was impotent, it now manifested a sudden energy. Warships and sailors were summoned from Kronstadt, regiments were put in battle position, and scores of propagandists were sent to meet and to demoralize the troops of Korniloff. The Bolshevist Ryazonoff was one of the busiest members of the High Committee, writing proclamations and issuing bulletins. One of the members observed: "Who would ever believe that Ryazonoff and Sorokin would ever be seen working together? Myself, I find this encouraging." But I did not feel particularly encouraged. My only thought was that revolution, like politics, sometimes makes strange bedfellows.

Korniloff's army continued to move on Petrograd, and there seemed grave doubts as to whether the disorganized troops of the Soviets would be able to cope with seasoned veterans. A revolutionary armed force is poor material against disciplined soldiers, and we trusted more to our propagandists than to our soldiers and sailors. Among the citizenry the approach of Korniloff aroused both hope and fear. Some regarded the General as a liberator and a savior, others looked upon him as a pitiless dictator. One after another the timid members of the Government, looking to their own safety, whichever party won, resigned their portfolios. Of Kerensky's most trusted lieutenants only Skobeleff and Avksentieff, Socialist Ministers of Labor and of the Interior, remained. All others simply deserted, some resigning, others leaving without formalities of any kind. I found Kerensky sitting alone in a corner of the Military Staff Headquarters, bowed with chagrin and disappointment. He looked like nothing but a deserted child, helpless and homeless. Yesterday a ruler, today a forsaken idol, he sat face to face with ruin and despair. I thought that now he regretted his many mistakes, and especially this last fatal mistake of his quarrel with Korniloff, Commander-in-Chief of all the army that remained to the once mighty Russia. In this hour I felt for Kerensky boundless pity, and I made my latest news as encouraging as possible, assuring him that all might yet be well. All that the Soviet could do would at least be done to save the situation.

Leaving the room, I met Avksentieff, Minister of the Interior. "Mr. Minister," I jokingly addressed him, "as one of your loyal supporters, I venture to beg your protection in case Petrograd is taken by General Korniloff. Meanwhile I should be grateful if you would assist me to some safe shelter for to-night and tomorrow."

"If I, myself, knew of such a place," he exclaimed, "I would seek it myself. Any moment I expect arrest."

"What about going home with me?" I asked. "There I think we shall both be safe for the night."

"I accept gratefully," replied Avksentieff, and at the spectacle of a Minister of the Government and the Secretary of the Prime Minister in such a plight we both burst into laughter. The night passed without event, and next morning Avksentieff went to his office and I to the Soviet. The High Committee had received information that our propaganda had been so successful that Korniloff's troops were already wavering and showing reluctance to continue the march to Petrograd. Two or three hours later came definite assurance that the Korniloff army was on the point of mutiny. Next morning General Krymoff, commander of the "counter-revolutionary" troops, came to Kerensky, and after a short conversation went straight out and shot himself dead. The whole Korniloff affair was to me a tragedy. His motives and those of Krymoff, his chief aide, were absolutely pure and patriotic. They were in no sense "counter-revolutionaries." Now the triumph of Bolshevism was merely a matter of time. The

Government, having lost the confidence of all non-Socialist groups, now hung by a hair and its downfall was imminent, although it still clung to the Democratic Conference as a last hope.

After that, things went swiftly to the devil. The Bolshevist leaders had been set free, their army was ready, and thousands of workmen and criminals daily marched the streets armed and equipped for battle. From Kronstadt, Viborg, and other places on the front, massacres of officers were daily reported.

The Democratic Conference was held, as planned, the Alexandrinsky Theater full of representatives. While the tempest gathered without, these men once again indulged themselves in endless polemics. As we listened to a debate between Tseretelly and Trotzky on the question of coalition or non-coalition with the bourgeois classes, I clasped my head and cried to myself: "Good God! Are we in the Academy of Sciences?" All around us men babbling party politics, and around us the hurricane!

By my side sat Marie Spiridonova who, in spite of greatest difference in opinions, is my friend.

"You are a conservative, but I like you," she said.

"I like you, also," I said, "but I believe you and the Bolsheviki are about to plunge the country in ruin."

"Why so? The dictatorship of the proletariat

and the abolition of capitalism is bound to bring happiness to the people. When you see how it turns out, I am sure you will join us."

"More likely, when you see how disastrously your policy results you will join us," I replied warmly.

The Bolsheviki, all through the Conference, behaved like hooligans, constantly interrupting speakers and keeping up a continual racket. This brought protests from the other side, and the Conference soon became like an anarchistic meeting without any pretense of order or system. While I was speaking, the noise became uproar and I finished amid wild applause on the one hand and yells of rage on the other.

Kerensky took advantage of the occasion to make one more of his famous blunders. Answering a Bolshevist speaker who accused him of restoring capital punishment in the army, he said: "Yes, the law restored capital punishment, but no capital punishment has been, up to this time, inflicted, and I assure you that no execution will in future take place. No blood is upon my head and no blood will be. I am stainless."

This speech accomplished nothing except to counteract the effect of a salutory law and it clearly illustrated Kerensky's readiness to sacrifice the interests of the State to his own cherished reputation as a humane and generous leader. Nobody who heard it was deceived. The Conference broke up after voting one more convention, this time a Soviet (or Council) of the Russian Republic, which would be a temporary Parliament until the opening of the

Constitutional Assembly. I was elected a deputy to this shadowy "Parliament," but I was not flattered. To the congratulations of my colleagues in the office of *The Will of the People,* I exclaimed: "To the devil with all these Councils of the Republic, Conferences, and Soviets! It would be better if we mobilized a hundred thousand good soldiers, under a strong leader, whose first act would be to shut us all up in lunatic asylums."

"You are angry because you are hungry," laughed Mr. Argunoff. "Let me present you with a loaf of good bread and then you will feel less pessimistic."

"I wish all the people had bread," I said soberly. "Then they as well as I would be more moderate."

"That is right, Sorokin, but alas, it is impossible."

"Then let us all be angry," I rejoined.

I have begun to study more intensively the great French Revolution. How history repeats itself. Who are we but Russian Girondists? What will be our fate? Their own? What will happen to the Fatherland? Probably the same horror of bloodshed and destruction, without any of the military glory that followed France's political and social upheaval.

I have to endure the sight of my wife and all our friends suffering from slow starvation. None complain, but by gay conversation we try to forget the

lack of food in our stomachs. Well, it is discipline
of a sort.

The Council of the Republic opened and from the
dignity of its first debates a foreign observer might
almost believe it a real Parliament. The Government participated in the opening sessions and in the
debates which followed. But to me the whole proceeding had the aspect of a drama of revolution with
half-grown children as the players. Sometimes,
listening to endless discussions of this or that trivial
question, I lost my temper and spoke angrily. But
to no effect. The Bolshevik delegates, after a declaration of their extreme program, left the Council
in a body.

"Our army can never fight again and the only
thing for us to do is to conclude peace as quickly as
possible." Such were the words of Minister of War
Verkhovsky, in the War Commission of the Council.
Like a pall the words fell upon the members of the
Revolutionary Democracy. Although some expressed condemnation of Verkhovsky, all knew that
he spoke the truth. Either by blood and iron discipline the army must be restored or the war must
be abandoned. "Democracy" will tolerate neither
iron discipline nor continuance of the war. Yet it
refuses to face the other alternative, anarchy.
"Democracy" is like that Russian hero standing at
the junction of three roads, one leading to the death
of his horse, another to the death of his wife, and
the third to his own death. It appears that we elect
the third road.

Again endless Governmental crises. Again sleepless nights in the Winter Palace and the Soviet. Just now it is a question of appointing a Minister of Agriculture.

"Who do you think might fill this place?" asks Kerensky.

"Well, if the man must be a Socialist, why not Oganovsky?" I suggest.

"Good! As a specialist in Agricultural Economy, and author of a book crowned by the Academy of Science, he is just the man. Please go to him at once and offer him the portfolio," says Kerensky.

I drive to the Soviet and seek out Oganovsky.

"No thank you," he says hastily. "Too much responsibility. But I might serve as Assistant Minister."

"Oh rubbish," I protested. "If I am in a position to nominate a Minister, surely the position itself is hardly bigger than that of a policeman in normal times."

"Nevertheless, I don't feel like taking it."

With this news I return to Kerensky whom I find reposing on a sofa.

"Well," he says wearily, "somebody has to be appointed. Make a suggestion."

"We might try Sem. Masloff."

"Sem. Masloff? Good. Go and convince him."

Again I get into Kerensky's motor car and drive to the Soviet. Masloff at first refuses point blank, but finally he yields to my persuasions.

"You must make one condition," comments a friend of us both who is present. "Masloff must cut his hair and buy a new cravat. Look at him. In such disreputable clothes he is an impossible Minister."

"A Revolutionary Minister may wear any cravat he likes," I declare with a laugh. "He may even dispense with a cravat altogether and appear only in his trousers. We shall all probably reach this stage very soon."

This whole performance is characteristic. In revolution, power lies in the street for anybody to pick up. My own position as a maker of Cabinet Ministers would be ridiculous if only it did not foreshadow a tragedy. Well, "on with the play!"

In all regiments the Bolsheviki have organized "Military Committees of the Revolution." This means new uprisings. I have bought a revolver, but would I shoot anybody? I do not know.

In view of the coming storm Kerensky has demanded of the Council of the Republic full and unequivocal support. The Socialist majority again has shown indecision. Instead of immediate action they begin their usual long debates, with the usual "inasmuch as." Hopeless! Hopeless!

Kerensky I cannot understand at all. He sees clearly the approaching Bolshevist revolution. He knows that the Government has no loyal troops, yet today he spoke in the Council assuring the members that "The Government is ready for immediate suppression of the revolt." Does this indicate utter imbecility or belief in his own lucky star? I am at a loss to know.

By thousands people are fleeing from Petrograd, and indeed why should they remain? They face starvation if not massacre by the Bolshevik mob.

"I advise you also to go," said a friend to whom I bade farewell at the railway station. "Get away as soon as you can, for a little later you won't be able to leave."

But leave Petrograd now I must not and cannot.

CHAPTER VIII

THE ABYSS

October-December, 1917.

The abyss has opened at last. Bolshevism has conquered. . . . It was all very simple. The Provisional Government and the first All-Russian Soviet were overthrown as easily as was the Czarist régime. Through their Military Committees of Revolution the Bolsheviki got control of the regiments. Through the Petrograd Workers' Soviet they became masters of the working classes. These soldiers and Petrograd workmen commandeered all automobiles in the street, occupied the Winter Palace, Petropavlovskaia Fortress, the railway stations, the telephones, and the posts. To destroy the old Government and to establish the new required only a bare twenty-four hours.

On October 25, in spite of illness, I set out for the Winter Palace to get news. In the streets I saw the familiar spectacle of speeding automobiles full of sailors and Latvian soldiers, firing recklessly as they passed; no trams, no droshkies. But so accustomed had all of us grown to this condition of things that I went on quite indifferently. Approaching the Winter Palace, I found it surrounded by Bolshevist troops. It would have been sheer folly to walk into their arms, so I turned around and sought, in the Mariinsky Palace, the Council of the Republic.

There I learned that while Kerensky had fled to the front to seek military assistance, Konovaloff and other Ministers, with the Governor of Petrograd, Rutenberg and Palchinsky, were barricaded in the Winter Palace defended only by a regiment of women soldiers and three hundred military cadets.

"This is outrageous!" stormed a Social Democratic deputy. "We shall certainly protest against such violence."

"What! Are we going to pass another resolution?" I asked.

"In the name of the Soviet, the Council of the Republic and the Government we shall appeal to the country and to the world democracy," he replied, offended at my levity.

"And what is that but another resolution?" I asked banteringly.

"We shall appeal to the military forces."

"What military forces?"

"Officers and Cossacks are still faithful."

"The same men whom the revolutionary democracy treated as counter-revolutionaries and reactionaries," I persisted. "Have you forgotten how you insulted them, especially after Korniloff's failure? After that do you imagine that they will be willing to defend us? I think, on the contrary, that they will be rather gratified at what has happened."

The Council of the Republic convened, and a proposal to protest against the criminal attack on the rights of the people and of the Government was made and debated. But the discussion did not last very long, for suddenly the Hall was invaded by a troop of soldiers who announced: "According to a decree of the new Government the Council of the Republic is dispersed. Leave here immediately or submit to arrest."

The chairman of the Council said: "The resolution of protest has been heard. All in favor raise their hands." The resolution was carried. Then the chairman said: "Under pressure of violence the Council of the Republic is temporarily interrupted." Such was the end of the first Republic, an end scarcely more heroic than that of the Duma.

With great difficulty I forced my way through the crowd to the committee of the Peasants' Soviet. Here also was great excitement. A minority of the Soviet, under the leadership of Spiridonova, Natanson, Steinberg, Katz, and, Schreider, were already preparing to join the Bolsheviki. The majority of the Soviet seemed rather helpless, but I perceived some signs of activity, for in one room the deputies were being furnished with revolvers and hand grenades. This at least was better than mere verbosity.

"Comrade Sorokin, have you a revolver?" the commander of our military section asked me, and on my affirmative reply he said: "Take another. You may need it."

It was decided that our members should meet that evening with the All-Russian Soviet, and as it seemed certain that the Bolsheviki, with the help of the Petrograd Soviet, would try to force the majority of the members of the All-Russian Soviet to join them, we agreed on the Municipal Duma, center of anti-Bolshevik activities, for rendezvous of this majority.

Lying ill all day on my bed, I listened to the steady booming of the cannon and the spatter of machine guns and crack of rifles. Over the telephone I learned that the Bolsheviki had brought up from Kronstadt the warship *Aurora* and had opened fire on the Winter Palace demanding the surrender of members of the Provisional Government, still barricaded there. At seven in the evening I went to the Municipal Duma. With many matters before us, the immediate horror that faced us was this situation at the Winter Palace. There a regiment of women and the military cadets were bravely resisting an overwhelming force of Bolshevist troops, and over the telephone Minister Konovaloff was appealing for aid. Poor women, poor lads, their situation was desperate, for we knew that the wild sailors, after taking the Palace, would probably tear them to pieces. What could we do? After breathless council it was decided that all of us, the Soviets, Municipalities, Committees of Socialist Parties, members of the Council of the Republic, should go in procession to the Winter Palace and do our utmost to rescue the Ministers, the women soldiers, and the cadets. Even as we prepared to go, over the telephone came the despairing shout: "The gates of the Palace have been forced. The massacre has begun. . . . Hurry! The mob has reached the first floor. All is over. Good-bye. . . They break in! They are . . ." That last word of Konovaloff from the Winter Palace was a broken cry.

Rushing out, we formed in some kind of an orderly line and in the darkness of the unlighted street we started, a few dim lanterns showing us our way. Never had Petrograd seen such a hopeless march. In absolute silence like phantoms we moved forward. Near Kazansky Cathedral three loaded automobiles full of sailors, machine guns, and bombs stopped us.

"Halt! Who goes there?"

"Representatives of the Municipality, the Soviets, the Council of the Republic, and the Socialistic Parties."

"Where are you going?"

"To the Winter Palace, to end this civil war and to save the defenders of the Palace."

"Nobody can approach the Palace. Turn back at once or we fire on you."

Nothing to do, we returned in ghastly silence to the Municipal Duma. There we made one more effort to communicate with the Palace, but the wires had by this time been cut. The firing had ceased and we knew that the massacre was probably in full swing.

Along pitch-dark streets I staggered to my home where I found my wife half-dead with anxiety for me. But I calmed her. "My dear wife, we must now be prepared for whatever comes. The worst, in all human probability."

Next day I went out to meet my unhappy associates. The aspect of things was horrible. At the corner of Zhamensky and Basseyny Streets I came on a crowd of soldiers plundering a wine-shop. Already brutally drunk, they yelled: "Long life to the Bolsheviki and death to capitalistic government!'' In other places similar scenes. Huge crowds of soldiers, sailors, and workmen plundered the cellars of the Winter Palace. Broken bottles littered the square, cries, shrieks, groans, obscenities, filled the clean morning. Many of those who entered the cellars could not get out owing to the press of those who madly pushed forward to get in. The cellars swam in wine from broken casks and bottles and many men were actually drowned in the flood of it.

The besieged Ministers had not been murdered but had been rushed off to Petropavlovskaia Fortress to join the Ministers of the Czar. But the fate of the women was even worse than our imaginations had been able to picture. Many had been killed, and those who escaped merciful death had been savagely ravished by the Bolsheviki. Some of these women soldiers were so vilely abused that they died in frightful agony. Some of the officials of the Provisional Government were also murdered with sadistic cruelty.

Oh Liberty, what crimes, what unspeakable crimes. In thy name!

The news from Kerensky was indefinite. The Central Committees of the Social Revolutionary and the Social Democratic Parties met, and some effort was made towards organizing a force of cadets from the military schools.

In the office of my newspaper I wrote my first article on the conquerors, hailing them as murderers, ravishers, brigands, and robbers. I signed this article with my full name, in spite of the protests of my colleagues and even the compositors. "Let it stand," I said. "We all face death anyhow." As a matter of fact my article had such a success that we had to print three times the usual number of papers. But while my friends lauded it, the mobs in the streets and even in private houses grew larger and more lawless. Murders, assaults, looting, especially of wine shops, increased. Passion for drink grew so great that the crowd risked even death to effect the immediate "nationalization" of the dram shops. In desperation citizens prepared to defend their homes. In the evening an armed band broke into our newspaper office to arrest all the editors. Fortunately, there was present only Lebedeff, formerly Minister of the Navy in Kerensky's Cabinet, and he managed to escape through a back door. My friends begged me not to spend the night at my home, and I decided to follow their advice. I consented also to change my appearance by ceasing to shave. Many are doing the same, clean shaven men appearing with beards, bearded men shaving.

Next day brought no news of Kerensky, but we heard of a fight near Gatchino, and of the massacre of all the cadets in Petrograd military schools. These young heroes fought like lions and died at last like true patriots. Everything is closed, schools, shops, banks, offices. Hunger is everywhere increasing.

Kerensky is defeated. The Bolsheviki have taken

the banks, State and private, and my former friend
Pyatakoff has been made Commissary of Finance.
From the front come new tales of horror. General-
issimo Dukhonin has been murdered with hundreds
of other officers. Our army is now a wild flying mob
which destroys everything that stands in its path.
German invasion is inevitable.

Clerks and officials of governmental and private
institutions have organized a strike as a protest
against Bolshevist excesses. Their sabotage handi-
caps the new rulers, who have begun a merciless
persecution of the people. Many are imprisoned.
In spite of all this, the strikers hold firmly. Today
I spoke at their meeting and just as I closed the
chairman cried: "They have come for you. Run
through this door." I reached the street and was
quickly borne away in an automobile kept for emer-
gencies by these simple heroes.

The play of cat and mouse has begun. Well, let
us be a mouse. We shall be caught, but until that
happens we shall do what conscience and duty still
dictate.

Today my colleague Argunoff, one of the founders
of the Social Revolutionary Party, fell into the
claws of the cat. Management and publication of
newspapers will now be carried on under difficulties.
Invasion of editorial offices and printing plants have
become an everyday routine. Bolshevik soldiers
destroy copy and even presses. As a matter of
form, we obey orders to cease our publications, but

they reappear immediately under slightly altered names. *The Will of the People* suppressed yesterday appears today as *The Will*, and later on as *The People, The Wish of the People*, and so on. The newspaper *The Day* appears as *Morning, Midday, Afternoon, Evening, Night, Black Midnight, One O'Clock, Two O'Clock*. What is important is that our newspapers are finally published. The readers who fail to get one in the morning read one at night.

Today again I narrowly escaped arrest. As I entered the courtyard of our building a band of persecutors followed me, some going to the office, others remaining at the gate. Fortunately, they did not know me by sight, and as it was dark I lingered outside devising plans of escape. One of our printers emerging from the doorway, I called him and explained my plight. "Just a moment," he said, and in a few minutes he came back with a certificate identifying me as one of the working force. "All right now. Let us go out together as though for supper." At the gate we were stopped and our certificates demanded. We showed them and the guard said gruffly: "Pass on." So again the mouse escaped. It is an interesting fact that this persecution is conducted by the very men who a few days ago were loudest in clamoring for a free press.

Our daily menu at home becomes exotic. There is no bread, but yesterday we found at a small shop a few tins of preserved peaches. For bread we prepare "cake" from potato skins, and find it not too awful to swallow. Long life to the Revolution which stimulates invention and makes the people more modest in their appetites and desires!

Elections to the Constitutional Assembly are being held all over Russia. These elections are a challenge of the country to the Bolshevist Revolution. If the Bolsheviki are right, they will get a majority of votes. Very soon we shall have the verdict of Russia. Of course, the Bolsheviki do everything in their power to block the elections, and all the hunted mice are doing their best to facilitate them. During the past week I have spoken at twelve meetings. The working people are in the first stage of "sobering off." The Bolshevist paradise is beginning to fade, and hostility to social patriots is disappearing. Three times the workers have saved me from arrest. At a meeting at the Trubochny factory a group of armed men came in and interrupted my speech, shouting: "At last we have caught you. You are arrested." I shouted back: "I am arrested if these workmen consent."

"Take your hands off comrade Sorokin!" roared the audience. While one crowd held back the soldiers another surrounded and hurried me to a safe refuge.

The first results of the elections have been published and the Bolsheviki are beaten. They, together with the left Social Revolutionary Revolutionaries are far behind the right wing of the party, and both are in a minority in the Constitutional Assembly. My name and those of other comrades in Vologda Province gained about ninety per cent of all votes.

Last night we celebrated in a most extravagant banquet, each of us having a bit of bread, half a sausage, preserved peaches, and tea with sugar!

The Bolsheviki are decisively beaten, but our situation becomes more serious, our responsibilities incomparably heavier. Had the Bolsheviki received a majority we should have submitted, but the votes of the people declare them an illegal Government. Yet we know that the Bolsheviki have no intention of accepting the verdict. As long as they hoped for a favorable vote they were willing for the Constitutional Assembly to meet. Now they will try to prevent its meeting. We must meet force with force. There is no other way.

"The Committee for the Defence of the Constitutional Assembly" has been formed. In the sphere of propaganda it does well, but in the assembling of military forces not so well. We have some troops, but obviously not so many as the Bolsheviki. Every day I speak, attend sittings of the leaders who are elaborating laws, decrees, and policies of the Constituent Assembly. In between I play the role of mouse against cat. Legally all deputies are immune from arrest, but the law is one thing, Bolshevist practice another. All roads now lead to prison. I am tired, exhausted, partly with work and excitement, partly with hunger. But I repeat the words of the poet: "Wait a little and you will have your rest." In prison or in the grave.

As an opening attack on the Constituent Assembly the Bolsheviki ordered all deputies to go to

Uritsky, an especially appointed commissary, to register their names and addresses and to offer documentary proofs of their election to the Assembly, the opening of which has been postponed from November 27 to January 5, 1918.

We declared this order illegal. The deputies of the people cannot be prevented from assembling by Uritsky, the verification of their claims being a matter for a special committee of deputies in which the Bolsheviki are fully represented. We object also to the arbitrary postponement of the agreed informal meeting of deputies on November 27.

November 27—

The legal opening day of the Constituent Assembly dawned beautifully clear. Blue sky, white snow, an auspicious background for the huge placards everywhere displayed. "Long Life to the Constitutional Assembly, the Master of Russia." Crowds of people, bearing these standards, welcome the highest authority of the country, the real voice of the Russian people. As the deputies approached the Tavrichesky Palace, thousands of people hailed them with deafening cheers. But when the deputies reached the gates they found them closed and guarded by Bolshevist Lettish soldiers, armed to the teeth.

Something had to be done, and at once. Climbing the iron fence of the Palace I addressed the people while other deputies climbed and scrambled after me. They managed to unlock the gates and the crowds rushed in filling the courtyard. Staggered

at the audacity of this move, the Lettish soldiers
hesitated. We attacked the doors of the Palace,
also guarded by Lettish soldiers and officers behind
whom appeared Uritsky and other Bolsheviki. Again
speaking to the people, I concluded by thanking the
Lettish soldiers for their welcome to the highest
authority in Russia and their apparent willingness
to guard its liberties. At last I even embraced the
commanding officer. The whole lot wavered in confusion and as a result the doors were opened and
we walked in, many of the citizens following. In
the passage Uritzky, an exceedingly repulsive Jew,
demanded that we go to his office to register, but
contemptuously we pushed him aside saying that
the Constitutional Assembly stood in no need of
his services. In the Hall of the Palace we held our
meeting and called upon the Russian nation to defend its Constitutional Assembly. A resolution was
passed that the Assembly, in spite of every obstacle,
should open on January 5.

To ensure its successful meeting, we hold daily
meetings in the factories and among the soldiers.
At the same time the leaders continue their work of
preparing fundamental laws and decrees, methods
of procedure, etc. These conferences are usually
held in my apartment. In the face of the great
crisis ahead we have at last buried all differences
of opinion and work in absolute accord. Yet there
are occasional signs of the old fatal weakness.

Today at a meeting of representatives of the
Petrograd Garrison, the subject under discussion

was the relation of soldiers to the Constitutional Assembly. Speakers of all parties were present. The Garrison was inclined to assume a passive attitude, not inimical of course, but not aggressively defensive. Exasperated by this cursed pacifism, I burst out, begging the soldiers to remember how many generations of Russian people had dreamed of the Constitutional Assembly as the greatest blessing that could ever happen. "Thousands of men and women," I told them, "have sacrificed their lives for the realization of this dream. Now when the great dream is about to come true, when the Constitutional Assembly is about to open, you dally with the idea of a Bolshevist paradise, you refuse to do your duty. Traitors to your country! If you cling to this mad delusion you will reap its certain fruits. Within a few months you will face starvation, tyranny, civil war, and horrors which you cannot even imagine. Remember then what voices warned you of what this treachery would certainly bring. That is all I have to say." Two regiments promise to be active in defending the Assembly. Of the others I have no hope.

The hand of the destroyer lies heavily on Petrograd. All commercial life is stopped. Shops are closed. In the factories discipline and authority have disappeared, the workers spending their time in vacuous conversation and oratory. Mounds of dirty snow block the streets. Night and day we hear the sounds of guns. Madness, plundering, and pillage lay waste the towns and even the country.

There exists no longer any army and the Germans can walk in whenever they choose.

This is the last day of 1917. I look back on the year with feelings of bitterness and disillusionment. The year 1917 gave us the Revolution, but what has Revolution brought to my country but ruin and disgrace? Has it brought us freedom? Has it bettered the condition of the people? No, the face of revolution unveiled is the face of a beast, of a vicious and wicked prostitute, not that of the pure goddess which has been painted by historians of other revolutions. I could pray that these historians themselves might live through a real revolution.

At New Year's we meet together, the Social Revolutionary leaders and deputies. Dull sorrow mingled with grim resolution to die fighting for liberty mark all our speeches. This mournful enthusiasm reached its climax after the speech of my friend K-, when we listened to the singing of the famous aria from Mussorgsky's opera, "Khovanschina" ("The Strelets Sleeps").

"My poor Russia sleeps; she is encompassed by enemies! Aliens are robbing her. Long years before it lay under the yoke of the Tartars, it groaned under the yoke of the aristocrats. My poor Russia! Who now will save you from your foes? Who will save you from your misfortunes? O loved and unhappy Russia!" The words moved us profoundly.

"We do not know who will save our Russia. But whatever sorrows lie before you now, dear country, you shall not perish. From these ashes you will rise, a great country and a great nation, a power among the powers of the earth. If for this it is necessary for us to lay down our lives, we are ready. May our Fatherland be forever blessed.'' Such were the words of the eloquent K- which closed our New Year's celebration. The prospects for 1918 are very dark, but come what may I believe in my country and its historical mission. Sooner or later we shall find the way out. Be blessed every day and every night my beloved country.

PART II

1918

CHAPTER IX

Trapped! At last the Bolshevist cat has caught his mouse, and now I shall have plenty of time for repose. My labors for the time suspended I can lie all day in my peaceful cell hearing from a safe distance the devil music of the machine guns. My arrest occurred on January 2, 1918. After a sitting of the Committee of the Constitutional Assembly, Mr. Argunoff and I went to the offices of *The Will of the People*. Arrived at our office on the third floor of the building we found everything apparently normal, but when we opened the door we were met by five or six men with leveled revolvers.

"Hands up!" they cried.

"What's the matter?"

"You are all under arrest."

"Members of the Constitutional Assembly are immune from arrest," I said, knowing well the futility of my words.

"Never mind. We are ordered to arrest you. That is all."

Glancing around I saw that every person in the room was a prisoner and that the whole place had been thoroughly ransacked.

"But most of these people are workmen," I protested, "and have nothing to do with politics. I insist on their release."

117

At last, yielding to reason, the ranking officer agreed to take only the editors, Argunoff, Stalinsky, Gukovsky, and myself, and from the business office Mrs. Argunoff and three clerks. The whole group was driven to the Chekha, this new terroristic organization. Here, confined in separate rooms, we waited. After about an hour a man came to my room and ordered me to follow him. In the office of the Chekha I met Mr. Argunoff who, with me, was put into a motor car and driven off at a rapid speed. Our body-guards were silent and the window shuttered, so we had no idea of our destination. A quarter of an hour later the car stopped, we alighted and found ourselves inside the walls of Petropavlovskaia Fortress, the Bastille of Petrograd.

In the office of the Commandant we found six or seven Bolshevist soldiers idly talking. For some time they paid no attention to us, but one, toying with his revolver, pointed it once or twice in our direction. Finally, we broke the silence.

"How long are we expected to wait? Is no one going to examine us?"

"The Commandant will be here in a few minutes."

"Can we get any food? We are hungry."

"There is no food."

"Are prisoners allowed to see their relatives and receive from them food, blankets, books, and linen?"

"Generally, yes. But for you, no."

"Why?"

"Because you deserve not only imprisonment but immediate execution."

"For what offense?"

"For attempt against the life of Lenin."

"Against the life of Lenin! Do you mean to say that we are accused of that?"

"You are under arrest for the attempted assassination of Lenin."

This was interesting news indeed. While we were digesting it the Commandant Pavlov, a man noted for his abnormal cruelties, entered the room, and after an icy glance at us, ordered the soldiers to lead us to number 63. A few minutes later a door of a cell in the Trubetskoy Bastion clanged after us. We were prisoners of Peter and Paul.

Number 63 of this celebrated Bastion was a small cell with one heavily barred window. It was cold and dirty, with streaks of half-frozen water on the walls. There were no chairs, no bed, and on the floor was simply a ragged mat of straw. Our eyes growing used to the half-light, we discovered the silhouettes of two men drawn in pencil on the wall, and underneath a scrawled legend: "In this cell were imprisoned the Rumanian Ambassador and the Attaché of the Rumanian Embassy." Some days before they had been arrested, and now we were in the cell where first they had been confined. "Some consolation, at least, to find ourselves in such aristocratic quarters," said Mr. Argunoff.

"Well," said I, "I have been a prisoner of the Czar, and now I am a prisoner of the Communists.

Out of this varied experience I should emerge a practical as well as a theoretical criminologist.''

"I should call you a recidivist criminal," suggested Argunoff jocosely.

"If so, I am in good company," I retorted.

Thus we jested, and when Argunoff mentioned hunger I reminded him that since the Communists were the most advanced people in the world, they must know what was good for us. After an hour of this we "went to bed" by huddling together on the damp and ragged straw mat. In silence and darkness our souls wrestled with secret apprehensions. I thought of my wife waiting at home for me in vain, her anguish when she learned the cause of my absence; the difficulties of the Assembly, the fate of our newspaper. These troubled thoughts, combined with cold, dampness, and hunger, murdered sleep. Suddenly my companion, also sleepless, began to laugh.

"Did any of us who prepared and welcomed the Revolution ever expect to be arrested by a Revolutionary Government?"

We both laughed and then I asked Argunoff: "How does this cell compare with your Czarist prison?"

"About as a country inn compares with a first class hotel," he answered truthfully.

"Ah, that proves you a counter-revolutionary."

Silence again, broken by the dripping of water from the walls and interrupted now and again by the staccatto of machine gun fire and the melodic chimes of the fortress, ringing every hour: "How

Glorious is our God.'' What hundreds of revolutionists of the past have listened to those chimes. What tragedies have been enacted beneath them. During two centuries these dumb walls have witnessed fever, despair, death, and execution. Within these fortress walls lie the bones of many revolutionists. Here, in the church of the fortress lie the mortal remains of the Romanoffs, beginning with Peter the Great and ending with Alexander III. Rebels and autocrats alike, their shades watch this hurricane of Revolution which furiously rages above their ashes. The Revolution will pass, its actors disappear, but the shades will remain, while new tragedies and comedies enact themselves upon the earth.

At seven the next morning the cell door opened and a warden appeared bringing hot water, a small quantity of sugar and a quarter of a pound of bread for each one of us. ''You will soon be moved to a more comfortable cell,'' he said encouragingly. ''At least, I shall try.'' And sure enough, in about an hour he returned with the cheerful summons: ''Come along.''

The new cell was indeed much better, warmer, and dryer, with two beds and a sort of table attached to the wall.

''How do you do?'' A voice greeted us through a small hole in the door. ''Could we ever have imagined meeting here?''

Looking up I beheld Professor Kokoshkin and Mr. Shingareff, former Ministers in the Kerensky Government.

"Representatives of the sovereign people, welcome to this shrine of liberty," said Mr. Avksentieff, former Minister of the Interior. Very soon other Ministers, Tereschenko, Kishkin, Bernatsky, Prince Dolgorouky, leader of the Constitutional Democratic Party, Palchinsky, late Military Governor of Petrograd, and Ruthenberg, now one of the principal organizers of the Jewish State in Palestine, came to our door and congratulated us. They brought us bread, tea, sugar, some books, and also news of the prison. Arrested immediately after the Bolshevist Revolution, these men had been in the Fortress for two months and were now old residents, privileged characters, so to speak. With them, in the most friendly spirit, mingled representatives of the old régime, Purishkevitz, leader of the Monarchists in the Duma, Shcheglovitoff, former Minister of Justice, and Sukhomlinoff, Minister of War in the Czar's Government. They all met us, and I imagine, saw with some pleasure members of the new Government in the same position as themselves.

At four o'clock we were taken out for exercise in the yard of the prison, and had the happiness to meet our friends. Their appearance had altered sadly, Kokoshkin and Shingareff looking really ill. Tereschenko, from a man very *comme il faut,* always cleanly shaven and exquisitely dressed, was transformed into a bearded man in shabby trousers and a sweater. Purishkevitz looked like a janitor, the work of which he really performed in prison. Walking up and down the small yard, our comrades warned us that our position in the fortress was extremely perilous. The wardens of the Bastion, Social Democrat Internationalists, were decent men, but the garrison itself was governed by Bolsheviki. In connection with the alleged attempt on the life of Lenin, they had issued a proclamation threatening a St. Bartholomew Night and a September Massacre of all prisoners of the fortress. "The sooner all these counter-revolutionists are killed the better," concluded this proclamation.

Later, we all learned the truth about this attempted assassination of Lenin. A tire of his motor car blew out and Lenin, terrified, took this for the report of a pistol. That was all there was to it. Kokoshkin and Shingareff proved to be in an acute stage of tuberculosis and were soon to be removed to the Mariynskaia Hospital. "Of course we are glad to go," said Shingareff, "but our happiness is clouded by the thought that you must all remain." Even in his weakened condition this man could not forget the misfortunes of others.

Little by little we adapted ourselves to the routine of prison. At seven o'clock we got up, received hot water, a little sugar, and a quarter of a pound of bread for the day. At noon we had our dinner, consisting of hot water with some cabbage and a bit of meat. At four o'clock there was afternoon tea—hot water, and at seven, supper—more hot water. In our dietary was too much water and too little anything else, but as we received a little extra food from friends, we did not actually want. The gloom of the prison was hard to bear. Even at noon

in our cell with its one high window looking out on
the fortress wall, it was difficult to read or to write.
In the morning and afternoon the place was quite
dark.   Sometimes the electric light was turned on
between six and ten o'clock, sometimes for not more
than an hour during the whole day.   Much of our
time had to be spent in weary idleness.   The hardships of life under the Revolution had, however, developed in us all a keener sense of humor, enabling
us to meet all new trials with a certain philosophy.

Talking with our friends during the half an hour
of exercise every day, exchanging news, cleaning the
yard from snow and ice, gazing at the blue sky, we
kept ourselves in fair health and spirits.   As long
as daylight lasted within doors we read and wrote,
and some of us studied English.   The adventurous
novels of Conan Doyle and of Alexandre Dumas
most entertained us.   Like boys, we devoured these
romances, adopting in our conversation the phrases
employed by our favorite heroes.   "Swear by the
five fingers of my hand," this expression from
Conan Doyle became a popular expression.

The dark hours of the late afternoon and of the
night were very irksome, lying down or pacing the
cell, and thinking endlessly of family, friends, and
the unhappy country.   It was a week after our
arrest before we had news of our wives.   Mrs.
Argunoff had been arrested with us, and I feared
that my wife also might have been taken.   Where?
If free how did she fare?   Life in Petrograd was
so full of danger that it is no wonder my mind was
distraught.

With great anxiety we looked forward to January 5, the opening day of the Constitutional Assembly. In newspapers brought us by the warden we read that all arrested members of the Assembly were to be allowed to attend the first meeting. We even read that Argunoff, Avksentieff, and myself, had been liberated on January 4 and that our speeches, the text of which was actually published, were well received by the deputies! With excitement we awaited reports of the first day's sitting. Intense firing around noon of the day disquieted us, but we tried to believe that it was only the every-day music of the Revolution. At eight o'clock word came, partly through the warden, partly through the evening newspapers he brought us. The Constitutional Assembly had opened. The ceremony of opening, election of the president, first speeches, turbulent behavior of the crowds in the galleries, and the calm behavior of the deputies facing terrible conditions, these we had expected. In the same newspaper I was astonished to read the speech I had planned to deliver at this first sitting. It was so fully reported that only those who knew I was in the fortress were aware that it had never been given at all. While this paper was being printed, the condition of the Assembly was extremely critical. That morning thousands of people had gone out to welcome it, but Bolshevist machine guns met them and killed and wounded many. The streets, we afterwards learned, were strewn with bullet-ridden bodies. Such was the reception of the Bolsheviki to the Russian National Assembly and to the unarmed citizenry who went out to see realized the long dream of the Russian people. "The dispersal of the Assembly and arrest of the deputies is only a question of hours," we agreed after reading and hearing this terrible news.

Up to this time all anti-Bolshevists had done their best to avoid civil war, but what was the use of such a policy when now these murderers were butchering hundreds and thousands of innocent people, forcibly suppressing the expressed will of the nation and handing Russia over to the German foe? Such were our feelings and the feelings of all loyal hearts throughout the country.

Next morning being the feast of Twelfth-Day, we were allowed to attend service in the Cathedral of St. Peter and Paul in the fortress. We listened standing among the tombs of the Russian Emperors, lying peacefully in their eternal sleep.

"The Constitutional Assembly is dispersed," we read that day in the newspapers. Utterly depressed in spirits, we met that afternoon in the prison yard, saying good-bye to Kokoshkin and Shingareff, who that evening were to go to the hospital. Next day one of the wardens, bringing our dinner, said:

"Have you heard of your friends?"

"No; has anything happened?"

"They were killed last night by Communists who broke into the hospital."

In utter horror we listened to the story. The plan for murdering Kokoshkin and Shingareff was made while they were still in the fortress, and by the connivance of Commandant Pavlov. "I have to tell you," added the warden, "that attempts may be made to kill you also. We shall try to prevent them, and the only thing for us to do, in case the men come in great numbers, is to open the doors of your cells and of this passage to the yard. Only there is no way out of the yard."

"At least do that," we begged. "It would be better to die in the open than inside like rats in a trap."

All during that half an hour of exercise we discussed our situation. Ruthenberg, nicknamed by us "Rinaldo-Rinaldino," for his ever-dashing and picturesque suggestions, was for disarming the wardens, leaving the Bastion, and fighting our way past the guards and out. The plan, of course, was hopeless. Purishkeich knew of an ancient underground passage leading from the Mint in the fortress grounds to the old house of Peter the Great, near the Troitzky Bridge. In what condition this subway was nobody could guess. But if the door were opened it might be possible to reach the Mint and try to make the underground way. We agreed to try it. Back in our cells, thoughts of Kokoshkin and Shingareff returned to torment us. Anything more wantonly cruel than this murder was difficult to imagine. Both men had devoted their lives to social and patriotic service, and now, sick to death, they had been butchered in their sleep as "enemies of the people." Night came, but we could not sleep.

About eleven o'clock we heard voices, the sound of opening and closing doors, the rattling of keys. "Don't be alarmed," said a warden at the door.

"It is only new prisoners who have just been brought in." Next day we met many of these prisoners, leaders of the Peasants' Soviet, members of the Central Committee of the Social Democratic Party, and deputies to the Constitutional Assembly. Arrests by wholesale were being made, they told us. Some prisoners were being sent to Kresty and other small prisons, while the most "distinguished" prisoners were being rushed to the fortress.

The Devil's Pepper Pot, an anti-Bolshevist newspaper published at this time: "The Winter season in the health resort of Petropavlovskaia Fortress has opened brilliantly. Prominent Ministers, statesmen, politicians, representatives of the people, writers and other distinguished gentlemen of the Czarist and Provisional Governments, members of the Soviets and of the Assembly, leaders of the Monarchist, Constitutional Democratic, Social Democratic, and Social Revolutionary Parties are taking vacations in this celebrated resort with its well-known methods of medical treatment by cold, hunger, and compulsory rest, interrupted at times by surgical operations, butcheries, and other excitements. There is reason to believe that in the near future this exclusive circle will become even larger and more brilliant. Other health resorts, especially Kresty and Gorokhovaia, are becoming quite crowded."

In some ways our condition became a little better. We received letters and twice a week were permitted visits from near relatives. From eight to ten every evening our cell doors were left open and we could thus mingle with fellow-prisoners. We exchanged news and were kept fairly well informed of what was going on outside. We even managed to edit our paper, writing articles and editorials which were taken out and published exactly as we wrote them. This reminded me of my first imprisonment in Kineshma, under the Czar, when our prison became the principal center for the revolutionary propaganda of the day. Such things, I am sure, can happen only in Russia.

The weekly meetings with my wife and with one dear friend were the happiest moments of my prison life. Once I was deeply touched by a visit from a peasant from Vologda Province who, being in Petrograd for a few days, spent a lot of time and energy trying to get permission to see me. At last he succeeded and came to the fortress bringing me half a pound of butter, all he had.

"Devils! What are they doing to you?" he cried furiously.

"Be careful, my friend," I warned, "they may arrest you."

"Let them arrest me. I am sixty-seven years old. What can these scoundrels do to me? Nothing."

If we had more such stout-hearted peasants, the present state of things would not be.

My wife and our friends have tried their best to effect our release. Up to this time their efforts have failed, but they are not altogether hopeless. The accusation of attempted assassination of Lenin has, of course, proven groundless, but now they have a new charge, "Participation in creating a psychical atmosphere favorable to attempts against the Bolshevist Government.'' The charge was general, no specific reason for our arrest being given. A month passed and we decided to send a protest against our confinement with a demand for our immediate release. This was addressed to ''The so-called Minister of Justice of the so-called Soviet Government,'' Mr. Steinberg. This extreme left Social Revolutionary and his Assistant Minister, Schreider, had been associated with us in the Social Revolutionary Party and in the Peasants' Soviet. Mr. Steinberg had become a Socialist only in March, 1917, but growing more and more radical, he rose in his career, and after the Bolshevist Revolution was appointed Minister of Justice. Schreider, nicknamed by the Peasants' Soviet ''the goat,'' on account of his long beard and his little wit, was a stupid but pretentious person. We thought our protest hopeless, but a few days after it was sent the door of our cell opened and in the half-darkness we saw the figure of Schreider. He stepped in and held out his hand, which none of us appeared to notice.

''How do you do, comrades!''

''Quite well, thank you, Mr. Minister of Justice, or Mr. Goat, which ever you prefer,'' said one of us. Others began to accuse him of arresting us without cause and keeping us under conditions unheard of in the time of the Czars. ''You were arrested by the Chekha, not by us,'' said Schreider. But we insisted that he and ''that fellow Steinberg'' were Ministers of Justice and therefore responsible, and we finished by telling him to go away and think it over—if he could think at all.

It was encouraging to hear, as we did at this time, that the murder of Kokoshkin and Shingareff had aroused such a storm of indignation in Petrograd that even Lenin realized that he had gone too far and that repetition of such atrocities was forbidden for the time being. Yet the bloodthirstiness of the soldiers and sailors did not abate, and the garrison of the fortress once more began to agitate for a general massacre of prisoners. One night four soldiers went to the guard's office and demanded the keys to the cells. The head guard, to his credit, absolutely refused, saying that he would relinquish his keys to no one except on written authority of the Minister of Justice. With a prophecy that this would soon be forthcoming, the "head-hunters" left. The Ministry of Justice was communicated with next day, and with the memory of the murder of Kokoshkin and Shingareff, and the fury which this produced fresh in their minds, the Ministers issued orders against any attempt on the lives of prisoners.

Everything has its end in this world, and our imprisonment in Petropavlovskaia finally came to an end. One evening a warden came to my cell with the abrupt announcement: "Your wife and a friend are in the office with an order for your release. Take your things and come along." The friend turned out to be a man quite unknown to me personally. He was an old Revolutionist named Kramaroff.

Now he was an Internationalist and was co-operating with the Bolsheviki. Nevertheless, he bravely opposed the methods of the Chekha, and when he heard of my arrest, he went vigorously to work to secure my release. Now, having been at last successful, he came in person to the fortress to see that I left the prison without violence from the guards.

Warmly I pressed the hands of those left behind in captivity, for the moment of liberation is always poisoned by the thought of those who cannot go free. Leaving the Bastion, we stopped at the office of the Commandant to have my order of release signed, and Kramaroff, addressing the brutal Pavlov, said contemptuously: "Well, rogue, when do you expect to be hanged?" These insulting words, far from offending the Commandant, seemed to please him. "Who the devil can hang me?" he asked laughing. Kramaroff replied that he knew plenty of men who would enjoy doing so, whereat Pavlov said complacently: "I know, but most of them are here now in my hotel."

Ten minutes later, after fifty-seven days and nights of imprisonment, I drove out of the fortress.

CHAPTER X

THE CAT AND THE MICE

AFTER about a week in Petrograd, my wife and I went to Moscow. The city of Peter the Great was dying, and with it was passing an epoch of Russian history, the period which during two centuries transformed Moscovia into the Russian Empire, created a true Russian culture, and achieved greatly in art, literature, and science. Now it was all passing. Thousands of Petrograd families, menaced with starvation and in deadly fear of the German invasion, which was rapidly nearing the capital, were fleeing the town. Even the Bolshevist Government was moving to Moscow. Settling my affairs as well as I could, and securing from the Government a positive pledge that my companions in Peter and Paul would be released, my wife and I, after incredible difficulties, secured tickets and places in the Moscow express. With deep sadness we left Petrograd, for behind us lay all our past, and before us lay we knew not what. In the filthy and over-crowded car, emaciated faces, suffering bodies, criminal countenances of Bolshevist agents, and all the vileness of the unrestrained mob surrounded us. We pressed our faces to the unwashed windows. Farewell, beloved city. Farewell, the monument of Peter the Great, still left standing in the Admiralty Gardens, to give us hope that neither Russia nor

133

the Russian people are utterly doomed. Now forward! Our hopes were still alive, our courage strong. Was it not said: "The Kingdom of Heaven suffereth violence and the violent take it by force?" And did not the founder of Petrograd say: "Know that the life of Peter is nothing to him. What is everything is that Russia may live and prosper." In this frame of mind we patiently endured the thirty-seven-hour journey to Moscow, a matter of fourteen hours in normal times.

Moscow! What the name means to a Russian heart. What emotions it awakens in the Russian soul. Yet now, if Petrograd impresses one as a dying capital, Moscow reminds him of a disturbed anthilloc. Throngs of refugees pouring into the town, Bolshevist officials trying to force communist doctrines on people who abhor them, peasants illegally bringing in and selling food and bread, and thereby saving the population from starvation, wrangling politicians and intellectuals, all these, together with the excited masses, give the impression of a furiously boiling pot. Many houses have been burned, many more damaged, many walls marked with bullets and bombs. Some streets, as Prechistenka and Nikitskaia, are completely wrecked. Upon my arrival, I called on a friend, formerly a rich merchant, and found him now "nationalized," all his property, even to his furniture and household treasures, "requisitioned." The bare walls of his house had been left him, and he had been ordered to leave the house within three days' time. I asked him what he intended to do.

"What can I do?" he asked patiently. "With my sick wife I am going temporarily to the home of a friend who has offered us a room. I am not so unhappy as you might think. Now I have no business for them to interfere with. As a free proletarian I can go about, look, and observe. The thing I most regret is that my wealth has gone, not for the common good but for the enrichment of scoundrels."

Next day I met other friends, scientists, scholars, and politicians, many workmen and peasants. The infamous Treaty of Brest-Litovsk leaving Russia in the hands of ruthless Germany, destroying the country both financially and morally, aroused in all classes the utmost rage and indignation. To Moscow flocked thousands determined to arrive at some constructive plan for saving the name of Russia from shame and dishonor. Something had to be done to stay the hand of destruction, and quickly, for the morale of the populace was beginning to break down. Crazed with hunger, peasants and workers had already begun to strike, riot, and plunder. The Bolsheviki did nothing to restore peace. On the contrary, after having broken up the Constitutional Assembly, they began to break up all newly elected Soviets which in any degree resisted their tyranny. The despotic nature of their policy became daily more apparent. While the autocratically appointed (not elected) All-Russian Conference of the Soviets held their meeting in Moscow, a meeting in which the American Red Cross Colonel, Raymond Robins, actively participated, while they were welcoming the "Power of the Peasants and

Workers," we renewed our activities. We knew
that the country was too exhausted, too demoralized
to fight victoriously, still we hoped that there was in
the social and individual life of the nation material
for regeneration. We therefore organized the
nucleus of a "League for the Regeneration of Russia," recruited from liberal parties, beginning with
Socialists and ending with the more radical members of the Constitutional Democratic Party. We
sought first to learn the actual state of mind of
people in all parts of Russia, and next to form plans
for military defense of the country against further
German invasion. All our meetings and conferences had to be held secretly, and old methods of
procedure which we had thought to abandon forever
when the Czar was overthrown were revived.
"Good habits always come in handy," said Argunoff, whose long experience in revolutionary
practices made him something of a leader in this
respect, even among revolutionists as experienced
as himself.

My personal connection with this new society was
curtailed by ill-health, caused by nervous strain, in-
tensive scientific work just before the Revolution,
by subsequent confinement, and finally by starvation. Rest and good food were ordered, and to get
both I decided to spend three or four weeks in one
of the Volga towns. One evening in March my wife
and I went to the Poveletsky Station, railway tickets
in our pockets, hoping to find places in the train.
Tickets in our communist country were not easy te
procure, but after two days of hard work and per-

suasion we got them. At the station nobody could tell us when the train would start, but a huge crowd was waiting to rush it as soon as it arrived. After seven hours it rolled into the station, and then ensued a spectacle quite indescribable. The whole enormous crowd rushed madly forward, jamming, pressing, fighting, shrieking, climbing one man on top of another, and finally seizing places, in the train, on top of the wagons, on the platforms between wagons, and even on the brake beams underneath. As for my wife and me, we got no places at all, but were obliged to go back to our lodgings. The next day we tried again, and I think we never should have left Moscow but for the resourcefulness of an experienced friend.

"I'll settle it," he said, and settle it he certainly did, for the next day, before the train had even backed into the station, we found ourselves comfortably installed in a sleeping wagon. We asked him how he achieved such a miracle, and he replied: "Why, you unsophisticated man, I simply turned the key which in our communist paradise unlocks all doors. I bribed a commissary." We felt that this method of getting an advantage over ordinary travelers was unethical, but we were so tired, and the compartment was so warm and comfortable that we had not courage to give up our places. We protested, but rather feebly. "Don't be foolish," said our practical friend. "To live with wolves one must learn to howl like wolves."

"Did all these people who have places get them this way?" I asked.

"Of course. How else?"

When the train backed into the station, we watched from our window the same shocking scene of crazed people fighting their way into the train, climbing roofs of carriages and clinging to brake beams. The cries of the injured and trampled were horrid, the yells of the stronger and more brutal frightful to hear. Half an hour after starting, the train stopped with a sudden jar which threw off two passengers clinging to platform rails. Their mutilated bodies were picked up and thrown carelessly into a luggage van, after which the journey was resumed. Several times the same thing happened, the vacant places of the victims being instantly occupied by persons having even less comfortable positions. At every station was repeated the wild scenes of pushing, fighting, and beating a way into the packed and stifling train. In vain, station guards and soldiers with rifles tried to hold the crowd back. At one place the soldiers actually fired on the people.

At last, through these torments, we reached Kozloff. Up to this time it had been impossible to buy any food, but here we found bread, real bread, with plenty of milk and meat. Passengers risking the loss of their places in the train made a mad descent upon that food. To understand it one must have known starvation. Like wild animals we fought each other, striking, gouging, kicking, grabbing what we could of that precious bread and meat, afterwards devouring rather than swallowing it. Ah! What joy to hold in your hands bread, real bread! To smell it, bite into it, chew it slowly, revel

in every morsel until you feel at last that you are
no longer hungry! Guyot was right when he said
that drinking the milk of Switzerland in mountains
sometimes gave one a sense of beauty no less grati-
fying than the reading of a perfect romance. People
who have never suffered hunger perhaps cannot
understand this.

Next morning we reached the Volga. Here also
the Revolution had left its bloody fingermarks, for
in the villages peasant riots waged fiercely. Communist troops taking from the peasants corn, milk,
and meat, they had tried to defend their property
by force, with the result that many on both sides
had been killed and wounded. At the moment of our
arrival at this Volga town the Communists were
gathering large forces to put down the peasants'
"anarchy." The mind of the towns, especially
among workmen, was intensely hostile to the Bolsheviki. A few days after our arrival were held
elections to the Soviet of the town and province.
The Communists received only a small minority of
votes, so they descended on the Soviet, dispersed it,
arrested all the majority members and appointed
Communist deputies in their places. The fury of
the population was so great at this outrage that a
general riot amounting to civil war was momentarily
expected. Gathering full particulars of these events
and helping to organize forces for future All-Russian movements against Communists and Germans,
I remained secretly in this town for about four
weeks. Having some free time, I resumed my interrupted scientific researches and began the first

draft of my "System of Sociology." Comparatively good food, rest, and a regular habit of life
resulted in rapid improvement of health and, recalled by urgent telegrams from Moscow, on May 4
I left my country retreat.

If travel from Moscow to the Volga had been unpleasant, the return journey was even worse. The
train was full of Meshechniks (bagmen), principally
peasants, bringing sackfuls of flour and potatoes to
sell in Moscow. This harmless business, persecuted
by the Communists as counter-revolutionary, was
full of danger to all those who carried it on. Trains
bore special troops for the purpose of confiscating
all foodstuffs and arresting the Meshechniks. But
hope of gain being stronger than fear of punishment, the Meshechniki continued their trade. By
bribes to Government officials and by all other
known expedients they went back and forth, and
the food they managed to smuggle into the cities
undoubtedly saved thousands from actual starvation. Markets and shops closed and all private trad-
ing forbidden, food-selling and buying persisted,
just as life itself persists. The Bolshevist agents
invaded our compartment and arrested one of the
Meshechniks, taking him to a wagon in the rear
where other "criminals" and "counter-revolutionists" were held. After a short time he returned,
and others asked eagerly: "What did you pay?"
And he replied, despair in his voice: "All I had.
Two pouds (about seventy-two pounds) of flour and
ten pounds of butter. Selling, I hoped to buy scythes

and some nails. Now I have neither scythes, flour nor butter."

"Never mind, old fellow," said one of them, "you may yet have good luck."

Soon two agents of the Government came again into our wagon, and the last peasant addressed them. "Look here, *tovarishi,* (comrade), you took everything this chap had. Don't you think that too much?"

"Silence!" roared the Bolshevist. "This is not your affair."

"Don't shout at me, *tovarishi.* I am not a dog. You ought to return this man half at any rate."

"Take him to the rear wagon," commanded the agent. But the peasant, smiling and stroking his beard, said pleasantly: "Don't be in such a hurry. I don't fear arrest, but if you do arrest me all your bribe-taking, all your profiteering, including those two pouds of flour and ten pounds of butter will be denounced, and perhaps we may find ourselves in the same prison. Wouldn't it be better for you to give half the flour and butter back?"

"Well—we'll see about it," grumbled the agent. And the Meshechnik did get back half his property. Two miles below Moscow all the food traders threw their bags out of the train, themselves jumping after at risk of breaking their necks. Only in this way could they avoid arrest at the station."

In Moscow the activity of all the anti-Bolshevist groups continued. "The League for the Regeneration of Russia," the "League for the Fatherland

and the Revolution," this headed by Savinkoff, the Social Revolutionary, Social Democratic, and Constitutional Democratic Parties, worked zealously together. Plans for a general uprising against the Bolsheviki and the Germans were being matured. Among the Bolsheviki themselves there was appearing friction, the left Social Revolutionaries resenting the abject surrender of the Bolshevist leaders to the Germans. Conflict between the Bolsheviki and the Czecho-Slovak Legionaires had also arisen. In a word, the Bolshevik leaders found themselves so discredited that they turned for support to their military forces, the Lettish troops, troops made up of German and Austrian war prisoners, Chinese and all kinds of adventurers and criminals. The real Bolshevist Reign of Terror began at this time and under this tremendous pressure of adverse public opinion.

As a result great changes took place within the Socialist Parties, many of those who formerly held extreme or doctrinaire views becoming much more moderate. Many, quite disgusted with what they had seen of Socialism in practice, abjured altogether the theory.

Immediately after my return, we began publication of our newspaper, *Regeneration,* and no sooner had the first copy appeared than Bolshevist agents raided the office, seeking to arrest the editors. They destroyed all copy, broke up forms and matrices, and smashed presses. Nevertheless, we went on writing, and for a month we issued regular editions. The cat-and-mouse game began all over again, and this time more ferociously. The resourcefulness of the mice included an elaborate system of danger signals, placed in all houses and apartments frequented by the editorial force. Special means of egress were provided in all buildings, and many were the hairbreadth escapes we made. I have no space here to describe them, but they were ingenious, picturesque, and sometimes positively perilous.

In Moscow at this time I met Kerensky, whom I had not seen before since the Bolshevist Revolution. Entering his apartment, I was met by a long-haired, bearded man wearing thick blue spectacles, the general make-up recalling the intellectuals of the 1860-70 period. In his six months of hiding, Kerensky had completely transformed himself and was now able to travel without being recognized by anybody. He told me that during those months he had written his own story of the Korniloff affair, and he wanted us to publish certain chapters of this in our newspaper. This we agreed to do. Quieter and more simple in his manner, Kerensky impressed me as an intelligent and sincere person, one who might fill the role of a teacher or a preacher. No stranger would have believed that this was the man who, a few months ago, had been virtually the ruler of Russia.

By the end of May a great many members of the Constitutional Assembly and the League for the Regeneration of Russia began to flee Moscow, and I decided that, for the time at least, it was imperative for me to work elsewhere. Spending two days in Petrograd, I left for Veliky Ustyug in Vologda Province, north Russia. The time of speechmaking and other preparation had passed. The time for action had begun.

In Archangel the most horrible terror was going on. The Bolshevist Commissary Kedroff executing people by hundreds and thousands. Victims were being shot, drowned, or murdered with unnamable mutilations. The peasants were being "nationalized"—that is, being robbed of most of their crops. Citizens, especially any who dared to protest against atrocities, were being searched, plundered, and arrested. Feeling the ground under their feet insecure, the Bolsheviki tried to strengthen their position by unrestrained terror.

In the Vologda Province the situation was somewhat better, although presage of the red terror was there. I had therefore to walk with caution and to conceal the real character of my mission, which was to organize Ustyug and Kotlas in connection with the planned overthrow of the Bolsheviki in Archangel. The district Ustyug-Kotlas was important to the plan. Located between Vologda and Archangel, at the mouth of three rivers, Vychegda, Sukhona, and Dvina, it was the center of concentration of enormous quantities of military supplies. Being a connecting link with anti-Bolshevist Siberia, this district had to play a very serious part in the re-establishment of the eastern frontier against the Germans, the overthrow of the Bolsheviki, and the re-establishment of the Constitutional Assembly.

Liberating the north of Russia—Archangel, Ustyug, Vologda, and Yaroslavl on the one hand and the Volga district and central Russia on the other—it was planned to form a union with Siberia, and in this way to surround the Capitals occupied by Bolshevist forces. The fact that Ustyug-Kotlas was my native place and where I usually spent my summers, helped me greatly in carrying out my mission in safety.

Meeting many people in Vologda who were engaged in the same political work, my wife and I started for Ustyug in a "nationalized" steamer, full of peasants traveling from the starvation districts to Ustyug in hopes of finding there bread and flour. Emaciated and in rags, they loudly cursed the Communists and all "communia." Strolling on the deck that evening, I was suddenly addressed by one of these peasants. "It seems to me I recognize you," he said. Recognition was not exactly what I desired on this trip, so I remained unresponsive.

"Don't you recall the meeting of representatives of the military regiments in Petrograd very shortly after the Bolshevik Revolution? Don't you remember how you warned us against the Bolsheviki? I was at that meeting and remember very well your words. Fools that we were! Blind and stupid sheep! We did not believe you then, but now we see that you were right. What we did not understand then we do now, but perhaps it is too late."

"Better late than never," I said.

"Surely. During these horrible months I have

thought many times of your words. If there are any
elections now, I will vote only for you. Because you
understand.''

"Please keep your recognition of me to yourself,''
I begged. And he promised.

Next day the Bolshevist commissaries examined
my papers and, not knowing me personally, passed
me. Once more the mouse slipped through, and un-
molested we landed at Ustyug. There we found a
bitter struggle going on between the Communists
and the Ustyug Soviet, the Municipality and the
District Self-government (Zemstvo). The Bolsheviki, unable to get a majority in any of these representative bodies, of course tried to disperse them,
but they, supported by the population, continued to
function. Sooner or later, however, the leaders and
members would probably be arrested by force. My
arrival became instantly known, not only to the national supporters but to the Bolsheviki, who spied
on me night and day. I pretended to be there only
on my annual vacation, attended no public meetings,
delivered no speeches, and declined all invitations to
participate in political activities. Tranquilly I pursued my studies, worked on my *General Theory of
Law,* visited friends, walked in the woods, and
bathed in the clear Sukhona. Such innocent conduct
weakened to some extent suspicions against me, mis-
led the spies, and gained the confidence of many of
the Communists who in former times had been my
students and friends. They did not wish to see me
arrested and my neutral attitude was therefore a
relief to them.

Needless to say, my neutrality was purely fictitious. My walks, picnics, bathings, and visits were really meetings in which were fully discussed plans and organization for the Bolshevik overthrow in Ustyug and Kotlas, and within two weeks after my arrival our preparations were almost complete. By the middle of June, however, the situation became complicated. The Central Government, dissatisfied with the conciliatory policy of the local Communists, sent a committee of Lettish, Jewish, and Russian Communists to enforce the liquidation of capital and the dictatorship of the proletariat. These newcomers bore themselves like conquerors among a vanquished people. They tried to dislodge the representative bodies from their halls, to arrest leaders and all merchants, to expel "capitalists" from their homes, to close the markets, and to extort huge taxes from the bourgeoisie. The local Communists did not dare protest against this wholesale communization, and on our part we decided that our only practical course was passive resistance. Before the overthrow in Archangel we could not disclose our plans, therefore we strove only to liberate the imprisoned people who had refused to pay the huge taxes. The peasants refused to close the markets, and the Municipality, the District Self-government, and other representative bodies, every day dispersed, simply reconvened. One order after another was issued by the commissaries, but they did not have forces enough on hand to carry out their edicts.

One day we went to a "picnic" near the old
Troitzky Monastery on the far side of the river.
In the middle of the meeting a friend from Ustyug
arrived with the news that a group of Communists
had broken into my house and into that of Zepaloff,
with orders for our arrest. Zepaloff was a young
poet and criminologist, the leader of the Social
Democrats in Ustyug, and before the Revolution he
had saved from arrest and had assisted financially
some of these very Communists. He was a talented,
generous, and most charming young man. After
the Revolution he, like many others, had shown himself a moderate and was now one of the strongest
adversaries of the Bolsheviki. It was necessary
now that we change our lodgings for new ones unknown to the Communists, and that night we moved
to a country house near the town. The Dvina has
many islands and on one of these we took refuge.
No boats being available, we undressed and, as best
we could, holding our clothes clear of the water, we
swam over to the first island. Still undressed, we
crossed it.

"Too bad we have no photographers to take our
pictures now," said Zepaloff. "Representatives of
the Russian people and a Russian editor on a revolutionary picnic."

"I never thought of the art of swimming as necessary to Revolution," I admitted.

"You must interpolate in the Constitutional Assembly a law that every serious politician must take
courses in athletics," said Zepaloff.

The wind, the sand, the beauty of the evening

put us in high good humor. Like children we laughed, joked, and enjoyed everything regardless of the dangers that threatened us. At last we swam the last sound, put on our damp clothes, and started to the country house. Next morning Zepaloff, who had been so gay during our flight, came down to breakfast pale and downcast. "It was a dream," he explained, "a frightful dream. I thought I was standing in the church at my wedding. But standing before the altar with my bride I suddenly saw myself on the guillotine with Mr. Vetoshkin" (once a friend but now a rabid Communist) "as my executioner. I tried to kiss my bride and my mother, but he thrust my head under the knife crying out: 'The gods are thirsty!' It is absurd of course to pay any attention to a nightmare, but I cannot help feeling depressed."

Zepaloff was engaged to be married, and this fact, together with the fact that he had been reading Anatole France's novel of the French Revolution, *Les Dieux Ont Soif,* seemed to account for his bad dream which we tried to laugh away. The loveliness of the day and the beauty of the meadows and woods in which we walked put him again into his usual good humor. From this time on we and the other "conspirators" began to live illegally continuing our work and looking forward to the success of our plans.

At the end of June Nicholas Tschaikovsky left Vologda on the steamer *Uchreditel.* Previously I had received an unsigned telegram bidding me try to get passage on the same steamer and go with

Tschaikovsky to Archangel, the telegram stating
that permission to enter the city would meet me
either at Kotlas or Ust-Pinega. This message disturbed me because it indicated that my vacation
might be suspected to be less innocent than I had
pretended. But as it represented orders, I altered
my appearance slightly and joined Tschaikovsky on
the steamer. He also was disguised, his long beard
and hair having been removed. Our journey was
an exceedingly dangerous undertaking. Inspection
of papers we knew would be very strict and the
only papers we had been able to secure were simple
statements that we were going to Pinega to investigate rural communes. Our documents lacked
official seals and signatures, but we hoped that their
very informality would keep us from being suspected. Once betrayed into the hands of the degenerate Kedroff, it was easy to foresee what fate
would await us. All our hopes rested on the permissions to enter Archangel which we were to get
in Kotlas. For the rest we relied on the stupidity
of the Bolshevist inspectors and on the word "commune" in our passports. Arrived at Kotlas, no permissions met us. But perhaps they would be at
Ust-Pinega. At all events we could only go on.

As much as possible we kept our cabin. Many
people on the steamer knew me, and if I went on
deck there might be some who would ask awkward
questions. So, on one beautiful evening we sat in
our cabin watching the broad Dvina gleaming under
the rays of the dying sun. Suddenly there was a
loud knocking at the door and two commissaries

entered demanding our papers. We gave them instantly, and the commissary scanning them, remarked: "Why is there no official seal on these?"

"What do you call this?" I asked, pointing to the seal of the Society of Economic Research.

"I know no such Soviet institution," said the man.

"Why," I exclaimed, "this was the society which first began the struggle against the Czar a century ago. Don't you know that Lenin himself as well as many other leaders have participated in its work? The certificates of this society are better than those of any other Soviet institution. Haven't you read the special privilege granted the society by Lenin?"

The commissary looked abashed. "You can't expect us to read all decrees," he said.

"Certainly not," I agreed sympathetically. "We are going to Pinega to organize the commune among the peasants. Russian Communism was not born yesterday you know. It existed many years ago, and that explains our present great success."

By this time the poor commissary was completely confused. "Excuse us comrades," he said at last. "So many counter-revolutionaries are everywhere that we have to be very careful not to miss any of them."

After two days we reached Ust-Pinega, but here again we were disappointed for at the post-office were no letters. There was nothing to do but send a telegram and wait in the village, which was about sixty miles from Archangel, for the answer. The

village was so poor that it was almost impossible
to get food, and besides, the peasants, suspecting
us to be Bolshevist agents, refused to sell us anything.

"Go to the commissaries," they said. "They
have everything while we have nothing."

Two commissaries, sailors from Kronstadt, soon
called on us with a demand for our certificates.
Again we lied successfully. A day passed, no telegram, and we began to ask ourselves what dreadful
thing had happened. On the second day the expected license came, but only for Tschaikovsky.
We agreed that he should go on and immediately
on his arrival at Archangel communicate with me.
My situation was very bad. Before the message
from Tschaikovsky could reach me I should have
been in the village at least three days. I, who was
supposed to be an agent going to Pinega for the
study of rural communes, was staying in a tiny
hamlet while steamers passed daily. I could not
long escape suspicion, and besides I was half-
starved. Nevertheless, I must justify my position
in the eyes of the commissaries, so I took paper and
pencil and began a house to house visitation, ques-
tioning the peasants about the organization of their
rural community, the forms of peasant self-government, the division and redistribution of lands, etc.
With the sailor commissaries I was quite friendly.
They invited me to their house where a good dinner,
tea, and even vodka was offered me. Plenty of food
and alcohol in the midst of a hungry population,
two mistresses to each man, besides violation among

village girls, such was the way of life of these protectors of universal equality and brotherhood. Listening to their brutal admissions, I felt horror and loathing, yet I had to play my role to the end.

The weather was beautiful, and I spent my time in "investigation," in walking and bathing, and in visiting an old church of the sixteenth century. Once, walking along the river I came on the body which had drifted ashore. He had been shot before being thrown into the water, but whether he was the victim of a brawl or of the revolutionary blood-lust I could not tell.

On the third day the expected message came. "Cargo is retarded. Continue the study of rural communes," the telegram read. This meant, "The arrival of English troops has been delayed. Return to Ustyug-Kotlas," I telegraphed to Ustyug: "How about the prices on furs?" Receiving the answer: "The same as before." By the next steamer I returned to Ustyug, where we continued our plans for the overthrow of the Bolsheviki as soon as the revolution in Archangel succeeded.

CHAPTER XI

The Bolsheviki were concentrating Red forces in Ustyug-Kotlas, the hand of Chekha fell more and more heavily, and arrests and searches were hourly occurrences. Ustyug took on the appearance of a place near the battle front, and the day of revolution in Archangel seemed very near. No information from our comrades reached us however, nor did my promised certificate arrive. What had happened? Was there misunderstanding among the leaders? At the beginning of August every sign of the overthrow at Archangel became apparent. The Communist authorities prepared to leave Ustyug and Kotlas and even went on board the steamers, taking with them many hostages from the towns and all the money and treasure they could lay hands on. Our quarters seemed safe, but one night a friend woke me from sleep, warning me that the twelve steamers of the Bolshevist "armada," defeated at Archangel, were approaching Ustyug. All members of the staff had been similarly aroused and we spent the rest of the night hiding in the woods.

What was to be done? We had received no word from Archangel or Vologda, and we did not know whether the 'armada," was being pursued by the Anti-Bolshevist forces or not. The "armada" we

learned, was in a panic, and we thought that our
small forces might possibly disorganize it. Praying
for reinforcements from Archangel, we prepared a
barge to be sunk in the Sukhona to prevent the
further retreat of the Bolshevist steamers. In the
afternoon one of the sailors of the "armada," a
member of our group, came to my shelter, begging
me to fly from Ustyug as the Bolshevists on the
steamers had sworn to shoot me. But I told him
to wait until they caught me.

That evening we reached the conclusion that our
plan for stopping the Bolshevist steamers was im-
practical, because our forces were too small to act
without support. Within a few days the situation
would be clearer. If the Bolshevist successfully
resisted us, the only effect of our work will be executions of hostages and a general orgy of blood.
Three days passed. No news. No signs of the
approach of our allies. The "armada" indeed recovered itself, new troops arrived from Vologda,
and a general increase of the terror ensued. No
further resistance on our part being possible, we
went into hiding in the woods bordering the wild
river. Hope had almost died from our hearts. At
last we heard that the anti-Bolshevist troops had
been stopped at Berezniki, about three hundred
miles away. This gave us assurance that they would
not approach Ustyug at all and that the only salva-
tion for us was now, by forced marches to reach
Archangel. Meanwhile preparing to go to Archangel, we decided to stay some time near Ustyug,
and so dividing in several groups, having agreed on

means of communication, and embracing each other we parted.

"Farewell, friends. May Russia live forever!"

"Farewell, farewell, until better days."

Alas, for many of us a next meeting never came. Bravely these patriots died for Russia and are now sleeping in eternal peace.

My first objective was a village where I spent two days with a peasant friend, and then went on to another village, beginning a long series of wanderings around Ustyug. To live secretly in a Russian village, where every stranger excites curiosity, is no easy thing. In the midst of civil war, when spies were everywhere, for a hundred friends might be ready to give you shelter, you never knew whether there might be some ready to betray you. Writing this history, I feel like expressing the deepest gratitude for those good and brave peasants who, at great risk to themselves, did shelter me and pass me on from one place to another. If my head at this moment is on my shoulders, it is because of these faithful "Ivans" who warned me of every danger, gave me every comfort they could, arranged communications between me and my wife—in a word, tried in every way to help me. Days passed with no news except a cheerful letter which said that while the Chekhists did not know whether I was in Ustyug or Archangel, they had broadcasted my photographs with orders to shoot me instantly if arrested. The terror in Ustyug had become more ferocious and the student Dvyjilny, one of the most energetic of our staff, had been taken.

"Poor Dvyjilny. God help you," I sighed. "I fear this finishes your drama."

On the morning of my second day's stay in the house of a peasant friend, a man came to the door and asked his way to Galueva. I could see that he was in disguise, but I gave him the directions saying: "Who do you want to see in Galueva? I am a teacher there and know everybody."

"Oh, I was told that it was possible to buy flour in Galueva, so I am going there."

"Better go to Voznesenie," I suggested. "Galueva is a very poor village and you can get nothing there. Where are you from?"

"From Gryazovetz," he answered.

Repeating my advice to go to the richer village of Voznesenie, I bade him good-bye and watched him walk up the road. My peasant friend who, like myself recognized the man as a Lett, followed him a short distance. When he returned I asked: "A Chekhist?" and he answered: "Certainly."

Putting a revolver in my pocket I hurriedly set off for the next village where in a schoolhouse I had arranged to meet my wife and a trusted friend. In the evening they came and we walked to a hamlet in the forest quite far from other settlements. Our friend, who had some relatives in the vicinity, introduced us as the engineer Daniloff and Mrs. Daniloff, who were in the country for rest and recreation after the excitement in Petrograd. For a week we stayed in this obscure place, walking, picking berries and mushrooms and reading Mommsen's Roman History and novels of Zagoskin. We had plenty of food, beautiful surroundings, and kind neighbors. After my wife and friend left, under the pretext of a visit to Ustyug, I remained intending to rest a few days longer. But in the evening a messenger came telling me that on the next day, if not that very night, the "head-hunters" would be there.

"Go to the village of X," he advised, naming a hamlet about fifteen miles distant. "At Y, seven miles from here, you will be given the address of a peasant in X who will shelter you. But try to reach there at night that no one may see you."

If the "head-hunters" were to reach my retreat that night I must not be found in the house, so I went to sleep in the bath-house which every peasant of north Russia attaches to his dwelling. In the middle of the night I was roused by a rustling sound, so with revolver in hand I crept out of the bath house and ran to the forest. But the alarm turned out to be a false one. The rustling I heard was that of a peasant trying to steal some potatoes in the kitchen garden. No doubt he had been as frightened as I. Early in the morning I started for Y where I was to receive the address of the peasant to whom I was consigned. I had plenty of time, and as I trod the pleasant forest path listening to the bird songs, I came on a huge anthill and sat down to observe their communistic labors. What a wonderful communist organization they had, to be sure, with a palace whose architecture outshown Egyptian pyramids, Greek temples, medieval cathedrals, Eiffel's tower, and even American skyscrapers.

Not from Marx or other ignorant ideologists, but from these ants should the Communists and Socialists have learned their theories. If they could but transform the human race into ants, stop the processes of evolution, and bring the many into absolute slavery to the few, what an ideal communistic society they would create. But as long as human beings love freedom and independence, as long as they insist on progress, communistic aspirations must forever fail.

About nine o'clock I came near the village of Y, but as I skirted the wood I heard voices, so I halted behind a fir tree.

"Have your peasants reaped their barley?" somebody was asking.

By his accent this was no local man, and I listened for the next words.

"We just begin to harvest," said a woman's voice. I peered through the branches and saw seven fully armed Lettish soldiers walking along the path. I waited a few minutes, considering my best move. I heard cow-bells tinkling, dogs barking, sheep bleating, voices of peasants—and then I heard a rifle shot. This meant that a guard had been left in the village and that I must keep in concealment still longer. It began to rain, my clothes were soaked through, and hunger gnawed at my stomach. Since morning I had nothing to eat but a few wild berries. I dared not light a fire or even warm myself by walking up and down. The only thing I could do was to exercise by squatting and rising, but this warmed me a little.

Three hours later I crouched down like a hare, hearing the tramp of the returning soldiers. "Escaped," I heard one of them say, but another replied: "What does it matter? If this counter-revolutionary is indeed here, he will soon fall into our hands."

I decided that I would wait a few hours and then tramp to another village where I had a peasant friend. About three the next morning, benumbed and very hungry, I cautiously crept out into the road and by daylight I was safe in the house of my friend. At once he sent his son to Ustyug with a note from me asking my friends to find me some shelter in the town. Then I lay down to sleep, but in spite of the fact that I had not slept for two nights I lay wide-awake. In my wet clothes as in a compress I felt myself growing feverish, and every few minutes I sat up in bed to listen.

When my friend's son returned it was with this message: "At midnight be in the wood near the cemetery where we met before." Midnight! Then I had but five hours in which to cross twenty-four miles of hostile territory. Putting on an old peasant coat, a dirty cap, an apron, and removing my glasses, I set forth. At two minutes before twelve I reached my destination but found no one there. I laughed softly, and quoted half aloud: "Just as the clocks struck twelve Monte Cristo appeared at the appointed place." The answer to this was a subdued cough, and from the gloom where they stood my wife and one of my relatives came into the path. We moved silently towards my asylum, my wife begging me not to make the slightest noise, not even to sneeze after we arrived. The shelter proved to be a half-destroyed miserable hut so near to two small houses that I understood her anxiety. Nearer my hut was the cemetery. The hut, after I had crept into it and closed the flimsy door, was so low that I could not even sit up straight, but on the floor my friends had laid a felt mat, so stretching out on it I tried to go to sleep. But feverish thoughts filled my brain. This then was the revolution for which so many thousands had worked and dreamed. And here was I, a revolutionist, like a Girondist of the eighteenth century, obliged to wander in dark forests and rest at night in a grave-yard.

"Crack!" Rifles. One, two, three. Executions. I remembered then that the place of execution was near by, on the other side of the cemetery. "Well," I said to myself, "this hut has the merit of convenience. It is so near the place of eternal rest that I shall not have far to walk."

In this feverish condition I spent the night. In the morning I found, to my comfort, that my wife had placed in a corner food, some books, and Bolshevist newspapers. Composing myself, I ate and read. But what frightful news! Four hundred and twenty-eight executions in Yaroslavl by Bolshevist-German forces. Fifteen counter-revolutionaries executed in Vologda. Seven shot in Ustyug, two of them peasants. "All who are not with us are against us. All are outlaws. Pitiless death for all capitalists, for all anti-Bolsheviki. Let us kill them all like poisonous snakes,'' I read.

The long day over I passed another sleepless night listening to the sinister crack, crack of rifles on the far side of the cemetery. It was clear that I could not remain where I was, and I though I might as well steal as far as Luza to the north where I would surely find shelter with the Ziryane people. From there I might possibly get through to Archangel. Next night I stole to the house of my wife and accompanied by her went into a wood near the town. Sad were our hearts on this rainy night. I was like one wandering in a circle without any outlet. My troubles were but increased by the anxiety of my wife and friends, but I could do nothing to lighten their grief. Lonely in the wet darkness we spent an hour discussing in whispers my plans. My idea of going to the Ziryane was voted down. To cross three hundred miles of territory where I was known and where in every village were Bolshevik agents arresting each newcomer, was clearly suicidal. What other solution of my problem was possible?

As though in answer to the question, the sudden bark of rifles interrupted our conversation. Oh, yes, this outlet could be, and perhaps it was the only one. Vainly I tried to console my wife, begging her to go home. Silently weeping, she embraced me and went away, leaving me alone and utterly desolate. The wood where I remained had been pretty thoroughly cut over, so I sat down on a stump and considered my desperate situation. In the morning people began to enter the wood to pick berries, hunt mushrooms, chop wood, and the devil knows what else. A boy spied me and stood still to watch. I pretended that I was a wood-chopper. The boy, however, did not leave. Was he a spy? Sleepless nights, anxiety, cold and hunger had brought me to such a pass that at last I put all fears aside and directed my footsteps to the house of my friend on the edge of the town. "If I am to be killed, let them shoot quickly," I said to myself.

"Good God! How is it with you?" exclaimed my friend. And then he gave me a glass of tea with cognac and prepared me a bed in his bath-house. After four sleepless nights I fell dead asleep and for some hours was troubled by neither dreams nor apprehensions. In the evening, my hair cut and ragged beard shaved, I was led to another asylum which had been prepared for me. This was in a low space between the floor and ceiling of an attic, without any window or even any door. Here I lay down on a bearskin, "like a king of old Scythia," as my kind host smilingly said. In this hole I could neither read, write nor do anything else but think. I turned my thoughts to the mechanism of human behavior, problems on which I had worked before the Revolution. "My present behavior," I thought, "represents a definite complex of reactions. What are their stimuli, or what devils have brought me to this behavior of a bear in a den?" Quite a proper reflection for a psychologist.

For an hour each evening I left my cramped

quarters to take food and to hear what news came through. Except for poor Dvyjilny, who was in prison, all the other conspirators were, like myself, in flight and in hiding. It seemed that I might as well try to join them in an effort to reach Archangel, but first it was necessary to prepare maps and to wait until certain of the fugitives reached our locality. We were to start separately from Ustyug, meeting at an appointed place in the forest. In early morning, after three days of concealment under the low roof, I started out disguised as a worker looking for flour in the villages. About thirty miles from the town I came on my fellow-fugitive, finding him in fairly good spirits and quite prepared, as I was, for whatever might happen. With difficulty we bought flour, onions, potatoes for four or five days, got an ax, a rifle, and a few cartridges, a porridge pot, a teakettle, tobacco, needles, and thread. These we put in bags with a change of linen, two or three books, and some canvas for sleeping beds. The night we spent in a corn kiln, and next morning we started to the forest, two peasants guiding us part of the way. In the afternoon of the same day a Red detachment galloped into the village to arrest us. But by that time we were far away.

CHAPTER XII

IN THE BOSOM OF NATURE

FOREST! Endless forest! Thirty miles to the nearest village. After danger a sensation of freedom. What happiness! Gayety filled us and we began to sing and shout at the top of our voices. There was a hut made by peasants who, in winter, came here to hunt squirrels, bear, and other game, and in it we settled down. Above us was a roof, around us rough walls, and under us moss, dry grass, and our sleeping bags. A goodly woodpile fuel, a brook of good water. The air was healthful, and above all there was no revolution, no "head-hunters," no reminder of the cursed lunacy of Communism. The incessantly falling autumn rain spoiled our comfort a little, but after all, very little. Time flew by. Cutting of more fuel, hunting, gathering berries and mushrooms, reading, writing, and conversation filled our time. Tired after a day of work, we slept all night like dead men. Five days passed thus, and it was time to go to the villages for food and information.

My friend knew the country better than I and had more acquaintances, so it was decided that he was to go first. We agreed that should he not return by Sunday noon—this was Thursday—I should go to look for him. Sunday noon came and my friend was still absent. I waited three hours and

165

then, shouldering a few necessities, I set out. After walking five or six miles I saw a man in the path. But was it he? Yes, it was indeed, but what a figure! Clad in a shirt and nothing more!

"Where on earth did you leave your trousers and boots?" I exclaimed.

"In the river," he answered cheerfully.

"Then let us be Communists and divide our clothes," I said, handing him my coat, boots, and trousers, and remaining in my under-garments. The man was fairly chattering with cold.

When we reached our hut he told me his adventures. In the first village he could get no food, so he crossed the river to another village, where he had a peasant friend. There they gave him supper and a bed in the bath-house. But just as he was falling asleep he heard voices and saw men at his friend's door. He took instant flight to the wood, hoping that the men would soon leave and that he could get his bag of food, but in the morning he saw that three saddled horses remained at the door of the house. Stealing out of the wood, he ran along the banks of the Sukhona to the place where there was a boat, but looking back he saw the Reds riding after him. At once he shed his clothes and dived into the water. They shot at him, but he reached the opposite bank without mishap. He stayed half-naked in the woods until night and then started for our shelter. The exposure, excitement, and exhaustion had told on him terribly. I made a good fire to warm him and went out to seek some game, but unsuccessfully. Berries and mushrooms were all we had for supper, and berries and hot water was our breakfast. It was absolutely necessary to get food, so we started for the villages. For three days we nearly starved, but as safety in this neighborhood seemed now so dubious we decided to push on to Archangel. In the evening we found ourselves, soaking wet, near the village from which we had set out.

In the darkness we cautiously approached the house of a relative of my companion, a peasant named Stepan; but frightened to death at our sudden appearance, he whispered: "Go away, for God's sake. Red soldiers are in the village. Go away!"

He gave us some bread, a pair of bast shoes and trousers for my friend, who had walked barefoot the whole distance, and we went off with the promise from Stepan that he would bring us provisions the next day. In the wood we ravenously devoured our bread and sat down to shiver under the shower until morning. "It seems to me that we take too many baths and too few meals," said my companion dolorously. But I reminded him that it was quite the other way with less particular people.

Morning came, hour after hour passed, but no sign of Stepan. About noon we heard someone swearing at his horse, which was a conventional method of announcing the advent of provisions. Five or six pounds of flour and about a hundred pounds of potatoes, this was all that Stepan could bring us. Putting it in our bags, we tramped off towards our new objective, the basin of the Low Jerga. Avoiding villages, we walked for five hours through the rain

carrying our burdens. It became quite dark. What
the devil! According to our calculations we should
have reached the river two hours before. In our
wanderings we must have lost the way. Coming to
a forest hayfield, we met another disaster. My friend
fell heavily and hurt his leg. As for me, I was feeling very ill. Fortunately, we found a hayrick and,
too exhausted even to prepare a meagre meal, we
burrowed under the hay and fell asleep. In the
morning, considerably refreshed, we found the
river, ate breakfast, and started to go farther and
farther into the wild forest, away from the hell of
the glorious Revolution.

Five weeks we spent moving from one place to
another through this endless forest. Coming to a
comparatively comfortable place, we built a sort of
a shelter with hewn trees, mosses, grass, and
branches. Two tree trunks set closely together made
us a fireplace. Potatoes, flour-gruel, and what berries we could find formed our menu. From time to
time we shot a little game, but we were obliged to
hoard our ammunition lest we should need them
against two-legged beasts. We tried fishing, but it
was an off season and we had no luck. By day we
kept ourselves busy, but in the evening when darkness came and we sat before the fire smoking our
primitive cigarettes, we talked and thought and listened to the symphony of the forest. Composed of
a thousand varying notes, this forest music was
always fascinating to me. Its pianissimo was full
of strange whisperings, mysterious voices, and low,
gloomy cries. In its wildest fortissimo, when all

around us were creaking, crashing, whistling, booming sounds, when branches and trees fell, the music was magnificent. But what I liked most was the moderato, when the forest, as though plunged in deep meditation, softly rustled its waving branches to and fro.

Our nights were full of dreams. Almost every night I saw myself walking along the streets of Archangel, of London or Paris. I met friends, and with them ate the most delicious food. Almost all our waking hours we were hungry; our bodies, and most of all, our feet in their bark shoes, were wet. We began to bloat and to feel strangely weak and tired. All the time I was trying to observe my dreams and my sensations of starvation from the psychologist's point of view. In vain. After a few minutes of concentration I always found my thoughts wandering from the psychology of starvation to plans of getting something to eat. Sometimes our hunger and exhaustion, with our anxieties about those we loved at home, threw us into horrible despair. At other times we felt indifferent, almost happy.

One day we came to a big marsh. For about five hours we walked through it in mud to the knees. Our bark shoes went to pieces, our feet were cut, our bodies ached, but still we came to no end of the cursed muck, no place where we could rest and eat. Everywhere we looked on a swelling, yellow-green surface with pools of open water, small and half-starved trees scattered here and there. Never shall I forget this damned moor. The water was so cold

that we lost all feeling in our feet. Often we fell
down and lay panting on beds of red huckleberries.
There were moments when we felt that we were
perishing, that the last breath of life was leaving us,
and that in that red, endless expanse we must cease
to breathe. Why not? Yet calling encouraging
words to each other, we managed to struggle on, and
at last, O happiness, the red nightmare was over.

Next day we were rewarded by coming on a hunt-
er's hut with a rude fireplace in it. Building a fire,
we took off our rags, washed them in the river, and
hanging them up to dry stretched ourselves out in
our Turkish bath. As we lay a wild duck flew by
and lighted in the water just below us. My companion grasped the rifle and fired. The duck was
shot, but the stream began to carry it away. We
ran out and threw ourselves in the river after it.
In this way we had a Turkish bath, a cool plunge,
and a delicious duck dinner into the bargain. Afterwards we treated ourselves to a cup of hot water
for tea, smoked dried-leaf cigarettes, and read Jack
London's *Stories from Alaska*. We felt perfectly
comfortable and happy.

So we wandered. A week later messengers, who
four times managed to bring us letters in the wilder-
ness, came with provisions, newspapers, and a letter
from some of the friends with whom we expected to
reach Archangel. This letter promised us maps,
without which we could hardly go on successfully,
but no maps came. Later we learned that they had
been sewn up in a lady's skirt and she, not knowing
anything about our plans, wore the skirt and the

maps to Petrograd. What to do? To obey instructions in the latest communication and to meet our friends in the place appointed we should have to move immediately. To wait until the maps came would make us a fortnight too late. That little mistake of the lady made it impossible to go on with the Archangel party, but alas, only two men reached their destination. The others were captured and shot.

We had about three hundred and fifty miles to walk. To travel that distance without stopping at villages for food was impossible. In every village we ran great risk of arrest. To pass from one place to another it was necessary to get permission from the "Communistic Committee of Poor Peasants." Red soldiers were patrolling the forests and special pickets watched all principal vistas. We thought of retreating into the deepest depths of the forest, building a hut and remaining there all winter. We considered also hiding in a house in a village, never appearing out of doors, and never speaking except to the master of the house. It sounds fantastic, but life is more fantastic than any fiction. Two of my friends saved their lives by that first plan and another by the second. This man lived for two years in a small house, never showing himself to anyone except his landlady, and in the end he escaped alive.

We continued to wander over the bosom of Nature, occasionally wishing we might see a little of civilization. In free moments we talked much about the Revolution, and doubts which had been born in my mind at the beginning of the upheaval grew to full size. In this wild forest the utter futility of all revolution, the vanity of all Socialism and Communism became clear to me. The catastrophe of the Revolution, the deep historic roots of Bolshevism, loathed by the majority, it is true, but having as its basis and its force the passive spirit of the Russian nation, overwhelmed me with its truth. Only when the people have suffered the fullest horrors of Bolshevism, only when they have passed completely through the tragic, perhaps the fatal experience of the Communist experiment, can their dreadful sickness be cured once and forever. Only then the poisons in which Bolshevism flourished would be purged from the organism of the Russian people. Only then would this damned passivity disappear and they be transformed from a people accustomed to tyranny to a self-governing nation.

Out of these meditations I wrote an address to my electors, sending it to my friends to be made public. I am no longer a revolutionist because revolution is catastrophe. I am no longer a Socialist, because Socialism is wrong. I released myself from responsibility as a member of the Constitutional Assembly, since the people would not support their own representative body. If they hope to have a "Government of the people, for the people, and by the people," they themselves must be active and must cease to lean on leaders who, without their support, are powerless. Such was the essence of my message.

Many dazzling illusions, beautiful dreams in whose reality I had once believed, I lost during my

meditations in the forest. They fled, I believe, forever. But I did not grieve over my lost illusions.
Life and the world are so beautiful, so wonderful
in their reality that illusions are necessary only to
the blind and deaf and lame, for mental, moral, and
physical cripples. Healthy persons have no need
of illusions.

CHAPTER XIII

As winter approached, our situation became much worse. Berries and mushrooms disappeared, and the fetching of food from the villages was attended with greatest difficulty. When snow began to fall, the marks of our footsteps made it easier for the "head-hunters" to trace us, and from merely haunting the country around settlements, they now extended their search far into the forests. Sometimes forty or fifty miles away from their detachments these men were killed, but oftener they succeeded in killing their victims. One group of seven fugitives had tramped from Vetluga to Ustyug, a distance of a thousand miles, enduring untold hardships, only to meet death at the end of their journey. All these things made it inevitable that we should leave our forest fastness and return to town. Concluding at last that we had no other choice, we informed our friends who hastened to prepare such refuge as was possible. On the eve of our exodus we moved cautiously a little nearer to the clearing. The next morning I buried my diary in the forest, discarded my worn bark shoes for my old boots, made myself look as much as I could like a local worker, and embracing my friend, who was to start the following day, set off. The distance to Ustyug was forty-seven miles, and I had to enter the town

174

between six and seven in the evening. At six it was dark, and after seven I should have to produce a certificate.

Vigorously I set out, knowing that when one's life depends on his feet they usually hold out. On the gray autumn road I met two Bolshevist Commissaries, and taking off my cap I greeted them as peasants formerly were accustomed to greet nobility, and they, conscious of their new dignity, responded quite in the old lordly way. Later on I fell in with two peasants, and naturally we began to discuss politics. Speaking of the Communist Government, which they cautiously alluded to as "Your Workmen's Government," I said: "Why do you say your Worker's Government? It is yours also, is it not?"

"Oh," said one of the women, "if this is a peasants' Government then I must be a princess."

"Well," I laughed, "if its a workmen's then I must be the Czar."

"Ah," said the other woman, becoming confidential, "when we had the Czar there was order, peace, and plenty of everything. Now people are starving and killing each other." Then sinking her voice, "Have you heard about the naked man?"

"The naked man?"

"Yes. You know how many people are wandering everywhere hiding from the Red devils. It seems that the Reds captured a man somewhere in the upper Sukhona. They were bringing him in a boat along the river. Two days ago they stopped for the night in the village to which we are going.

Well, they put the man in a hut on the bank, took off all his clothes and tied him hand and foot. Three of the Reds went to the village and the fourth was left to watch. What happened no one knows, but in the morning the guard was found butchered and the man was gone. Last evening one of our lads met a naked man in the wood. He was very frightened, but the naked man seized him, took his coat, trousers, and cap and left him, saying: 'I am sorry for what I do, and if I live I will pay you.' God help that unhappy one now." And she devoutly made the sign of the cross.

Carefully avoiding all villages and hamlets, I made my way onward and at a quarter before seven I was safely in the appointed house. Ah! What pleasure after weeks in the wild to wash one's body, to put on clean clothes, to sit at a decent table, to lie down to sleep between smooth sheets! The first part of my revolutionary adventures was over. What was to come was mercifully hidden behind the veil of destiny.

An absolutely noiseless life, the existence of a fleshless phantom, I lived in the place of refuge. Never laugh, never cough, never approach a window, never leave the house, be ready at the slightest warning to fly to the lumber room, then remain motionless and still as long as a chance visitor remained, to listen night and day for untoward sounds —these spelled the price of existence. I was like a hermit who has taken vows of perpetual solitude and silence. One day followed another and the more I thought of it the more inevitable seemed the end to my confinement. I knew they were looking for me, knew that my presence in the village was suspected. Sooner or later they would get me. Finally, I came to a desperate resolve.

"My friends," I said that evening as we sat together, "I see no use in continuing this frightful existence. I know that I shall be soon arrested, and to stay here longer simply puts this whole household in jeopardy. It is not right for me to go on risking your life and safety. So I am going to put an end to it all—my suffering and your danger."

"What are you going to do?" they asked.

"I am going to do what our northern hunters do as a last resort when they are fighting for life against a bear. They thrust one fist into the bear's mouth and with the other hand they try to stab him to death with their small knife. Something like this I intend. Tomorrow I am going to walk into the jaws of the Chekha."

"You are mad," cried all my friends. But against all their persuasions, I showed them that my present situation was intolerable and that it did not even promise more than a few days' additional safety. I admitted that I had no more than one chance in a thousand, but that one chance I was determined to take. I hope I shall never again in life have to go through such a scene of farewell as we endured the next evening. Good-bye, when it almost certainly means good-bye forever, is a terrible thing to say. A mother sending her son into battle knows something of what my wife and I and our faithful friends felt that night. Twice I said good-bye, and twice I turned back. Last good-byes, last kisses and embraces, last stifled sobs, last signs of the cross on my forehead, last looks, then in my ragged pockets they thrust a few cigarettes for comfort and let me go. As I stumbled into the darkness the thought crossed my mind, "there is yet time to return." But no, the die was cast and on towards the dread Chekha I went.

Two Lettish soldiers in top boots, each with three revolvers stuck in their leather girdles, met me in the anteroom. Pale faces with red lips and dull eyes that seemed to see and yet not see me, a thick odor of alcohol, this was my first impression of the Chekha.

"My name is Professor Pitirim Sorokin," I announced. "Please let them know that I have arrived."

In the dull eyes of the executioners something like astonishment awakened. After a moment of silence one of them rang a bell. At once four armed men entered and stood staring at me. I lighted a cigarette. After an interval one of the soldiers beckoned and I followed him into the office of the head of the Chekha. The house, and even the room, I knew very well. Many times I had been there as a guest. But instead of a comfortable study with books and pictures it was now a filthy den with ragged tapestries, broken furniture, and on the table a pile of dirty dishes and a litter of bottles. Pictures of Lenin, Trotzky, and Lunacharsky decorated the walls. At the table sat Sorvacheff, for the moment head of the Chekha. He was one of the local Communists, not a particularly bloodthirsty person, but weak before the higher authorities.

"Sit down," he invited, "and allow me to ask you some questions. Where did you come from?"

"From the forests."

"From which forests."

"From the Dvina," said I, indicating a direction I had not been.

"How long have you been in the forests?"

"About two months."

"With whom?"

"Alone."

"Where have you been before?"

"In the villages."

"In which villages?"

"That does not matter."

"You must name them."

"I will not name them."

"I insist."

"You may insist as much as you like, I will not give any name."

"Well. Why did you go to the forests?"

"Because your agents paid me too much attention. Besides, I like to be in 'the bosom of nature.'"

"Have you been in Archangel?"

"No."

"Have you participated in the organization of the Archangel counter-revolution?"

"No."

"We have some evidence you did."

"I say no. Let me see what sort of evidence you have."

"This does not concern you."

"Well."

"Why did you come to us?"

"To know why I am persecuted and to learn what you are going to do with me."

"I think you know well why you are persecuted, and as to what we will do with you, I think you know that also. Personally, I would be ready to set you free. But your fate does not depend upon my desire. You will have to be shot immediately. But as you are too big a bird for us, and as your principal activity was carried on in Petrograd and Moscow, we must ask the Central Chekha what we shall do with you. You may be sure, however, that this only postpones your execution for a few days," he concluded.

"Thank you for your candor, at least," I said.

"Now I shall send you to the prison."

A few minutes later, accompanied by four armed men, in the darkness of night, I strode to the prison. Approaching it, I looked in the direction where I left my dearest people and sent to them my last "good-bye."

"*Lasciate ogni speranza voi ch' entrate.*" "Take leave of all your hopes, you who are entering here," I remembered Dante's words above the gates of the hell, as I entered the gates of the prison.

I was in the Kingdom of Death.

CHAPTER XIV

THE RED MASS

AGAIN in prison! A little too much for one man in one year. Revolution takes no account of human sufferings. Well, then, should I bother to complain or repine? Let come what must. For my part, it seemed better to be an optimist and to regard all things from their brighter side. The mental attitude of Voltaire's "Candide" is sometimes quite convenient. Why, for example, can't I imagine that this prison is a "communistic hotel," I myself a traveler, and my feelings similar to those who in freedom read of prison? In fact, I don't know which is better, this prison or a wet stump in the wild forest. I think a bed on the dirty floor of a prison is, after all, rather more comfortable than the wet ground. In order to divert my attention from this harassing problem, I will write these notes. Writing will help me to kill time. As my fate is apparently decided, I need no longer fear being arrested because of what they may read in my diary. The man who is already submerged has no fear of getting wet. In other countries liberty of speech and press exists outside of prisons; in our communistic paradise it exists only in prisons. Therefore, let us now make use of this situation and exer-

cise our "rights of a man and a citizen." Perhaps
these soiled pages will survive me and fall into the
hands of someone. If not, it does not matter.

In the cell of the prison in Veliky Ustyug, where
I am confined, there are about thirty men. Some of
them are known to me. There are three students,
who took my course in the University of Petrograd,
two teachers, three priests, two lawyers, four merchants. Most of the others are peasants and workers. The population of Russia outside of prisons is
horribly diminishing, but inside of prison walls it
is wonderfully increasing. Before the Revolution
in this prison there were scarcely thirty prisoners;
now there are more than three hundred. In addition there are about two hundred in the cloister,
which has been transformed into a prison. Is this
not striking progress in the direction of Freedom?
Some of the prisoners are lying in their rags on
the floor. Some are sitting and hunting for insects.
When I arrived, questions were hurled at me. In
what way, why, and when was I arrested? What
were the news and prospects for the future?

"In the usual way, for the usual crime," was my
answer.

"But we don't know why we were arrested," ob-
jected some of them.

"You have been arrested in the name of the Revolution. You have been told that the Revolution is
God and God cannot be questioned." I spoke in the
humorous tone of a prospective gallows-bird.

Poor fellows! Especially the peasants and workers! The "bourgeois," students, lawyers, mer-

chants, and priests know they are imprisoned as "hostages," but these laborers cannot understand why they are arrested by the "Government of the workers and peasants."

"What do you think they will do with us?" asked some of them.

"Probably you will be liberated very soon." But I did not explain what I meant by this "liberation." Let them think they will soon return to their homes, wives, parents, and children. If at the hour of their liberation, instead of the joyful faces of those they love they see the tragic face of Death, the final agony will be comparatively short. It takes just an hour to go from here to the place of execution; another hour perhaps, awaiting one's turn to be shot. It is far better to suffer these two hours than to live many days and weeks as a man condemned to death.

I lighted a cigarette and offered the rest to my fellows, leaving two for myself. Two cigarettes I will keep for a special purpose—to smoke on the way to the execution. It seems a little strange, but human psychology is generally strange. Therefore, my intention is a natural one in this incomprehensible center of human suffering. Here in the prison all is *commune*. Here exists a real Communism more effective than Communism introduced by force outside the prison. Food brought to this or that prisoner from outside is divided among all. Here complete equality is recognized. Death is the common fate of all of us. Our standards of life are the same. Inequality exists only as regards psychology and anatomy; and even these differences may be diminished by long imprisonment. Living under these conditions for any length of time would transform anybody into a kind of idiot. Equality in idiotism and death can easily be achieved by the Communists.

Long life to Communistic equality in madness and death!

However, in spite of Communism and equality, all prisoners are starving. Myself, as well. Many months of starvation have left me permanently hungry. But even this has its compensation. It gives me again a chance to continue my study of the psychology of starvation. I see that under any conditions it is possible to be an optimist. Everything depends upon the point of view.

"Dinner" is served. I am a "newcomer," therefore no dinner is prepared for me. However, my fellows invite me to partake of their repast. One-fourth of a pound of bread which bears but slight resemblance to real bread, some hot water with a few potatoes compose "dinner," "lunch," "breakfast," and "supper." This "ration" differs a little from the quantity and quality of calories regarded by physiologists as necessary for a man in the course of a day. But these physiologists are "bourgeois" physiologists; therefore, their conclusions have no value in a communistic society. I think that for the transformation of sinful capitalists into communistic angels, such a diet is in fact both suitable and effective. Most of my comrades greedily eat their portions at once. Some try very hard to leave a little for the evening. But they cannot. Only for a half-hour can they resist the temptation. Their "bourgeois" habit of satisfying their hunger overcomes their good intentions. Only four men in the cell are free from the sin of gluttony. They lie in a corner and pay no attention to the eating. Being in the delirium of typhus, they are unconscious of their environment.

Strange thing! My companions not only do not try to keep away from these poor creatures, but rather strive to be near them.

"My comrades, be careful and keep yourselves farther from the typhus," I warn them.

They smile. "It is not so bad to have typhus," says one. And they all agree. Very strange fellows indeed!

Night! My God! I feel as though I shall not be able to keep myself under control. My calmness has disappeared. Perhaps writing will help me to recover myself.

About eight o'clock the people in the cell all "went to bed." That is, they stretched themselves out on the floor and became silent. I followed their example. In the silence and probably because of the insects, to which I have not yet become accustomed, my thoughts and imagination became active. In spite of my desire not to think of my position and of the future, my whole brain insists on thinking of these things. The nature of the inquiry in the Chekha today and the concluding remarks of the examiner did not leave any doubt as to my fate.

Though they had no definite evidence of my participation in preparations for the "counter-revolution" in Archangel, they had suspicions, and my crimes were so numerous that there could be only one decision. I am to be shot.

I accepted the sentence quietly—if the term "quiet" may be appropriate for such an occasion—but only my reason comprehended it, not my whole consciousness. Now, in the dark night, I feel all its dreadful significance.

After the prisoners had fallen asleep, the door of the cell suddenly opened and nine or ten communists came in. The head of the executioners, a Lett named Petersen, gruffly commanded:

"Petroff, Diakonoff, Tachmeneff, Popoff, Sidoroff, Constantinoff, put on your overcoats and follow us."

"No, you don't need to take your things," he said to the peasants, who, supposing that they were to be freed, wanted to take their "property."

With pale faces, half-mad eyes, quivering hands, the victims tried to put on their rags. All their movements were feverish. They moved like hypnotized somnambulists. Only two of them, the student, Popoff, and the peasant, Petroff, kept to some extent their tranquillity of mind. They shook our hands, and Petroff said: "Good-bye for ever, my comrades. Don't bear me any ill will. If you come out alive, remember me to my family and give these things to my wife. Overcoat and boots are no longer necessary for me; for my children they may

be useful.'' He crossed himself and genuflected:
''Good-bye for ever!''

Popoff kissed the other students and me; ''Long
life to Russia and death to the communistic hang-
men of the Russian people!'' he exclaimed as he
started out.

''Be silent, rascal!'' roared Petersen, and struck
the student's face with his revolver. A tiny stream
of blood flowed down the face of Popoff.

''Long life to Russia and away with the communistic torturers!'' shouted the student again.

''Then I will teach you, counter-revolutionary
scoundrel!'' said the executioner, pointing the revolver at Popoff.

''I am not afraid of your revolver. Fire!''

One, two, three shots thundered. The student
fell. One life destroyed! Horrified silence suddenly
fell upon us, but after a few moments it was broken
by a wild and purely animal cry; a cry of terror and
pain; a roar; a savage groan trailing off into murmurs of dead sadness. Tachmeneff fell into a fit of
hysterics and writhed with convulsions.

''Take this body up and follow us!'' ordered
Petersen.

The executioners and their victims disappeared.

Then deep silence in the cell once more. How terrible this silence! And how terrible the pale faces
of my comrades and their feverish looks! At last
one of the lawyers spoke:

''All that has to be shall be,'' said he. ''All that
must not be shall not be. Let us not think about
this.''

Then the prisoners began to talk in low tones. A priest was on his knees in a corner, continuing to pray. After some time they "went to bed" again, but nobody can fall asleep. Death is too near to every one of us for us not to feel its presence.

"Today was their turn; tomorrow will probably be mine." This everybody thinks.

I have tried to visualize my own last moment. Do I fear it? I do not! It is not fear I feel, but a sense of outrage! I picture the way to the hill of execution. The place is well known to me. How many times have I stood on that lovely hill covered with beautiful pines! How often I have enjoyed the splendid view. How peaceful was this sight then, and how terrible it is now! Probably I will be led out with other victims, surrounded by twenty or thirty Communists. On the way I shall smoke my two cigarettes. I shall have to cross the street near my house where my wife and brother are. Will they feel my last approach? Will their hearts tell them I am near? Perhaps! Perhaps they will come to the road and perhaps I will have the happiness of giving them one last look. In half an hour after that we will arrive at the hill. Then we will be commanded to dig our own graves. I shall refuse to do it. Let the Communists themselves dig my grave, if they want to bury me. For my body I have no sentiment. It may lie in a grave or on the top of the ground for all I care. After that they will order us to take off our overcoats and boots, which they will appropriate as their "revolutionary perquisites." At last they will make us all stand up. If the number of victims is large, some of us will be obliged to await our turns and to watch the others die. Then will come our turn. They will give the order to fire. I wonder if I shall hear the firing before I lose consciousness. There probably will be a sharp pain, but if they shoot straight all will be finished; if the shooting is bad, it will be necessary to suffer for some time. But do I fear this suffering? Not at all. Why, then, does all my organism, all my soul, all my "self" protest against this? Why do I feel so upset? Why? Not because I fear, but because I want to live!

I want to hear, to see, to experience all the wonders of life! I want to do what I have to do, and so much that I have not yet done! I want to see my friends, and above all, I want to see her, my heart and love! Good God! What must she be living through! My sufferings are nothing in comparison with hers. She will be thinking of me every moment and wondering whether I am alive or dead. She will be wanting to help me, knowing herself to be absolutely helpless; knowing that she may not have a chance even to say good-bye; to give me a last glance; knowing that she may not even see my dead body! All this is too much for anyone! Where is she now and what is she doing? Perhaps she is wandering somewhere around the prison in the hope of seeing me, wanting to know whether I am alive or dead. And my friends? My country? My scientific works? No, I wish to live and I must live! Escape, run, run, run away! But how? I ponder over this matter. But no chance! No possibility!

The prison is too closely guarded. The doors are too strong, the walls too high. Impossible! Oh, if it were possible to fall asleep and forget everything! But alas, I cannot! In the cell is half-darkness. On the floor are lying many bodies, the flesh of the Revolution. Silence! Only from time to time deep sighs and delirious exclamations from the men sick with typhus break the silence! Typhus? I begin to understand why my fellows do not fear typhus. Indeed, it is not so bad to be in a delirium. All is relative in this world.

Seven men—young and healthy, though emaciated —were brought in today. Fleeing from Vetluga, after terrible sufferings, having traveled about a thousand miles they were caught in the places near which we wandered. Their mothers and relatives, their wives and sweethearts will wait for them in vain. Their lives are over. If not tonight then to-morrow they will be executed. They know it. Three of them are silent. Having knelt in a corner, they are praying. This prayer is the last deepest token of Life, and the highest and purest manifestation of Spirit. Their "self" is now only spiritual, their eyes see the depth of Truth and their bodies are nothing but garments seen by the others and felt not by them. Good Heavens! To whom, for whom, or for whose advantage is the destruction of these young men, these strong men, who have not yet lived half their earthly life! "Their death is necessary for the happiness of Mankind and for the perfect well-being of future Generations!" I wish I could see these happy generations who will build their happiness on the blood and sufferings of previous generations. I think if they have even elementary morals they will not dare to be happy. If they can know even any peace they will be the greatest Egotists that ever existed. However, these happy and perfect generations are nothing but an illusion created by the miserable cripples who have never tasted the wonderful beauty, the mysterious miracles, and the endless happiness of real Life. This ideal of a perfect world is created by beasts who, holding in contempt every real Man's life and Happiness, are cloaking their bestial impulses in the garments of sonorous slogans. If among the people there are criminals dangerous for their fellow-men, surely they are these ferocious brutes styled "saviors" and "liberators." . . . Stop! I begin to philosophize. This is not quite proper now in this "Communistic Academy of Hell."

I have been removed from the common prison room into a lonely cell. It seems that my case is approaching its end. Here in loneliness my thoughts are turning still more urgently to the question "to be or not to be." "My present behavior, from the behavioristic point of view," I say to myself, "is merely an expression of the instinct of self-preservation." For a moment my thoughts are drifting in the direction of scientific curiosity. I begin to analyze my situation, thus stimulating my reactions. I observe my pacing to and fro, my restlessness, my general sensations. It would be interesting now to investigate my physiological processes and to photo-

graph my movements. Probably they are a little
unusual. Probably I look now quite unlike myself.
I have not seen myself in a mirror for many weeks,
but I can imagine how I must look in these rags;
unshaved, bloated from starvation, pale, and disordered. Probably not very different from a real
idiot.

But only for a few moments my attention is concentrated on these scientific problems. Very soon
I catch myself in the thought that no scientific processes can have any interest for me now or ever
again. Wherefore, since my life is almost finished?
I pace to and fro in my cell; listen to voices; from
time to time I peer through the little hole in the
door and think, and think, and think. About what?
I cannot say. My mind is disordered. Through the
little hole I hear a whisper.

"My friend, how are you?" I look out and see
my friend, Zepaloff. "My God!" I exclaim, "you
also here!"

"As you see."

"This means that your crossing the Red frontier
was unsuccessful."

"I was caught."

"It means?"

"It means that in a few days I shall be dead. It
would be nice if we could be shot together, would it
not?" He said that.

Then his nightmare was really prophetic. His
bad dream was about to come true. God help him.

A day or two later the warden told me that my
friend had been shot. "He walked out crying:

'Long live Russia and real democracy,' and on the wall of his cell he wrote, 'The gods are thirsty,' " said the warden.

One more valuable life gone. I wish I might see Smilga, Vetoshkin, and other Bolshevist leaders whom he saved from arrest, and to whom he gave such generous help. They thanked him then. Murderers!

Seven men from Vetluga died tonight. This voracious monster, the Revolution, cannot live without drinking human blood.

I am still alive. All my preparations are finished. My last letters to my wife and friends are written. My last address to my countrymen, also. They are in the hands of a friend who will forward them when the time comes. In this cell time is passing very slowly. I sleep badly. Each morning I try to read and write, but with little success. Only for a few minutes can I hold my attention to the pages. Beginning at six o'clock in the afternoon until midnight I watch and listen feverishly to the sounds and to heavy steps in the prison. This is the time when the Red "popes" of the Revolution come for the daily sacrifice to their God. For me, or not? When the steps are gone, I say to myself: "It is not yet my turn!"

Today the door of my cell suddenly opened and the Commissar of Public Instruction came in. I had been told that he was a worker from Petrograd and a comparatively decent man. He carefully closed the door behind him, and in a low voice said to me: "Citizen Sorokin, you are our enemy now, but I remember your lectures for us in the workers' school in Petrograd, before the Revolution. Then you gave us a great deal and you really helped the workers."

"I fear that I taught you very badly if you, one of my students, are with the Communists."

"Let us not dispute in vain," he replied. "In spite of your present views, I think you may be useful to the country as a scientist. We have to do a great deal in the sphere of public instruction, and we have very few men capable of instructing. According to my opinion, such men as you must not be executed."

"Well, what do you want from me?"

"Would you agree to participate in the organization of public instruction if you were saved?"

"I have worked as an educator for many years and, of course, I am ready to perform this duty now as I understand it ought to be performed," I replied. "But I have no reason to think that such activity on my part will not again be regarded as 'counter-revolutionary.' "

"I cannot deny it. However, I will do my best to save you, though I have no serious hopes. Don't tell anybody about our meeting. Good-bye."

The door closed. An odd little "comrade" he is, this worker-commissar! At any rate, he is a brave man. If his friends in the Chekha should learn of his visit to me, he would soon be in my position.

Through the little window of my cell I can see a part of a field beyond the wall of the prison. Many hours I have stood at this window, hoping I might see a friend or my wife, and today I was splendidly rewarded! Standing at the window I suddenly saw her. What happiness! I shouted and waved with my dirty towel to attract her attention, and I succeeded. My poor dear! A few minutes we gazed at each other. That was all we could do, but what happiness! Thanks to Heaven!

The first anniversary of the Bolshevist Revolution—November 7—has arrived. Yesterday the Red priests gave their glutton god an extraordinary feast of human flesh. Twelve lives were sacrificed at once. Now we are told that for three days there will be no more executions. In the official newspapers this is announced as an "amnesty." Well, then, we all have three days to live while the Revolution is digesting its last heavy meal. After that the god will probably be so hungry that it will demand extra rations.

I am back again in the common cell. Why? I do not know. I find many changes. Two have died with typhus; one man was liberated; about twenty-five others have been "liberated" on the hill of execution. In their stead, new prisoners, principally peasants, have been brought in. It is the "sacred place of Revolution" and it ought not to be empty.

Three days of comparative quiet.

Three days passed over. My apprehensions concerning the hunger of the Revolution were justified. Today at about ten o'clock the worshippers of the god of Revolution again came for the food. But instead of three or five men—the average daily portion—they took sixteen at once. The high priests of the Revolution entered at the moment when the prisoners were praying. But the prayers were rudely interrupted. As usual, the names of the victims were read. All submissively began to put on their overcoats, and to shake our hands. All but one. He did not move, but continued to lie on the floor. "I will not go," said he. "If you want me, you will have to carry me."

"Then, comrade, perhaps this will make you move," said the same Petersen, putting his revolver to the man's head.

"Fire! It is more convenient for me to die here than there!" stubbornly answered the prisoner.

"As you wish! Carry him out!" shouted the Communist.

Again the old terrible silence in the cell. Then: One, two, three, four shots in the prison yard!

"Great God, do not forget his soul in Thy blessed kingdom; give him peace and eternal life," prayed an old peasant kneeling and crossing himself. All the prisoners fell on their knees and began to cross themselves.

"We have no help, we have no hopes but You, O Mother of God," a priest began to sing. "Help us," joined in all the prisoners in full voice. "We have hope in You. We pray to You, we praise

You! Don't leave us, poor creatures of the earth!"

This was real prayer. Never have I heard such. In the voices echoed all man's love of life, all despair, all suffering, and all belief in the God of helpless human souls.

"Sorokin, put on your overcoat and follow us." This was the command today of four Communists who came into our cell. My turn had come at last. Well, I was ready. Only inside of me, I felt as though something had suddenly snapped, and a cold shiver ran through my body. "Courage, my friend, courage," said I to myself. "Noblesse oblige." So with all my courage uppermost, without haste, I shook hands with my fellows. "Good-bye, my friends. . . . Good-bye." I went out to the yard of the prison, preceded and followed by my guard.

"Come here." One of them pointed to the door of the prison office. I entered.

A man with a long nose, probably a Jew, invited me to sit down. I sat.

"Is this telegram known to you?" he stretched forth a bit of paper to me. "On Thursday N. Tschaikovsky is starting from Vologda by the steamer *Uchreditel,*" I read.

"No, I don't know it."

"Have you received such a telegram?"

"Never."

"Nevertheless, it was addressed to you, was it not?"

"I might with equal justice claim that it was addressed to you."

"You may persist in denying an evident thing,"

said the inquisitor, "but it is all in vain. Your participation in the Archangel counter-revolution is known and your sentence has been passed."

"If that is final why trouble me further?"

"Take him back."

It would be interesting to know just why they keep taking me to that office instead of to the place of execution. Though these interviews may have some meaning for somebody, I should prefer to die without any more of them. They are too exhausting, too nerve-racking. Congratulations met me in my cell, but they gave me no hope. Today's examination tells me that my drama is approaching its end.

The days crawl like lice one over the other. Every night the same summoning of victims to the slaughter. Our suspense grows almost unbearable. It would be easier to walk out to death than to die thus slowly from day to day. It is difficult to keep one's outward calm for weeks together. If one knew that in two days—three—five—. But weeks, weeks! It is very difficult even for the bravest. I try to take cold, to contract typhus, anything to hasten the end. All the others, I observe, do the same. There is actually competition among us to get nearest the typhus patients. Some of the men pick lice off the unconscious and dying and put them on their own skins.

Today seven victims.

Today three.

Today only one.

Today nine.

Death hovers over me but does not touch me yet. Today three more. My God! How long will this torture keep up? I am remembering descriptions of the French Terror. This is quite like it. History repeats itself.

Sixty-seven new prisoners, among them five women and four children, have just come in. They are peasants of the Nicholsky District, who had the temerity to resist when the Communists came to "nationalize" all their corn, cattle, and other possessions. Artillery and machine guns were sent to the village to put down the revolt. Three villages were razed and burned, many peasants were killed, and more than a hundred arrested. The sixty-seven who joined us here are in horrible plight, arms broken, flesh lacerated, black bruises. The bitter weeping of little children is heard now in our prison. I wonder how long they can live in this hell. If they survive they will be, no doubt, good Communists in future. The education of the new generation of Communists has begun, and probably will not be soon forgotten. Good God! If the fathers must suffer, why should these sinless little ones be punished? The prison is overcrowded now. Would that the babblers who used to sing revolutionary songs could be with us.

We are less crowded today. Most of the peasants have been executed. One of the children is left without father or mother. Also new cruelties are

beginning, reminiscent of the last moment reprieve
of Meseneff. This afternoon a merchant was led
out for execution. He witnessed the shooting of
four men, and then came his turn.

"Tell me where you have concealed your money
and I will let you off," said the Chekha executioner.

"I have no money left."

"All right, then. Fire!" he commanded.

The rifles cracked, but the merchant did not fall.

"This round was blank," explained the executioner, smiling. "But I am sure you will not wish a
repetition of the experience. You'd better tell
where your money is hidden."

They brought him back to the prison, speechless
and half-crazed. In a few hours he was a gray-
haired wreck.

We have a very interesting new prisoner, the
former commissary Kkapkoff. This man, previously a clerk in the Northwest Transport Company, had been ardent in arresting counter-revolutionaries, but still more ardent in appropriating
"nationalized" wealth, and in the violation of girls
and married women. "If you don't come with me
for the night, your relatives will all be arrested. If
you come they will go free." Such had been the
method of this apostle of the new millenium. It
seems that at last he carried his bestiality so far
that even his fellows could stand him no longer. In
prison he behaves with revolting cowardice. Some
of us want to kill him, but we agree that it would be
too bad to soil our hands on such a beast.

Blessed be this day! For the first time I was permitted to go with some of the others to saw wood on the banks of the Sukhona. This great privilege was hitherto permitted to all save myself and one or two other politicals. In a group of about sixty I went out, heavily guarded. The prisoners greedily picked up from the streets cigar ends, cabbage leaves, and rotting potatoes. Some friends recognized me as I passed and hurried to inform my wife and one relative. An hour later, at some distance, I saw them, those beings so dear to me. During two hours of hard labor I had the bliss of gazing at them. As we filed back to prison we passed close to them. Tears streamed from their eyes. In my rags, unshaven, dirty, prison-pale, I must have been a sad sight for them to look upon. Yet I bless the day that gave me the unspeakable joy of seeing them once more.

CHAPTER XV

TODAY, December 13, I am writing, not in prison, but in the railway station of Luza. Yesterday about three o'clock I was again ordered to go to the office. I entered the room. My wife! What does this mean?

"Please, Professor Sorokin, will you sit down?" This was my inquisitor, only today there was in his voice a note of servility. "This article in *Pravda* may interest you." It was Lenin's article about me, the main theme being that men of my kind, representatives of the little bourgeoisie, the middle classes, the peasantry, in their origin and previous activities democratic, and only by unhappy chance becoming enemies of the Communists, deserved special attention. The task of the Communists should be to convert them into allies. To have intellectuals and educated men in Communist Russia would be good for the country.

"We have received an order from Lenin himself," and the Chekhist emphasized the last two words, "to send you to Moscow, where you will be at the disposal of the Central Chekha. Tomorrow morning you will start. We will arrange whatever is necessary for you."

"May my wife go with me?"

202

"No, she will have permission to join you within two or three days."

"May my wife bring me clean garments? These," pointing to my filthy rags, "are a little soiled."

"Oh certainly."

Next morning, followed by Petersen and a Russian Chekhist, I was driven to the Luza station. A clear winter sky was over my head, a clean, cold wind blew in my face. Life, wonderful life, summoned me again. I tried to imagine how the miracle came about, but I gave it up. In one village we had to change horses. Petersen rushed into a house and pointing his revolver at a terrified peasant bellowed: "Horse, in five minutes, or you will be shot." The peasant rushed out, but not without casting a look of deadly hatred at this representative of the Government of the Proletariat. Never in my life have I seen such treatment of peasants by Czarist officers.

The train arriving at Luza, we entered a wagon of "Special designation," to quote the legend on its walls. This was a comfortable international sleeping wagon appointed solely for agents of the Government, while the people travel in, on top, on platforms, or above the wheels of trains. While the other travelers fast, the apostles of "equality" sit comfortably in their compartments eating caviar, meat, good bread, and drinking wine. Equality indeed!

For three days, closely guarded, I traveled with these Chekha officials. Quite casually they told me

how they had hunted for me among the villages,
how many people they had killed, among others
naming some of my friends. "Some of them died
quietly," said Petersen, "but some cried, screamed,
and tried to get away. They caused a lot of trouble,
those people. Often we were forced to shoot them
on the way, or at least out of their turn."

"How did Zepaloff die?"

"Oh, quite bravely. He was a perfect reactionary."

"What do you do with the bodies after execution?"

"We take off the clothes and throw them into the
graves. In this way we once detected a perfect
scoundrel. When his boots were jerked off, we
found a hammer that this thief had stolen from the
prison." Petersen's voice, as he told this tale of a
prisoner's criminality, was full of indignation.

"Is there a physician to certify to the death of
those who are shot?" I asked.

"Ah! Such a bourgeois formality does not exist
with us. The proletariat kill their enemies. But if
a few are buried alive—the result is the same. The
only thing that is important is that they die."

On the morning of December 16, 1918, we reached
the Central Chekha, in Moscow. There I found,
among other prisoners, Professor Kaminka, just
down from Petrograd. Soon the rooms began to
fill with "fresh fish," newly arrested girl and boy
students, a priest, two literary men, workmen,
profiteers, professional thieves, and two prostitutes.
There being no chairs, we all sat on the floor. Most

of the "fish" were depressed, but two students, two girls, and a boy who told us that they were anarchists, were in high spirits.

An agent of the Chekha appeared, and addressing Professor Kaminka and me, said: "Do you want dinner?" Half an hour later came potato soup and two small morsels of bread were given us. The others got nothing. About seven in the evening the agent again entered the room and said to me: "You are free to go when you like."

Concealing my intense excitement, I followed him to the office, and while papers were being signed, I looked around at this center of the terrorist machine. There was a pretty woman in the room, exquisitely dressed and adorned with many jewels. Merrily chatting, she worked at a pile of papers. The others addressed her as "comrade Peters," from which I inferred that she was either the wife or the sister of the great head terrorist Peters. I could not keep my eyes off this beautiful women, this lady of the terror, participating in the bloody work of the Chekha. Any woman outside the Chekha who went into the street in such clothes and such jewels would have lost all her finery, her liberty, perhaps even her life. Her relatives would have been arrested. Apparently the Communists, if they could not bring about universal happiness, were looking well after their own.

At last my papers were handed to me, and clasping them to my heart I walked out into the streets of Moscow. The thought that I was saved, that I had actually risen from the dead, quite overwhelmed me. I wandered along for a time unconscious of where I was going. Recovering myself with difficulty, I turned towards the house of an old friend. But in answer to my ring a stranger came to the door. He had no idea of what had become of my friend, so I went on to another apartment. Strangers were in his home also. The third visit brought to the door an intimate friend who at first sight failed to recognize me. When I spoke my name he cried: "My God, but you have changed. You look twenty years older."

"It is the times that move so quickly," I laughed. "In a few months of this glorious era of progress one lives twenty years. Now please give me some clean undergarments. Mine are full of lice."

He gave me a room in which to bathe and change. The water was icy cold but I enjoyed the bath, and afterwards the hot tea over which we discussed my adventures and those of our friends. Three days later I had the happiness of meeting my wife and also the friend with whom I had wandered so long in the forest. The day after my departure he had left and had safely reached the house of a friend in Ustyig, who hid him in the bath-house. One night he heard sudden cries and rifle shots, and looking out through a knothole, he saw many armed Communists chasing a man who was being led to execution. The man had made a desperate attempt at escape and was headed straight for the bath-house. If he had reached it there would have been two executions instead of one, but the fugitive fell in the road and the Communists, running up, plunged their bayonets in his prostrate body. With the help of his friends, my friend got himself registered as an unemployed workman and finally the Bolshevist Labor Exchange gave him permission to go to Moscow.

A few words about my unexpected reprieve. It was the work of my old student, the commissary, who visited me in prison. He spoke of me to two Bolshevist leaders, who were friends of mine in our student days, and the three of them, old memories being not quite obliterated, went to Lenin demanding my liberation. Lenin, hoping to get credit for his magnanimity, wrote that *Pravda* article about me and ordered my release.

As I was not on parole of honor, I felt myself free to act as my conscience dictated. Therefore, if my activities since my resurrection have not entirely pleased the Bolsheviki it is their affair, not mine.

CHAPTER XVI

FIRST STEPS IN THE COMMUNISTIC PARADISE

AFTER a few days in Moscow I went to Petrograd. What I saw from the Nicolaevsky Station was the abomination of desolation. It was as though a devastating plague had swept the town. No trams, no droshkies. No shops open. Broken and dirty windows revealed dark emptiness. All sign boards had been torn down. The streets were indescribably dirty, and in many places the pavements had been torn up. Here and there fragments of torn flags and red placards made the desolation seem more complete. And the people!—in rags, with emaciated and pallid faces, the few pedestrians plodded along as though crushed by poverty and grief. Old men and women sat on the pavements from time to time stretching out withered hands in vain. "In the name of God, a crumb of bread." But no one gave them anything. As I turned into Basseinaia Street I met a man and a woman drawing a sled on which lay a rough coffin.

Very hungry myself and sickened by such sights, I looked everywhere for a shop where I could buy a morsel of food. I found none. I went to my own apartment on Nadejdinskaia Street and found it occupied by a Jewish family. The woman politely explained to me that my lodging with all its furniture was "nationalized" and had been given to her family by the Soviet authorities.

"Might I at least get my books and papers, my linen, clothes, and personal belongings?" I inquired.

"Some of your books and papers are over there in the corner. Please take them. As for your clothes and other things, we found nothing like that here."

Except a few books and papers, all my property had disappeared. Some volumes lying close to the stove indicated the use to which others had been put.

"Please excuse us," said the woman. "We didn't know whether you would ever return. Besides, it was so cold and we had no fuel to burn."

"Well, please don't burn what is left," I entreated. "Tomorrow I will come and get them."

My precious books burned, my papers, all my clothes gone. Dressed in borrowed undergarments and in the torn boots and overcoat I had worn in the forest, I went to the home of old neighbors. As usual, I was greeted with: "How terribly you have changed."

"Look at yourselves," I retorted. "You are changed, too."

Mrs. D. laughed. "Oh yes, my daughters and I wear our clothes several sizes smaller now." And having heard of my homeless plight she said: "Do take one or two rooms here. We are to have two or three Communists quartered on us, and it will be ever so agreeable to have you instead."

Now it was only necessary to settle the problem of daily bread. My friends gave me what they could, but they had so little that I could not possibly accept anything from them. Private commerce being forbidden, it was also impossible to buy food.

"You must get cards. Meanwhile, if you have any money left you may get a dinner at this house on Konyushennaia Street. Tell them we sent you, otherwise they won't dare admit you," said Mrs. D.

Next morning early I went to the Commissariat of Dwellings to get permission to live in Mrs. D's house. After about an hour I got it. Then I went to the Commissariat of Supply for food cards. After standing four hours in line the crowd of hungry people were told that the office was closed for the day. Half-starved, I went to the "illegal" dining saloon and rang the bell. The door was cautiously opened by a lady who gave a quick glance at my rags and asked me what I wanted. I told her my name and said that Mrs. D. had sent me.

"Come in," said the lady smiling. "I beg your pardon, but you see I took you for one of the 'tovarishi'." In an inner room to which she led me I found about twenty men and women "illegally" dining. Among them I saw Professor Rozin, my old colleague in Criminal Law and Criminology, who was now vice-president of the University. Warmly he greeted me, saying: "You will now have a very interesting book to write about crimes in Communistic Society. Only under Communism is eating in a place like this, in dead secrecy, counted a crime."

"I shall certainly write that book," I assured him. "Not forgetting to point out that without committing crimes against a Communistic Government one would die of starvation.''

Being given a bowl of millet gruel, I began criminally to eat. In fact, I could criminally have eaten two or three portions without entirely satisfying my hunger.

Next morning, two hours before the opening of the Commissariat of Supplies, I joined the long line of waiting people. About noon I got, not cards, but an order for cards. I walked a very long distance to the designated district office, but finding there a very long line, I knew I should get no cards that night. Again I sought the secret dining saloon and criminally ate another small bowl of gruel. It was two days before I got the desired bread card, food card, tobacco card, fuel card, and clothes card. As a professor I received cards of the second category. First category cards were issued only to Soviet officials and some workmen. Third category cards were issued to "bourgeosie" and "exploiters." These last, as Zinovieff said, gave just enough to enable the holders not to forget the smell of bread. In fact they gave nothing. Professors, as a "semi-parasitic group," got second category cards, which meant barely enough to keep them alive.

"At last I have finished my damned card collecting," I told my friends. "Yes," they answered, smiling sarcastically, "but to have cards for food, clothes, and fuel is one thing. To get the food, clothes, and fuel is another. As far as that is concerned, you may as well throw away the clothes and fuel cards. But keep the other, and something you may get with it." A whole week I had spent getting those cards and now I had to throw them away. Adaptation to the Bolshevist paradise I found was going to be difficult. I remembered the old Socialistic formula: "To everyone according to his needs," now became "To everyone according to his cards." But cards, unfortunately, one cannot eat or wear. The real rule was "To everyone nothing unless he gets it by transgressing laws of the Communist Government." But if during that first ten days in Petrograd I had not found means of transgressing I should have died of starvation.

Having finished my card collecting, I visited the University of the Psycho-Neurological Institute to let my colleagues know that I was alive and to find out what had happened to my University position. Busy with civil war, the Bolsheviki had not yet annihilated all University life. My old professorship in University and Institute was offered me and after Christmas it was arranged that I should begin again my lectures and seminars. I was elected also professor of Sociology in the Agricultural Academy and the Institute of Public Economy, and I accepted both, because it was necessary to have the extra allowances. At the same time two large co-operative organizations, not yet nationalized, asked me to write them textbooks in law and sociology.

Visiting the University dining-room, I met another publisher, a literary man of great talent, who asked me how much longer I was going to postpone writing my System of Sociology. I told him that all my material, gathered over a long period of years, had been lost. The subject was not fresh in my mind and I felt I could not write the book. But he urged that his Society needed it and that I should know from experience how foolish postponements, in our circumstances, were.

"Today one is alive, tomorrow dead. It is better to publish a needed book even if it has some defects," he said. "Begin your *System* at once, and I will publish it."

I knew he was right, so I accepted his offer. Soon my wife arrived from Moscow and we settled down to live and work in the bosom of Communistic culture.

On the night of December 31, 1918, we held a New Year's meeting with Mrs. D's family and a few other intimate friends. Each had a little piece of bread, some cakes made from potatoes, and a glass of tea with a morsel of sugar. It was so cold in the room that all sat in wraps and hats. Midnight struck, the hour for congratulations and speeches in other days. Now just one speech was made.

"The terrible year is over. Let us be thankful that it has gone. Let the memory of our dear friends who perished during its mournful months live forever. From the coming year we expect neither peace nor joy. If at its end we, our relatives and friends, are alive we shall be happy. May we have courage to meet the coming trials."

We sat silent and mournful. Each thought sadly of those who had died and prayed fervently for those who were still in the jaws of the Red monster. One mother mourned her son, who had just been beaten to death. Vera, the beautiful daughter of Mrs. D., was moody and distraught. Her betrothed was in prison. This, together with other horrors she had known, had affected her seriously. Her mother feared for her life, and I knew that her apprehensions were not unjustified.

PART III

1919-1920

CHAPTER XVII

IN THE BOSOM OF COMMUNISTIC CULTURE

"THE TROGLODYTES," we called ourselves. Not that we lived in caves, but I am sure that the original cave-dwellers enjoyed more comforts than did the ninety-five per cent of the population of Petrograd in 1919. Mrs. D's apartment, for example, had eight large rooms, but in that bitter winter only two of them could be used. Mrs. D. and her two daughters lived in one, my wife and I in another. We always spoke of this as our "winter concentration." In Communistic society everything had to be "natural," and we certainly had a natural temperature in our dwelling, which was heated principally from our lungs. We had fuel cards, but no fuel. We did use the cards themselves for fuel to some effect— that is, for boiling water and for very primitive cooking. The water supply of Petrograd at this time was so full of typhus and other disease germs that it was impossible to drink a drop of it without boiling, and this is how we managed. We got a small iron box, often used by the very poor, and called a *"bourgeuika."* This had one hole on the upper side and another at the back. In the latter we inserted the pipe from our samovar, and by stuffing the box with useless fuel cards, we got from it enough heat to boil water. Sometimes we succeeded in buying (illegally, of course) some fuel. More

often we went to the Neva and more or less successfully ripped boards and timbers from barges sunk
in the river. We also tore planks and palings from
fences, but mostly we had to burn chairs, tables,
books, and papers. Often when, after waiting days
at a time, people received directions from the Commissariat of Supply as to where to get wood on fuel
cards it was simply some wooden house that was
being torn down, I suppose, as part of the Soviet's
program of destroying capitalism. Small wonder
that house furniture and even fuel cards seemed
more practicable, especially in view of the fact that
when amateur house wreckers attempted to get fuel
from the condemned houses, they were frequently
injured and sometimes killed by falling beams and
timbers. In 1919 the most valuable present one
could give or receive was a piece of firewood.

As for sanitary conditions, they are simply not
to be described in the language of decency. All
water pipes cracked under the intense cold of un-
heated houses, and in the upper stories people could
neither use toilets nor get water. We had to use
the courtyards for our physical necessities, and get
what water was running in the first floors of our
own or neighboring houses. In the spring and summer water began to run, but as the pipes were all
burst, the water and filth that leaked through ceil-
ings made lodgings still more unlivable. Above us
lived a group of those sailors whom Trotzky had
hailed as the pride and glory of the Revolution.
The living habits of these men were so filthy that

when the winter thaw began—but I really must draw the line somewhere in these descriptions.

"This is communia," said a plumber, invited in to repair the disaster to our rooms. We experienced communia in many other departments. Broken window glass had to be repaired with rags. To wash or to take a bath was almost beyond anyone's power. The laundry, a bourgeois institution, disappeared. Soap was included in food cards, but it was never given. There being insufficient fuel at home to heat water for baths, we sometimes went to public baths, but that meant standing hours in line on the one or two days of the week when the baths were open, and it meant also running fearful risks of contracting disease or becoming infected with lice, an almost certain way of contracting typhus.

What was perhaps hardest to bear was the darkness. Electric lights were turned on only for about two or three hours in the evening, and very often it was not turned on at all. Everyone knows that in that northern latitude it is quite dark at three o'clock in winter, so our blindness of vision may well be imagined. We could get almost no kerosene. In fact, the best thing we could do was to make what we called a *"nedyshalka"* (which means "don't breathe") lamp out of a bottle filled with kerosene or wood oil, and having a crude wick in it. This lamp made darkness visible, but it did not permit either reading or writing. It did not even permit much moving around, for the *nedyshalka* was well

named; it went out at a breath. Most evenings were
spent in doing nothing at all, for even when the
electric lights were turned on we knew it was for
the purpose of making house searches and arrests.
Also more "nationalization," for when the Chekhists visited a house they took everything they
pleased.

Our food cards gave us daily from one-eighth to
one-half a pound of very bad bread, and sometimes
we received even less. We used to go to "dinner"
at the Communistic dining-room at the University,
but even here we had only hot water with a few bits
of cabbage in it. We went in spite of the fact that
Professor Vvendensky, as a real scientist, accu-
rately computed that we wasted more strength in
walking and in waiting there than we received in
vitamines and calories from the food. The words
dinner, and "I have dined," had a pleasant sound
and gave a sort of an impression that we were still
getting something to eat. But we were always hungry. Our dreams were always full of eating, especially eating pounds of butter and other fats. Those
people who formerly had suffered from indigestion
and sugar excess became cured of indigestion. They
became extremely emaciated. We, on the other
hand, grew bloated, pale, and weak. This bloating,
however, was a temporary symptom. In time all
grew thin. Many began to lose their memories, developed starvation psychoses and delirium, and
died. Had it not been for "speculators" and
"profiteers" there is hardly a doubt that the entire
population of Petrograd would have died in a

month. All except the Communists. Risking arrest
and death every time we did it, we used to steal to
certain apartments, particularly to that of the Communist sailors, and buy potatoes, gruel, bread, and
even sometimes a little butter. From time to time
friendly peasants, "meshecniks," came to our
apartments and illegally sold us food or exchanged
it for silver and gold objects, watches, clothes, cur-
tains, linen, even pictures, anything they fancied.
Many people took their valuables, including old
clothes, and went to the country to barter. But
often after they had succeded in getting a few
pounds of potatoes these were seized by the guards
and they themselves were arrested. Some died in
prison of typhus, some were shot.

Day and night all apartment house dwellers had
to do guard duty at the doors of their own houses.
Sitting or pacing up and down, we looked out on a
dead Petrograd. From midnight until six in the
morning it was forbidden for anyone to leave his
home without special permission from the authorities. Therefore, the only thing that broke the
monotony of these night watches was an occasional
fire alarm, funeral sledges being drawn over the
snow, firing squads going out with prisoners for
execution, or Chekhists on searching parties. There
was one other interruption of which it is difficult
calmly to write, and that is the noisy and obscene
exit of drunken Communists from an orphan asylum
of girl children next to my lodgings. Sometimes
these unhappy children came to our house, to the
apartments of the sailors overhead. I could not

stop them because they were not counter-revolutionaries. I could not stop them because they were so
hungry, and in the apartment of the "pride and
glory of the Revolution" was abundant food. Besides, sexual purity had been declared by the new
nobility to be more bourgeois prejudice.

Getting up each morning, one of us began preparing "breakfast" while another ran off to get a
place in the bread queue. These damned queues
took two or three hours of our time each day, but
gave us almost nothing in return. Our existence
was filled with queues; queues for bread and salt,
queues for herrings and tobacco, queues for
"coffee" and gruel, queues for registering our address, as we had to once a month, queues for any
official certificate we might require, queues for
everything imaginable. They became a perfect
nightmare. The real scientific definition of Communism, based on experience, is queues, endless
queues.

While one of our household was thus haunting
queues, the other split wood—if there was any wood
—carried up water, lighted the *bourgeuika*, and
with eyes streaming and throat half-choked with
smoke, prepared breakfast—that is, hot water with
a little saccharine, a morsel of bread, and if we had
had very good hunting, a little rye gruel. For dinner
we had what I have described, and for supper more
hot water and bad bread. After breakfast we
cleaned our room as well as we could, and then if
there was no compulsory public work, no guard
duty, no more queues, no sick or dead friends to

attend, I tried to write on my *System of Sociology* or to prepare my University lectures. I sat with all my wraps on, gloves on my hands, and my feet rolled in rags. From time to time I got up and exercised to limber my half-frozen limbs. In the afternoons and evenings I went to my work, walking from one Institute to another, from eight to ten miles a day. Exhausted from these exertions and from constant hunger, I went early to bed—unless it was my turn to stand guard all night. So we lived in the "Russian Soviet Federative Socialistic Republic"—"Russian Surely Fantastic Soviet Republic," we called it.

Depression overcame me everytime I went to the University. Entering the campus, you heard no more the sound of young voices and laughter. The place was dark except in the physics building where, by some miracle, Professor Khvolson managed to get enough kerosene to keep his laboratory windows alight. Lectures were given only in the evening, because all day the students were struggling to get a living. As I walked through the familiar halls and rooms I heard only the echo of my own footsteps. All lectures and seminars were held in the students' dormitory, which was no longer crowded. Official Communist statistics record that the number of students increased from nine thousand before the Revolution to twenty thousand. But where were these twenty thousand? Neither I nor any of my colleagues ever saw them. In the whole University were no more than three or four hundred.

Passing the office of the University at the end of

the main building, I often read, by the flickering gleam of the "don't breathe" lamp, the following announcement:

"By order of the Petrograd Soviet there will be, tomorrow and the day after, compulsory work for professors, assistants, instructors, clerks, and other University people. The work will consist of transportation of timbers from one place to another. Persons whose names begin A to M must be at the Admiralty Quay tomorrow morning at ten o'clock. Others must be at the same place at the same hour on the following day. Those who disobey this order will be arrested as counter-revolutionaries."

These compulsory labors troubled me little as I was young and strong, and had been accustomed to do manual work. But what a pitiful sight other University people presented, old professors and women who had never in their lives done other than intellectual work. Having neither strength nor skill in handling heavy timbers, within a few minutes they were exhausted, sore, and wounded. Covered with mud and blood, in their threadbare clothing, often falling under their burdens, they were like nothing so much as Egyptian slaves working under the lash of a merciless Pharaoh. This likeness was increased by the presence of Communist bosses, fat and healthy, who enjoyed themselves watching the sufferings of the bourgeoisie, or "idle parasites" as they were called. Often I burned to strike these brutal overseers in the face, but of course that would have been worse than foolish. I may say truthfully that this compulsory labor served no purpose whatever, and for the old scientists and scholars who toiled under the lash, it was slow torture. For Zinovieff and the social dregs who now ruled it was vengeance and nothing more, although they represented it as "Protection of Science and Arts, Scientists and Writers," these words greatly impressing foreign visitors to Russia, who took them on trust.

My classes in sociology at the University became the largest and most closely attended in the whole institution, not because I was such a talented lecturer, but because sociology had now become such a vitally important subject. Not only the students, but the University clerks and the public attended my lectures. I knew that many Communist spies also attended and regularly reported my utterances to the Chekha. Very soon after my release from prison, Lunacharsky and Kristy—Commissaries of Public Instruction and Education—had offered me the position of Commissary of the Universities and Institutes of Petrograd. They thought that Lenin's scheme for converting me and others into allies of the Communists—that is, making us tools in their hands, a feasible matter. But if my colleagues and I were powerless to stop their physical and moral suffocation of our country, we had conscience enough not to encourage or to participate in their murderous activities.

In my lectures I never "played politics." I did not directly try to undermine the existing system, but I did give scientific data, regardless as to whether it supported Communist theories or not.

When I described the social organization of Ancient Egypt under the Ptolemies, of Ancient Peru and Sparta, of the Roman Empire in the Third and Fourth Centuries A. D., it was hardly my fault if the audience burst into laughter and shouted: "This is just the same as our Communist régime." Nor was it my fault when they went out agreeing with each other that no Communistic organization in history ever gave liberty and equality, ever resulted in improvement of the masses or mitigated the exploitation of the toilers. If my scientific data had favored the Government, I should not have been sorry, because it would have made my lot much happier, but I had to present facts as they were. Being a sociologist under such conditions was a damnable business, but I had to be honest. I can hardly describe the difficulties under which I continued my work, which I knew might any day cause my arrest. I lectured in the dark to an audience almost invisible. When I was obliged to consult my notes I would ask: "Is anyone rich enough to loan me a candle end?" Usually someone produced a tiny inch of candle, which I blew out as quickly as possible, for the students, who took their notes in darkness, needed a little light whereby to study. In spite of all obstacles, including constant hunger, these students managed to make almost normal progress. I am speaking of the old students who had returned to the University from the War. We had a new class of student sent up by Lunacharsky, who ruled that a son of the proletariat needed no examinations in order to matriculate in the University. Zero students we called them, and organized special classes for their benefit.

In the daytime, as I have said, the students worked for a bare existence. The faculty visited the University only for meetings and conferences. In our reading-room, as everywhere, desolation reigned. We had no new books or magazines, no scientific journals. Cut off from the whole world, we knew nothing of what our colleagues abroad were doing. We were absolutely cut off even from our colleagues in other Russian Universities. When we met for dinner, the professors, standing in line with dishes and spoons, which everyone had to bring from home, were like the beggars' line at church doors in former times. After a half hour wait these professors, many of them world-famous, sat down to a dish of hot water with a little potatoes and cabbage boiled in it. No bread, no salt, unless someone could contribute a little from contraband stores. As we ate we talked, or tried to talk, of ordinary topics or of our work, but mostly the conversation turned on who had been arrested that day, who had been executed, who had died. Sometimes our conversation was of a timeliness rather ghastly. Professors Vvedensky and Swere enlightened us as to the number of calories in the food we ate, of its chemical composition, and told us about how long human life could be supported on such a diet. Professor S. told us of the dogs that had died of hunger in his laboratory and of their conditioned reflexes. Dr. L. gave us the chemical composition of the brains of twenty men and women who had died of want. Psychologists and psychiatrists gave us their studies of revolutionary psychoses and neuroses. We could not record very many of these discoveries because we had almost no paper, pens, or pencils. We had to give them to each other orally.

When we finished our dinner and our talk we went home. "Good-bye, I hope you will be alive tomorrow," was our usual parting. As the days went by fewer and fewer of us were left to say it.

CHAPTER XVIII

"MEMENTO MORI"

From my journal—

THIS afternoon we buried the academician, Lappo-Danilevsky. A week ago when I visited him he looked like a living skeleton. Smiling feebly, he told me that going to the Academy a few days before he had fallen down and slightly hurt his leg. Three days later I saw him in a hospital after he had undergone a surgical operation. Lying on his bed, a dying man, he was reading *The Phenomenology of Spirit,* by Hegel. "Never had time to study it attentively," he whispered, "begin now." The next day he died.

Yesterday Mrs. D.'s beautiful daughter, Vera, threw herself out of the fifth-story window of our apartment. When we picked her up from the pavement she was alive, but unconscious. Lying on the bed we could see no blood or bruises on her lovely body. Even her half-open, unseeing eyes were brilliant and unclouded. Two hours later she was dead. Vera was like a flower that could not live in this soil of cruelty and bestiality. She lies now on the table in the next room.

To die in Russia in these times is easy, but to be buried is very difficult. Four days elapsed, all of us standing hours in line, interviewing dozens of officials before we could get permission to bury Vera. Finally, we swore to one commissary that unless he gave us a permit we would bring the body to his office. Tomorrow we shall bury her. Meanwhile, we must carefully watch Mrs. D. Crazed with grief, with nothing to look forward to but poverty, suffering, and memories of this horror, she runs about dumb and half mad.

"Ca ira!" Some days ago Professor Khvostoff hanged himself. Yesterday Professor Inostrantseff took potassium cyanide. So dies a great philosopher and the first geologist of Russia. During the last weeks both he and his wife have been very ill. At last, unable to get food or medicines, unable even to call for assistance, they ended their lives. When we entered the dirty, cold apartment to see what we could do to relieve their sufferings, we found two dead people, and near the bed of the geologist traces of potassium cyanide.

Professor Rosenblatt has just put an end to his life. *"Ca ira"* has a meaning somewhat different, I fear, from the old French Revolutionary song. "Why do they commit suicide?" asked Professor Shimkevich, cynically. "One can be sure of a quick death without it." Our intellectuals are stubborn in their counter-revolutionary spirit. They prefer death to life in a Communist paradise.

Professors Rozin, Diakonoff, two Volkoffs, Vilieff,

Kapustin, Pokrovsky, Batushkoff, Kulisher, Ostrogorsky, Karpinsky, Arsenieff, one after another have died, and others are dying. Dying from typhus, influenza, pneumonia, and cholera, from starvation and from all the seventy-seven plagues of Egypt. A friend one sees alive today is dead tomorrow. Our faculty meetings are now little more than mournful memorials to our colleagues. Closing one of these meetings, the Rector, Shimkevich, addressed us with grim humor. "Gentlemen," he said, "I beg you not to die so rapidly. In dying you find relief for yourselves, but you cause us a great deal of trouble. You know how difficult it is for us to get coffins for you; you know that there are no horses to transport your mortal remains to the cemetery, and you know how expensive it is to get graves for your eternal slumber. Please be considerate of your colleagues and try to live as long as you can."

To get coffins is indeed so difficult that most people simply wrap their dead in mats. Some rent coffins in which to carry bodies as far as the cemeteries. Three days we spent in getting a coffin for Professor K., and when the Soviet kindly granted us one it was too small. Only by the expert help of one of our professors of medicine did we succeed at last in cramming poor K. into his box. We drag our dead friends on sledges to the cemeteries. For few of them can we afford an individual grave, the majority of people now being buried in a collective ditch. Not even in death can we escape Communism!

In today's *Pravda*—we have only official papers now— there was published an editorial praising the creative energy of Communism. The author refers to the decision of the Government to build a crematory, the largest in the world. The author is ignorant of the ironical significance of his article. A giant crematory is the most suitable monument a Communist Government could possibly conceive. However, I doubt their ability to construct even a crematory.

This afteroon Professor L. burst into my room in almost insane agitation. "I can't, I can't endure this nightmare longer," he wept. "My sister is dying, all our friends are dying. Around us we see only death, death, death. I cannot do anything. I read, but I do not understand what I am reading. There is no light—there is no end to these horrors!"

I have to remind myself that only those with very strong nerves do not go mad and commit suicide.

Even this triumph of death is not enough for the builders of the new society. The machine of the Red Terror works incessantly. Every day and every night, in Petrograd, Moscow, and all over the country the mountain of the dead grows higher. Shchepkin and one hundred and fifty others, many professors among them, have just been executed in Moscow. More than a hundred in Kronstadt. Hundreds of victims are reported in Kiev. Everywhere people are shot, mutilated, wiped out of existence. In a few years from now the soil along the Irinovskaia and the Finlandskaia railroads, behind Okhta and in the yards of the Chekha, should be very fertile. Ten thousand men and women have fertilized that soil with their bodies. Every night we hear the rattle of trucks bearing new victims. Every night we hear the rifle fire of execution, and often some of us hear from the ditches, where the bodies are flung, faint groans and cries of those who did not die at once under the guns. People living near those places begin to move away. They cannot sleep.

So many arrests are made daily that cloisters and schools are being transformed into prisons. Getting up in the morning, no man or woman knows whether he will be free that night. Leaving one's home, one never knows whether he will return. Sometime a neighborhood is surrounded and everyone caught out of his house without a certificate is arrested. An automobile standing in front of a house is an almost sure sign that someone within is being arrested. Life these last days depends entirely on luck. In forty-seven provinces of Soviet Russia the population has diminished by eleven millions. Everything around us bids us *"Memento Mori."*

"Do not interfere with this great experiment of the creation of a new and perfect society," writes a foreign humanitarian after visiting Soviet Russia. To us this means, do not interfere with the murder of one hundred and fifty million Russian people. If these babblers could be included among the murdered, it would not greatly afflict us.

Today I caught an insect on my body. Is it a typhus louse or not? Let us wait a fortnight and see. If it is typhus, that means the end of me. I am too weak to live through the fever. If I survive this, I am sure that neither I nor any of us will in after life know such a thing as fear. We daily face the ultimate fear.

CHAPTER XIX

In the spring of 1920 we removed to Czarskoe Selo, once the residence of the Czars, now the center of children's colonies. In the Agricultural Academy of Czarskoe Selo my wife and I had work, and given two small rooms and a bit of land for a kitchen garden, we were much more comfortable than we had been in Petrograd. The beautiful parks of the old Imperial town, if badly neglected and cut over, were still beautiful. The palaces, built after Rostrelly's wonderful plans, still charmed our eyes, and recalled to my wife and me the grandeur of our once great Russia. In free moments I wandered in the silent and desecrated parks, peaceful in spite of chopped down trees, scum-covered ponds, and obscene scrawls written by Red soldiers on arbors and bowers. Everything spoke there of the long and glorious reign of the Czars, and everything spoke also of the tragedy of the Revolution.

Sometimes I visited the Alexander Palace, the home of Nicholas II, and Ekaterina Palace, the residence of the older Czars. Neither luxury nor very good taste were shown in the apartments of the late Czar and Czarina. They were like the rooms of rich bourgeois, nothing more. In the boudoir of the Czarina there was a fine Gobelin showing Marie Antoinette with her son, the fated little Dauphin.

Did Empress Alexandra never look at this tapestry with a premonition of dread? On the walls of her sleeping-room were hundreds of religious pictures —ikons—revealing her deep religious nature, perhaps her fanaticism. As a contrast, the tapestries in her bathroom showed designs of a Pompeiian character. In the Czar's study I looked over his library, finding only military works and a few books of humor in cheap and popular editions. Everything in his apartments suggested a certain mediocrity. Tender father and loving husband, sincere man and faithful patriot, what a good citizen he would have been. But to be Czar of one hundred and eighty million people, at the most critical period of Russian history, this was as terrible a tragedy for him as it was for the nation. Nicholas II did not even have in his character ruthlessness enough to be Czar in such times.

The personal valet of Nicholas, now one of the guardians of his old palace, said to me: "The Czar's kindliness was the cause of his fall. He was too soft. He shook hands with everybody. The Czar should not do that. His father, Alexander III, ah, there was a real Czar! He knew what he wanted and he always kept the reins strongly in his hand. Oh, yes," repeated the servant, "that was a real Czar!"

The Czars who made their residence in the magnificent Ekaterinensky Palace were the monarchs, the "Little Fathers," as they existed in the Russian popular mind. Splendor, luxury, exquisite taste,

and marvelous beauty, such were the surroundings
of the autocrats in the days of their grandeur.

"What does my palace lack?" the great Catherine
once asked a French Ambassador.

"Only a casket, your Majesty, nothing more,"
was the courtly reply.

He was perfectly right, this Frenchman, for
Catherine's palace was a real jewel. I wandered
through the silent rooms gazing at their magnifi-
cence and dreaming of the past. Yes, the despots
who lived here, and who now look down from their
gold picture frames, were sometimes cruel, sometimes vicious. Millions of people they exploited.
Many lives and much suffering paid for this jewel
of a palace. But are not the defects of these autocrats in some measure balanced by the power and
the energy they displayed in building the Russian
Empire? Now that despotism is dead, will the
world see another such creation as this palace, the
symbol of their greatness? Comforts men will have
under democracy, but not the enchantment of romance. General standards of decent living are the
aims of democracy, and this is right. Only the
poetic dreams of despotism, disregarding reason
and humanity, creates for its own prestige the
deathless beauty on which the eyes of future generations love to dwell. I thought of these things as
I walked through the silent palaces of the Czars.

Outside the hideous reality of Communistic
despotism met my eyes. Wooden houses half-destroyed for fuel, broken pavements, filthy streets,

weak and emaciated people, Red soldiers in ragged uniforms, and starving children of the Communist colonies, monuments to this new "democracy." On all sides one hears such comments on democracy as these: "When there was the Czar we had plenty of *swinina* (pork), now there is Lenin and we haven't even *conina* (horse flesh)."

"Down with Communists and Jews. Long life to Russia!"

"Russia has had three thievish Gregories. Gregory Otrepieff, Gregory Rasputin, and Gregory Zinovieff. Two Gregories were killed, and the third will be killed also."

"Under the Czar we had only one Rasputin. Now we have thousands."

"Under the Czar we were robbed only by a few of our own people. Now we are robbed by scoundrels of all countries."

"Don't worry. They will all die the death of dogs."

Words like these were scribbled on walls and on arbors in the parks—the only free newspapers left to the people.

Whenever I looked on the children of the Communist colonies, these words found an echo in my heart. I had seen these houses and these children too closely to be deceived by the one show colony kept for the admiration of foreign visitors. Conditions in the ordinary colonies were terrible indeed. Cold in winter, frightfully dirty at all times, no linen, even on the beds, almost no food, such were the visible shortcomings of these "homes" of children of the new aristocracy. Our investigations showed frightful physical deterioration of the children. Their growth was retarded, their bony and lymphatic systems abnormal. In all respects they were much worse off than children not yet "nationalized." The moral conditions of the colonies were very bad. In two colonies every child had gonorrhea. Boys and girls living together were sexually depraved, some of the boys acting as panders between other boys and their own "mistresses." Maddened with hunger, all the children stole from each other and from the administration. Communists being free from bourgeois prejudice against such peccadilloes made light of these things, and of course, no moral or religious education of the children was allowed.

"They are destroying not only the bodies but the souls of the young generation," said several conscientious teachers in these institutions, "and we can do nothing to prevent it."

"I have plenty of such material," answered Maxim Gorky when I implored him to do something to end this appalling condition of affairs. "But I can't help it. The Communists are already angry with me for my interference. They wouldn't even publish my articles about it in *Pravda*."

Later I happened to read articles by foreign writers, enthusiastically praising this "wonderful achievement of the Bolsheviki." If the children of these writers could be placed in these colonies for a year or two—but no, I could not wish them such a fate, not even as a just punishment of their fathers and the lies they have spread abroad.

Not long after taking up residence in Czarskoe Selo, my *System of Sociology*, after many delays, was published. How I ever managed to write those two volumes I have often wondered. Financially, I profited little, but otherwise the publication gave me considerable satisfaction. In a few weeks the edition was sold out, and in spite of many defects, which I frankly pointed out in the preface, my colleagues commented most favorably on the work. I was elected head of the Sociological Department in the University, vice-president of the Sociological Society, and head of the Department of the Social Reflexology in the Research Institute of the Brain. "We are reading your *System* secretly," said two Communistic students from the Workers' Faculty. The factory workers had often in former years invited me to lecture before them. Now their expressions of appreciation, though privately offered, are grateful to me.

Roses of authorship have their thorns, however. "What! Aren't you shot yet?" exclaimed my friend, Professor R. "For certain pages of your *System*, page 142, for example, I think you deserve, under our admirable Government, several executions. No one has published such an audacious criticism of the existing order as you have."

"Well," I answered, "since executions are the general custom, I would rather be shot for something than for nothing."

Later, the books were forbidden by the authorities, but by that time they were all in the hands of readers, so I did not mind. Neither did I object to denunciations which appeared in the Communist press. "The ideologist of counter-revolution"; "The leader of the most implacable professors and intellectuals"; "It is time to crush, once and forever, such persons"; "How long will the Chekha stand this man's activity?"

The Chekha did not mean to stand it very long. One of my students, after his liberation from an arrest, told me that he had seen in the Chekha office a special brief entitled "The University," and under the title "Active Anti-Communists," my name was prominently displayed. The ice beneath my feet became so thin that I did what many others did at that time. First, I neglected to register my address in Czarskoe Selo, but continued to live there illegally. If my room in Petrograd were searched I would have time, being warned by friends, to disappear. With this necessity constantly before me, I provided places into which to disappear. In all these places, and in my lodgings, a system of signs and warnings was arranged by my friends, both for my protection and their own, for when the Chekha searched for a man and failed to find him, they usually set an ambush and arrested everyone who ventured into the place. In this way tens of thousands of innocent persons were arrested. The best thing a wanted man or woman could do was to disappear successfully. The Chekhists had so many people to arrest that they sometimes forgot all about a victim and went out after others instead.

In October, 1920, the "night visitors" went to my
Petrograd address and demanded "comrade" Sorokin. Truthfully my friends told the men that I no
longer lived there, and that they did not know where
I was. When they asked for what crime I was
wanted the men answered: "For banditry."

"That is impossible," exclaimed my friend. "I
have known Professor Sorokin for years, and I
know he is a professor of Sociology in the University."

"All professors nowadays are bandits," replied
one of the Chekhists.

Next morning my students read the announcement: "On account of sudden illness, the lectures
of Professor Sorokin are interrupted. Notice will
be given of their resumption." Such announce-
ments were so frequent that the students quite
understood. For two weeks I peacefully reposed in
the apartment of a friend pursuing my studies. As
soon as I "recovered my health" I went back to my
lectures, but these sudden illnesses became more and
more frequent between 1920 and 1922. After a public speech or the publication of an article, it became
my habit never to spend the night in my own home.
Always on going to bed I asked myself, "Will they
come for me tonight?" I became accustomed to
this, as man accustoms himself to anything.

CHAPTER XX

"THE remuneration of the foreign press," said a prominent member of the Soviet Government in 1920, "requires a considerable sum of our money." This was evident from the number of foreign correspondents, foreign writers and other celebrities who visited Russia at this time, and the character of the information they spread abroad. The English Labor Delegation, H. G. Wells and Bertrand Russell, like other foreigners, saw principally what the Communists wanted to show them; they came in touch with few non-Communists, nor would they have been able to speak with many such had they so desired. They simply swallowed what ever bait the Soviet leaders offered them and went home impressed with the dictatorship of the proletariat, "endless Communist enthusiasm," and the devotion of the people to the Soviet Government. I did not meet Bertrand Russell, but friends of mine did meet him and made what efforts they could to enlighten him as to the true condition of affairs.

I was present at the meeting in the Palace of Labor, from which most real laborers were excluded, and I saw something of H. G. Wells who, from his arrival, was placed under the constant guardianship of Gorky. Wells visited the Academy of Science, but he could not talk with J. Pavlov or other distinguished academicians. Gorky did not take him through the University, but showed him only its one decently equipped building, the physical laboratory. A dinner was given Wells in the House of Arts, with clean table cloths, clean dishes, and better food than any of the intellectuals had seen in years. There was even meat on that table. But to give it a proletarian appearance, the spoons were of wood. To create a truly liberal atmosphere, a number of University professors and literary men were invited, although most of the guests were Communists, and two Chekhists were on hand to watch the counter-revolutionaries. Indignant at the betrayal of truth by these men, I decided to make a speech, although I could not then use the English language. Addressing Wells, but really speaking to the Communists, I explained the real situation and the appalling campaign of murder which was being carried on in the name of liberty. I spoke moderately, for one does with the hangman in the room, but I must have spoken to the point, for Gorky suddenly interrupted, saying that such speeches were inadmissable.

"Then why are we here?" I asked. "Are we invited only to assist in deceiving this great English writer?" At this several celebrated Russian writers, to show their indignation, rose and left the room, crying: "We refuse to be classed with liars."

Amphitheatroff, an eminent novelist, remained, saying to me: "I am going to try to finish your speech." He did manage to speak briefly, but Gorky made him take his seat, declaring that what he was saying was "improper." Gorky's own speech was a sweeping defense of the Communist Government, and made him very popular with them. But it cost him the respect of the intellectuals, many of whom after that evening would never take his hand. As for me, even before the dinner to Wells was over, I left the hall and once more, for my "health's sake," disappeared.

In 1920, when all these famous foreigners were reporting so enthusiastically on the new democracy, the mortality of scientists and scholars increased so frightfully that the Soviet Government began to fear that in a few years all Russian scientists would be dead. A special "scientific ration" was therefore established, giving each family of scientists a monthly allowance as follows: forty pounds of bad bread, two or three pounds of sugar, five pounds of salted fish or meat, five pounds of groats, one pound of salt, two to four pounds of butter, half a pound of "coffee," a poor substitute for the real thing, half a pound of tobacco, and five boxes of matches. We were also permitted to organize a House of Scholars, where we might hold meetings and conferences. For these concessions we were grateful neither to the Government, which had done so much to increase the sufferings and death of the University people, nor to Gorky, who all along had played the rôle of a cunning broker, displaying a generosity which cost him nothing. We were grateful to the foreign scholars and scientists who sent us additions to our poor fare. Every half pound of sugar or bit of soap we thus received was a treasure; and once when we received in one parcel, from some Czecho-Slovak professors, ten pounds of sugar, we felt like millionaires.

The increased ration of course gave us great joy, and once or twice a week when we visited the House of Scholars to receive it, we gladly stood hours in the queues. "Beggars of all the World" we called ourselves, watching world-famous scholars like Pavlov and Markoff waiting in line with rucksacks or baskets; Karpinsky, president of the Academy of Science, falling asleep from happiness when he received his first basket; others, almost as well known, asking each other like paupers: "What are they giving this week?" The House of Scholars became a pleasant retreat also when foreign journals and magazines began to be sent us, H. G. Wells being among the donors. Unfortunately, no new works on social science or economics, psychology or history, philosophy and law, were included in these. We had *The Outlook* for 1919, some copies of *The Edinburgh Review* for 1917-18, two old copies of *The Economic Review* and one of *The Historical Review,* nothing more. In 1922 I received a few sociological works from Czecho-Slovak scholars and from Prof. E. C. Hayes, and these were most eagerly read by all of us.

As our economic situation became ameliorated, our status in other respects became lowered. At the beginning of 1921 a decree was published, signed by the commissary Rotstein, that "Liberty of thought and scientific research is a bourgeois prejudice; that all professors, teachers, and writers should teach and write in full accordance with

Marxian and Communistic theories; and that those who would not do so would be dismissed." To this we replied with a declaration saying that liberty of thought was a condition without which no science could exist or develop; that science recognized no dictatorship except the dictatorship of truth, and that no real scientist or professor would or should obey a decree so absolutely dogmatic and anti-scientific.

Some University professors were instantly dismissed, while others, forbidden to teach, were removed to the Research Institute, "where they would not be harmful to students." The autonomy of the University was utterly destroyed, the elected deans being replaced by Communists, the dismissed professors by Red professors, and a special commissary—a freshman, Tsviback—was set over the Rector and academician Shimkevich. A sailor of the Baltic Fleet, one Serebryakoff, was made dean of the Faculty of Law and Social Sciences. It is enough to say of the Red professors that at one of the faculty meetings the students appeared with the following petition: "As many new professors have been appointed whose scientific works and University activities are unknown to us, we beg the faculty to require the new deans and new professors to publish a list of their scientific works and a short *curriculum vitae* to show their University career." The Red deans and professors got out of this delicate situation by arresting some of the students' representatives, and declaring that they held all bourgeois sciences in contempt.

The students prepared a new petition in which they declared the lectures of the new professors revealed ignorance of their subjects inadmissable even in freshmen. They gave us stenographic reports of these lectures to prove their charges, and they begged us to organize special courses in which they could be trained. Of course, we could neither dismiss the new professors nor organize special courses, and the Rector told the students to take their complaints to the Government—that is, if they were anxious to be arrested.

The new commissary of the University, the Jew Tsviback, took away from the Rector, Shimkevich, the most prominent zoologist in Russia, all his seals and declared that he was now the University head. For the contemptuous manner in which he treated professors and students alike, this man was caught one night by students and severely beaten. But that did not drive him from office. In 1921-22 the Rector was dismissed and most of the professors dismissed, banished, or executed. This policy of the Government was a clear trial of the moral and social spirit of Russian scholars, and I can testify that most of them withstood every trial and temptation to which they were subjected. A very few of those in the lower ranks of the scientists, Svyatlovsky, Gredeskul, Engel, and Derjavin, for example, preferred the benefits of the Government to sacrifice for truth. One of the greatest, J. P. Pavlov, showed to what heights moral and scientific ideals soared in Russia in those terrible days. For no other reason than foreign propaganda, the Soviet Government in 1921 issued a decree giving Pavlov special consideration, providing for publication of all his works, and giving him a committee consisting of Gorky, Lunacharsky, and Kristy, to care for him and for his laboratory. The answer of Pavlov to this decree was this declaration: "I am not a broker, and I do not sell my knowledge for your rations. The dogs in my laboratory may eat better food if you give it to them, but I will not accept any privileges or benefits from hands that are destroying Russian science and culture." Another distinguished intellectual, the writer M., refused even to accept the "scientific ration," and though he was in an advanced stage of tuberculosis, he declined to go to a Soviet sanitarium. "I prefer to die rather than accept anything from the murderers of my country," he said.

Such acts of heroism, such devotion to ideals, in the face of all temptations, have been every day occurrences in Russia during the Soviet rule. Between these moral heroes and those men who have shown themselves cowards, there have been intermediate types, among them three or four scientists who, while hating Communism, adopted a policy of "*captatio benevolentiae*," flattery and servility to the ruling powers. The great majority of intellectuals have simply endured and, when endurance failed, died. Let anyone looking for moral heroism turn his eyes to the thousands of people in Russia who, for years, from day to day, from night to night,

in spite of persecution and temptation have stead-
fastly replied to the Bolsheviki: "Man does not
live by bread alone," and "Thou shalt worship the
Lord thy God, and Him only shalt thou serve."

PART IV

1921-1922

CHAPTER XXI

THE AVENGERS

In January, 1921, I was obliged to go for three weeks to Tambov. Traveling was a dangerous thing, as in a train one could hardly protect oneself from disease-bearing insects. Still, as our daily existence was a permanent duel with death, one extra danger seemed hardly worth noticing. With some difficulty I got permissions and tickets, a mandate from the University certifying my scientific mission, and with all these safeguards I left Petrograd. It took almost three days to get as far as Moscow. By this time my clothes were, as I had expected, covered with insects. That they were of the virulent kind I could not doubt, for on the journey three passengers fell ill with typhus. These unfortunates were simply taken out of the train and left on the platforms of way stations. My neighbor in the compartment was a teacher from Moscow, and on the second day of the journey he handed me a paper with his address, and begged me in the name of God, to let his relatives know in case he, too, were put out of the train. "I know my turn has come," he whispered, "but I shall try not to show my illness. Perhaps I shall be lucky enough to reach Moscow, but if I am discovered and put out I shall certainly die." He was lucky, but if he lived after reaching Moscow I never heard.

After the train left Moscow, the picture became more and more terrible. Rails buried in snow caused the train to move very slowly and to stop almost every hour. At each halt we went out and tried to clear the rails, but what could we do with only two shovels? Near Bogoyavlensk we were halted for almost two days, those two days and nights being quite beyond my power to describe. Few passengers had any food, and as there was no village near, they began to starve. Many fell ill with typhus, and during all the time delirious talk and laughter, moans and cries, oaths and obscenities, mingled with the howling of the winds. In the darkness of the night, in that train full of sick and dying people, devoured by insects, I had a vision of hell itself. When the train finally reached the next station, a dozen typhus cases were left on the platform to die. At all stations the sick had been abandoned thus, and at towns between Bogoyavlensk and Kozloff, I saw dead bodies piled up like stacks of firewood. I even saw abandoned dead along the railway between stations. Seeing them, I remembered an utterance of Lenin: "Either Communism will conquer the insects or the insects will conquer Communism."

Somewhere between Kozloff and Tambov an incident happened which shows how bitterly the Communists are fighting for their lives. The train suddenly stopped and three men in soldiers' uniform entered our car, ordering everyone to remain quiet. All obeyed, but one young peasant, who had entered the train at the last station, stood up and said to the newcomers: "In this wagon only those two are suspicious." As he spoke he pointed to a man in a leather jacket, and to another who, in his conversation, had shown himself a Communist.

"Your papers," the newcomers demanded curtly.

Searching the man in the leather jacket and finding a revolver, they glanced over his papers and said: "A Communist. Take him out." This was done by the young peasant and one of the men in uniform. The other man, who had talked Communism, now began to protest that he was not at heart a Communist, but that he was a clerk in Commissariat of Finance only to keep his family from starving.

"So? Let us see. Have you a cross on your breast?"

The trembling clerk pulled out a cross, and the uniformed man said: "That alone saves your life. I advise you to leave your Commissariat and to babble no more Communistic nonsense." Then, addressing the passengers, "Good-bye, you fellows, go home and tell what you have seen, and try to do what we are doing. Tell your friends that Antonoff sends them his greeting. Death to all Communists, and long life to Russia!"

"Antonoff's boy!" exclaimed the passengers as the man left the train.

At the moment the young peasant returned. "Not a very rich haul this time," he said, "but we caught a few big fish in the wagon of special designation ahead. Look out, my friends, and see what happens."

We looked, and saw a dozen Communists ranged

along the rails. A sudden blaze of rifle fire and the detachment, mounting swift horses, rode away, leaving the bleeding bodies on the snow.

For a few minutes the passengers were silent, some frightened, some smiling. "Not badly these boys of Antonoff are doing," one old peasant exclaimed. Then everybody began to talk of Antonoff, his energy and boldness, and it was evident that in this neighborhood Antonoff was a hero. At Tambov I left the train. Airplanes were hovering above the town, many Red soldiers strolled about, and on the walls I read this announcement, signed by Tukhachevsky, one of the chief commanders of the Red army.

"Villages actively participating in banditry will be burned, the peasants shot, and the women and children arrested. An entire village is held responsible for every bandit, and if a bandit happens to belong to the village where he is caught, every tenth peasant will be shot, his house burned, property confiscated, and his wife and children arrested." In addition, a large reward was offered to anyone who delivered Antonoff, dead or alive, into the hands of the Government.

Even as I read I saw a group of peasant women, old and young, some with babies in their arms. Clad in dirty rags, exhaustion and despair whitening their faces, they walked dumbly on. To prison, of course. I perceived that I was in one of the centers of the Russian "Vendée," not the Vendée of the nobles, the aristocracy or the white generals, but the Vendee of the peasants. Under the leadership of Antonoff these peasants, for more than a year, had waged ruthless war on the Communists. Led by Antonoff, they had been paying back cruelty for cruelty, blood for blood. This Antonoff was a revolutionist whom the Revolution of March, 1917, had liberated from a Czarist prison. He was appointed Superintendent of Police in Tambov by Kerensky, and bore himself so well that the place was soon cleared of criminals. Soon after the Bolshevist Revolution he made the mistake of arresting for murder two Communists. In revenge for this audacity the Communist authorities shot Antonoff's wife. He promptly shot the two men who did it and disappeared.

In that district the requisitions and the beastly cruelties of the Communists soon became unbearable. Not only did the agents take from the peasants all their corn and their poor belongings, often arresting or shooting them afterwards, but sometimes in the dead of winter they chased the peasants naked out of their houses, and threw water on them until they were living icicles. Once or twice a peasant turned on a Communist and murdered him. In retaliation the Communist agents mutilated peasants before shooting them, cutting off the ears, hands, legs, and pudendas of their victims, gouging out their eyes, or violating their wives and daughters in their sight. The peasants caught some of the agents unawares and mutilated them in similar fashion. Some they killed by binding their legs to the tops of two bent trees, letting the trees slowly straighten. Others they tied to the tails of horses and dragged to death.

Antonoff reappeared and organized these peasants into disciplined and systematic avengers. Antonoff's bands, as they were called by the Government, began to attack and to murder Communists in villages and small towns, in trains and even in their offices. Soon many districts were cleared of all Communists. Some were killed, others fled in terror. Liberating these districts, "the Avengers," welcomed by the people, introduced a democratic system of government and proclaimed themselves partisans of a government of the people, for the people and by the people. The movement grew. Against it the Soviet Government sent one regiment after another, but all were defeated. About four provinces were involved in Antonoff's movement, and in others there shortly appeared peasant organizations under similar leaders. The Government then gathered an immense military force and sent it to crush "banditry" at all costs. Artillery, airplanes, cavalry, infantry, and the international regiments were thrown against the peasants as "enemies of the Workers' and Peasants' Government." Many villages were destroyed, many peasants killed. For months the peasants bravely resisted the Red army, but the odds were too great and at last the Soviet trained army began to get the upper hand.

At the time of my arrival in Tambov this war was at its climax. In spite of airplanes and overwhelming numbers, no small group of Communists ever dared go out alone. Once Antonoff with some of his "boys" went to the Communist headquarters in Tambov, and showing false papers, received ammunition, rifles, machine guns, and provisions. That same evening five Communists were found dead, and on their riddled bodies was this message: "This is my thanks to the Communist Government for their gift of ammunition. Antonoff."

In the house of a friend in Tambov I met one of these "Antonoff boys." A tall, fine-looking peasant of about thirty, he impressed me as a very intelligent man. "It may be that we shall be crushed, or for a time, forced to suspend our activities," he said to me. "But someone had to begin to bring these mad dogs to their senses, so we started to do it, and something we have accomplished. If we all die it matters little, because this sort of life is too frightful to endure. What does matter is that we have set an example. The people are waking up, and sooner or later they will rid themselves of this damned communia."

He went out, putting on his head a cap with a red star. "As you see, we disguise ourselves to look like them. In my pocket are plenty of false certificates. In this way we make fools of them. Good night."

Tens of thousands of these avengers perished and are still perishing in Russia fighting against the Communists. If the communistic program was abandoned in 1921, if foreign capitalists have been granted some concessions, and if some property rights are now secure under Bolshevism, this is not due to the sensibility of Lenin or the Communist Government, nor to the intervention of foreign politicians and capitalists. It is due, first of all, to these Antonoff "boys," to the thousands of Russian peasants, and to others who have died and are dying "to bring these mad dogs to their senses."

CHAPTER XXII

EXPIATION

"CAN you, comrades, point to any other country in the world where the Government gives to the working people food, clothing, lodging, and everything free from any charge as we are doing in our Communistic Russia?" So spoke Grishka (Gregory) the Third, otherwise Zinovieff, at a meeting of workmen early in 1921.

"I can," cried a voice from the audience.

"Then pray do."

"In the old Czarist galleys food and clothes, lodging and everything were free, just as in our Communistic society. Only they were better," shouted the man.

"Good! Perfectly true," laughed the audience.

Grishka tried to speak again, but he was interrupted.

"Sit down! We have heard enough, you fat devil!" And as the workers' patience, long suppressed, broke all restraints, Chekhists with revolvers surrounded Zinovieff. The shouts continued, personal insults were hurled, and Grishka the Third disappeared.

Scenes like this are not reported in the censored news which leaves Russia, but they have been common for at least three years. I was in Novgorodskaia Province when two Communist agents, requisitioning corn, butter, milk, and meat, tried, like Zinovieff, to represent the Soviet Government as a purely beneficent institution. An old peasant was the voice of the despoiled *muzhiks*. "Listen, you comrades, to what I tell you," he declared. "The land is ours, it is true, but all the harvest is theirs. The forests are ours, the cattle are ours, but the trees are theirs and all the milk, butter, and meat are theirs. That is what the Government has done for us. Let them take the land back and eat it themselves." Turning to the Communist agents, he continued: "Before we began to lend to your proletariat we had plenty of plows and nails. For three years we have been lending you all we raised. You have taken everything without payment, and now there are no plows and no nails. I think it is time for us to stop lending."

Other voices rose, some threatening, some conciliatory, but all of the same tenor.

"Stop this counter-revolutionary talk," commanded one of the Communists angrily. "Tomorrow morning you must pay the *prod-razverstka* (food tax), that is all. Every man who does not pay will be arrested."

"So!" exclaimed a stout peasant, " 'the comrade peasants' suddenly become in your sight counter-revolutionists. You are worse even than a Czarist tax collector. Then listen, there is God," pointing to an ikon, "and there is the door. Get out."

"This is open rebellion," cried the Communist. But in the ensuing scrimmage the two tax collectors found themselves no match for the crowd of peasants, who seized their revolvers.

"Go in peace," said the head peasant, as they threw the Communists out of the door, "but if any of us are arrested you will lose your heads."

By 1921 the destructive consequences of the Communist program became clear to even the dullest peasants. Their fields lay untilled and weed-grown. The peasants had no seeds to sow and they had no incentive to industry. In the towns everything was slowing down to a death sleep. Nationalized factories, having no fuel, stopped operating. Railways were broken down. Buildings were falling in ruins. Schools had almost ceased to function. The deadly noose of Communism was slowly choking the people to death. But Russia did not want to die, and in one sudden, desperate uprising the whole system for a time was smashed. But the Communists were left alive. In some ways that is unfortunate for them, for if they had all been killed by their enemies they would have lived in history as martyrs who tried to establish a new order but perished before their experiment had time to prove itself. Instead a different end is destined for them, an end of slow disintegration. Their destiny is to destroy their own ideal with their own hands, to exhibit it to the world in all its rottenness and horror; to plunge themselves deeper and deeper into the mire of corruption, cupidity, crimes, and bestiality; to erect higher and higher the mountain of the slain. And what end could be more terrible?

When that destined end comes, the cross which

Russia bears will be taken from her shoulders, in spite of those moral bankrupts abroad who ignorantly or otherwise support the hands of the stranglers.   Let these foreign theorists go on as they have been doing.   They cannot help what will finally come, and what was foreshadowed by the terrible events of 1921 in Petrograd.   By the middle of February in that year the factories had practically ceased production, railway traffic was paralyzed and could no longer transport food supplies to starving Petrograd.   Stormy meetings were held in the idle factories and at one of these Zinovieff, spokesman for the Government, was badly beaten.   Rumor told us that neighboring towns and cities were in rebellion and that peasant riots were increasing.   Even in the Red army defection was spreading.

On my way to the University on February 24 I witnessed a demonstration of workers from the Laferm factory on Vasilievsky Island which was strikingly akin to the scenes of the March Revolution of 1917.   The same cry for bread, the same demand for liberty of speech and of the press, only this time the banners read "Down with the Soviet." Children running around merrily sang popular songs satirizing the Government. A popular parody of "The International" ran thus:

"I am sitting on a barrel
Barrel turns about . . .
The Chekha makes us quarrel.
Let us send it to the devil. . . ."

On the Nicolaevsky Bridge the demonstration met Communist troops, which opened fire and dispersed the workmen. The next days the riots were renewed. The crowds were larger and more defiant, and it was plain that the people were trying to get together. Many were arrested or killed. But the movement grew, and as Russians in the Red army refused to act, the Government brought up the ever-faithful forces, principally Lettish, Bashkirian, and International troops, and restrained the mobs. On February 26 a great demonstration occurred in the center of the town, on the Nevsky Prospekt, and this time so many people were killed that it seemed that the Government had completely suppressed the uprising.

The next day, February 27, we heard that the Kronstadt sailors, formerly ardent supporters of Communism, had revolted. This turned out to be true, and had that revolt succeeded, had we had even one free newspaper to support their revolt, it would have been the end of the Soviet Government. Plainly we heard the cannonade from Kronstadt, and plainly we saw the panic of the Government. Within twenty-four hours a proclamation appeared announcing the New Economic Policy (NEP). According to the proclamation, requisitions from peasants were to be replaced by definite taxes; trade and commerce were to be re-established; many factories would be denationalized; people would be allowed to buy and sell food; special conferences of non-Communist workers would be organized to improve living standards. In this way Communism was liquidated and "NEP" was established.

The effect on the half-starved population was to weaken their spirit of rebellion. The bribe of meat and butter, potatoes and bread, even more than the presence of the Chekhist troops, caused the people to cease their attacks on the Government. Thus the resistance to the Kronstadt rebellion was strengthened, the Soviet Government promising the army Kronstadt and its entire population if it would suppress the sailors' revolt. For three weeks we listened to the constant sound of guns, our hearts melting with joy in the hope that the sailors would win that life and death duel.

At that time both my wife and I were seized with pneumonia. She went to the hospital first, and next morning, although I was suffering, I attended a private meeting of six professors, two lawyers and two priests, with whom I discussed plans of action in case the Government fell; plans of organization of a new Government, reorganization of the courts, the police force, and so on. There was no conspiracy, but simply practical discussion. I mention this because later, for just such discussions, many people were executed.

The next day I was so ill that my physician ordered me to the hospital in Czarskoe Selo, where my wife fought with pneumonia. In normal times that hospital would have been counted a dirty place, but at least we had hot water, clean linen, food enough, and very few insects. My temperature not being very high, I lay in my bed quite happy. In the same room lay five or six workmen, two Soviet clerks and a University professor. Boom! Boom! echoed the sound of canon from Kronstadt, and we whispered to ourselves: "Brave boys. God help them." In the darkness of the night I was awakened by what I first thought were the delirious ravings of one of the patients. But it was only one of the workmen on his knees, crossing himself, and muttering: "God help them. Great God help them. Deliver us from these sufferings." Many hearts throbbed with prayers like that during those days and nights.

A week passed. The cannonade still went on. Boom! Boom! My wife and I progressed through the crisis of pneumonia and began to mend, still to the sound of guns. But on March 18 the firing died down and a dead silence fell over Petrograd. Joyful excitement left the hearts of the people and fear took its place. The duel of Kronstadt was over. The Communists had conquered.

Woe to the vanquished! For three days the town was at the absolute mercy of the Red troops. For three days the Lettish, Bashkirian, Hungarian, Tartars, Russian, Jewish, and International dregs, free from any restraint, mad with blood lust and alcohol, killed and violated. Men, women, children, young and old, strong and weak, all alike suffered untold tortures before death released them.

In the days of their Communist madness those Kronstadt sailors had committed many crimes. They too had murdered and violated. But for what they had done they now expiated most horribly.

The Government, which had been raised to power principally through their support, had no mercy upon them. When the bloody feast in Kronstadt was finished, thousands of the "pride and glory" of the new régime were in prison or dead. About ten thousand were shot and almost as many were sent to places where they could not long survive. This was done in spite of guarantees of the Government that those who surrendered would be given immunity.

At the end of March, passing along Millionnaiai Street, I saw a group of workmen walking with bags of potatoes on their backs. Near the Hermitage we met a large group of sailor-prisoners being taken from the Chekha to Predvarilka prison. When they saw the workmen they began to revile them. "Traitors! You sold our lives for the Communists' potatoes. Tomorrow you will have our flesh to eat with your potatoes. Eat, and choke yourselves!"

The workers stopped, looking after the prisoners. Soon they passed with their guards and disappeared around the corner. The workers started slowly to walk on, but one man ran to the Neva and threw his bag of potatoes into the water. "I can't eat them now," he said bitterly. "Those boys are right. We betrayed them, and their blood is on our hands."

Three days after that the people of Czarskoe Selo living near the Kazanskoe cemetery had a sleepless night. Endless discharges of rifles were heard and seemed to strike them in the very heart. Five hundred sailors were shot that night near the cemetery.

The regular executioners could not do it all, so the Union of Young Communists was mobilized to help them. This was represented as a part of their party obligation. But the Young Communists had not had much rifle practice, and possibly, too, their hands were shaking. Next morning people passing the cemetery heard groans coming from hastily filled-in graves. From our window we saw motor trucks of jackets and trousers, caps and shoes of the executed sailors. From other suburbs of Petrograd we heard of similar sights and sounds. "NEP" was dearly bought by these men of Kronstadt and by thousands of peasant heroes now lying in eternal peace. If the politicians ever forget that, Russia will remind them in the future.

CHAPTER XXIII

NEW BUTCHERY

THE dreadful days of revenge passed. The machine of the Red terror still worked, but now it exterminated lives by tens and hundreds instead of by thousands and ten thousands. The New Economic Policy, forced on the Communists, began to have a revivifying effect on the country. As in a fairy tale, the dead land seemed to come to life. The limits of our freedom were narrow, it is true, but individual initative and responsibility did assert themselves. Shops and stalls, private offices and workshops, very poor and primitive at first, were opened. Wonderful it was to see exhibited in shop windows bread and meat, butter and vegetables. Just to enter without any permission, without any waiting in long queues, and to buy the little one could afford gave the most intense happiness. Those who have never known starvation, who have never experienced our fruitless wanderings from one Communistic office to another, cannot even faintly imagine how happy we were now.

Little by little Petrograd began to assume the outward aspect of a European city. People were repairing their houses, taking some care of their dress and appearance. The marks of death and desolation which had rested on us like a pall for two years, by September, 1922, had almost been obliterated. Luxurious hotels, restaurants with signs, "Everything as before," tram cars running, droshkies, theaters, and movies, decently dressed people, such was the outward appearance of the town. Inwardly the change had not been so great. Buildings left without any repairs were still in bad condition. The canals were foul, the water supply bad. Much poverty existed. But the busy streets, the shops and restaurants, and above all, the prosperous appearance of the Communists and "nepmen" (bourgeois of the New Economic Policy) gave the city a thriving appearance. These people showed an endless cupidity and desire for luxury, not for the people, of course, but for themselves. They displayed a fierce desire to make money, any way they could, by fraud, extortion, bribes, gambling, or theft. They seemed devoured by passion for luxuries, debauchery, mistresses, and their contempt for the welfare of the people was hardly concealed. These destroyers of capitalism were now ardent defenders of sacred private property—their own. By this utter selfishness, even more than by their former blood-thirstiness, they discredited in the eyes of the people Socialism and Communism.

In the spiritual life of Russia a great revival awoke. While all other buildings were left to decay the churches were repaired. Religious services, little attended between 1917 and 1920, now became crowded. On May 21, 1921, the Communist demonstration was participated in by only a few thousands, but a religious procession, held on the following day, was attended by about three hundred thousand people. This procession was so big and so impressive that the Communists themselves were obliged to take off their hats in respect. Those who did not remove their hats had them knocked off, and certain of the commissaries were attacked and beaten. Intellectuals and students, previously atheistical to a degree, now became religious. Professors Losky, Grevs, Karsavin, and others, began to preach in the churches, a thing never heard of before. The traditional ideology of the Russian intelligentzia, materialistic, Socialistic, and revolutionary, seemed to have been consumed in the conflagration of the Revolution, and in its *experimentum crucis,* and a new and quite different ideology born.

The anniversary of the University foundation was celebrated in a solemn and impressive meeting. About five thousand professors and students, besides those of the Institutes, were present at this meeting on February 3, 1922. After the Rector Shimkevich delivered his address, I spoke. In my speech I pointed out the new guide-posts which would be followed by the young generation. Old idols of Socialism and Communism, atheism and revolution, had fallen and should be forever abandoned. Old teachers of life, Marx, Engels, and others like them, had lost their authority and should forever be forgotten. They had led us to the edge of the abyss. Individual freedom, individual iniative and responsibility, co-operation, respect for liberty of others; reform instead of revolution; self-government instead of anarchy—these were now and should be our social ideals. Instead of the internationalism which had made our country the hunting ground of adventurers of all countries, the standard of nationalism, not inimical to other countries, but devoted to the welfare of our fatherland, is erected and will be upheld by the new generation.

Next day the Communist papers attacked me furiously, but the only result was that my speech was sent broadcast over the country calling forth many plaudits. Communist attacks had exactly that effect. Whatever their press condemned the people praised. Whatever it praised the people condemned. A free press even began to appear. At the end of 1921 a group of economists, sociologists, and historians started the publication of a scientific journal, *The Economist*. In spite of its high price, it sold readily. And the more the Communist press assailed its articles, its editors, and contributors, the more popular it became. When Zinovieff and Lenin attacked me personally for my article, "The Influence of War Upon Population," the journal was sold out in a week and a new edition had to be published. The Communists could stop the growing popularity of *The Economist* only by suppressing it altogether and by banishment of its editors, and this would have been a little difficult, as no issue was published without preliminary permission of the censor. Some of the articles they suppressed, however, were in some mysterious way rewritten, copied, and circulated all over the country by the people. Scientific works and non-Communist books and magazines were also circulated in the face of the censors.

Communist censorship deserves a little description, since nothing like it ever existed under the Czarist régime. A certain novel was suppressed because in it a Red sister of mercy was described as smoking a cigarette while chatting with Red soldiers. Said the censor: "A Red sister of mercy, under our discipline, could not smoke or chatter. Change it into a white sister of mercy and the novel will be permitted." An article by Professor Kisevetter on late publications of Russian historians, absolutely academic in tone, was forbidden because "the author praises these books while our Communistic historian, Professor Pokrovsky, disapproves them. Since Professor Pokrovsky places on them a low value no favorable criticism can be allowed."

Nevertheless, the Communistic straitjacket no longer held the people in confinement. They became courageous and openly satirized the ruling powers. The revolutionary title "Tovarishi"— "comrade"—made obligatory, was now despised. If anybody was addressed as "Tovarishi," the chances were that the reply would be "go to the devil." Many satiric poems and songs were circulated in manuscript. One of these poems, "The Adventures of the poor fellow, Karl Marx, in Communistic Russia," described how Marx had visited Russia, was arrested and condemned to death by the Chekha as a counter-revolutionary. How he stood in queues for food, wandered in commissariats, suffered in nationalized factories, was forbidden to teach or to publish his own views, was graphically described. Finally, in the poem, he burned his books, cursed Socialism and Communism and fled without his clothes.

People even began to deface and destroy monuments which the Communists had erected to their glory. In Odessa one morning the monument of Karl Marx—that is, the mouth and beard of the German prophet, were found plastered with millet gruel, and on the monument was written: "We have eaten plenty of it. Now eat it yourself." The population of Odessa had subsisted for more than a year on millet gruel, and the stuff at last became so disgusting to them that it could not be digested. In Petrograd one night the monument of Kogan-Volodarsky, a Communist leader killed in 1918, was blown to pieces and on his grave a dungheap was left, with a red flag on which were written these lines, after a poem of Pushkin:

"I erected a monument not made with
human hands, quite worthy of myself."

In 1922 Communism in Russia was practically dead and the Government was in a condition nearly of collapse. It was kept alive by terror, which was effective only because the people were physically exhausted, and it retained power only because of the terrible famine which had devastated Russia in 1921. This famine it was that gave the Soviet Government courage again to drench the country with blood. Even while the famine threatened the terror began.

"Comrades, the hydra of counter-revolution is raising its heads again. Either these heads must be cut off or we shall be devoured by the monster." Thus spoke Zinovieff at a meeting of Communist officials soon after the great religious demonstration of May 2, 1921. "We must demonstrate that the machine of the Red Terror still exists and works efficiently," he concluded.

Very soon after this more than a hundred people, mostly scholars, writers, and priests, were arrested. In their lodgings, as usual, were left Chekhist guards who allowed no one to go out and who arrested everyone who for any reason entered. The morning after these arrests Professor Tagantzeff, eighty years old and the greatest criminologist in Russia, came to consult with friends about the arrest of his son, the geologist Tagantzeff. We met in the apartment of Professor N. Lazarevsky, leading authority in constitutional law. In the lodgings of the arrested Tagantzeff, after he and his wife had been taken away, were left only two children, whom the Chekhist guards, of course, felt under no obligation to feed. If we did not send food to the children they would starve. If we did send it, it would mean the arrest of the person who went. Too well we knew the practice of the Chekha, to "catch the enemies of the people" by holding their children foodless in hopes that sooner or later someone would come to their rescue. Finally old Professor Tagantzeff determined himself to go. He went and was arrested. Unfortunately, that day we were unable to get very much food, and after a few days another one of us had to volunteer to go with supplies and be arrested.

"I suppose I shall be arrested also," said Lazarevsky, "because Tagantzeff's son and I have been friends from boyhood and in his lodgings must be many of my letters."

I begged him to disappear, but he said that as vice-president of the University he felt he could not afford just then to leave. "Let us wait and see what happens," he said.

Some weeks passed. More people were arrested and a few were released. Among these were the venerable Professor Tagantzeff and his grandchildren. In July, Lazarevsky received a summons from the Chekha to appear before it as a witness in the affair of the younger Tagantzeff. In spite of the advice of his friends, he went, and was detained, "only as a witness and for a few days," as the Chekhists explained to his wife. Lazarevsky himself wrote to her: "Don't be alarmed. I am in no danger, and in a few days I hope to be free."

At the beginning of August, however, *Pravda* published an article about a "new Tagantzeff plot, just uncovered by the authorities." The tone of this article convinced us that all the arrested persons were in great danger, and every one of us, professors and writers, friends and relatives of the prisoners, began work in their behalf. The elder Tagantzeff went to Moscow to see Lenin, to beg him to forbid the threatened butchery. But he was not allowed to see Lenin. Then he wrote a letter to the Dictator, reminding him that years ago he had risked his position of Senator and Judge of the Supreme Court, in an effort to save the brother of Lenin from execution, and how, failing in this, he had illegally arranged a last meeting between the condemned man and his mother. "In memory of this service, which you well remember, and in memory of your brother, as a father and a man, I beseech you to prevent this butchery of my son and his wife, and of other innocent people." Thus wrote the great criminologist. The letter was given to Lenin, but no reply was sent. Lenin and his companions needed a new reign of terror to frighten the people, who were becoming over-bold. Relatives of the arrested ceased altogether to hear of or from them.

"This silence alarms me greatly," Mrs. Lazarevsky told us. "I fear something terrible may happen to my husband."

We feared also, but in spite of vague rumors nothing was really known of the intention of the Government. On the morning of August 23 I called on Mrs. Lazarevsky to console her and to hear if she had received any news. While we were talking, the postman came in and handed her a bundle of letters.

"Five letters at once from my husband," she exclaimed with beaming face. "What happiness." Reading them she told me: "All goes well. He tells me not to be anxious, the affair is approaching an end, and he will soon be home."

I do not know why I was so disturbed by those letters, but after congratulating her I went out. The

House of the Scholars was very near the Lazarevsky
home, and on the house next to it I perceived a
freshly glued copy of *Pravda*. Strangely alarmed,
I stopped and read it. "The Tagantzeff Plot and
its Suppression" was the heading of the article
which met my eyes.

"By order of the Petrograd Soviet the following
persons were executed yesterday for participation
in a counter-revolutionary plot." Horrified, my
eyes ran along the list of names badly printed on
dirty gray paper.

"Tagantzeff, professor, for organization of the
plot.

"Mrs. Tagantzeff, his wife, for participation and
for failing to denounce her husband.

"Lazarevsky, professor, pro-rector of Petrograd
University, for composition of a project of a new
electoral law.

"Tikhvinsky, professor, for writing a report adversely describing the present state of the Soviet
oil industry.

"Goumileff, writer and poet, for his monarchist
opinions.

"Ukhtomsky, painter and scholar, for giving information about the museums.

"Gissetty and wife," and so on, more than fifty
names, each with a short account of their "crimes."
Some of these offenses were merely described as
"counter-revolutionary." At the end was printed,
"And other counter-revolutionaries."

"Five letters at once from my husband. . . .
He will soon be home." These words of Mrs.

Lazarevsky burned in my brain. Now I knew why
I had been so disturbed. To keep those letters for
many days and send them to a wife after her husband had been shot! What a hellish deed!"

"Hush! Don't express your opinions so loudly,"
said an acquaintance who passed at the moment. I
had not known that I was speaking aloud. My first
thought was to go back to Mrs. Lazarevsky, but I
literally could not do it. Let someone else tell her
of her "happiness."

Shot for adversely describing the state of the
Soviet oil industry! The oil industry was indeed
in a deplorable state, but the report of Tikhvinsky
was written for the Soviet by order of Lenin
himself. Shot for giving information about the
museums! Shot for writing a project for a new
electoral law! I remembered our private discus
sions during the Kronstadt riots, about the reorganization of the Government, the courts, and the police,
should the Soviet Government fall. Lazarevsky said
then that he would try to outline a new electoral
law. This outline, falling in the hands of the Bolsheviki, had condemned him. Shot for his monarchist opinions! Not the fact that Goumileff was one
of the greatest poets in Russia, not his bravery in
the war, which had been rewarded by the order of
St. George, not the discretion of his daily conduct
were enough to save him. He had monarchist convictions. In this "plot" were involved people who
had never even known each other, and all of them
had been denied even an open trial. If in a
"bourgeois" country such a mockery of justice had

been accorded Communists or anarchists, what a roar would have been heard all over the world against the merciless cruelty of "capitalism."

But this was not the full extent of Communist cruelty. When Mrs. Lazarevsky and relatives of the other victims of the bloodthirsty god requested the Chekha to give them the bodies of their beloved for burial, the Chekha insolently answered: "What bodies? Those persons have been sent to Archangel prison." Most of the relatives knew this was intended as an added torture, but two, not really believing, and hoping that their people were still alive became insane. Visiting old Professor Tagantzeff, I found the aged man utterly crushed with grief. "It is time for me to die," he said weeping. "All is over for me. But my grandchildren—they have sent them to an asylum for young criminals. Why could they not permit those innocents to be brought up by our friends? I thought once that they were human, but now I know that they are worse than devils." In 1922, soon after my own banishment, poor old Tagantzeff died.

"This proletarian justice once more shows our enemies our power," Grishka the Third declared in a speech. "Let them remember this lesson."

We remember. If ever we are given opportunity to do justice to him and his companions, may God help us not to be too soft-hearted.

CHAPTER XXIV

S. O. S.

WHAT we feared most of all for Russia in 1921 happened.

Looking over a map of the whole country, with provinces marked by harvests bad or totally lacking, we said: "Twenty-five million people, at least, are fated to die of starvation this winter unless the world comes to their aid."

We said this long before the Government and Maxim Gorky issued their wild appeal to the nations of earth to help the starving masses. Who or what was to blame for this terrible Russian famine? We have a proverb which says: "A bad crop is from God, a famine is from the people." There was a drought, it is true, but it did not cause the famine in all its horror. The Communistic policy of plundering the peasantry, thus leading them, in self-defense, to reduce the area of cultivated land almost by half; the requisitions of corn, even to seed corn, in the dry areas; this policy must be held responsible for the most catastrophic features of the famine. Had the Soviet Government not pursued this mad policy, and had it not so wrecked the railroad system that transportation of food and systematic relief was rendered impossible, that most appalling famine of 1921 would not have

282

occurred. When it came, there was no remedy. No provinces had necessary surpluses of corn. Even if it had been willing to act, the Government was powerless.

Although they knew that they risked arrest, the intellectuals of Petrograd and Moscow immediately offered their services in what relief work was possible. The Government at first allowed them to organize a Committee for Famine Relief, but very soon, as we feared, the committee was arrested for "counter-revolution." Their obsession of "plots," and their desire for their own self-protection at any cost of human lives will stand forever as the hallmark of Communistic tyranny.

Having published my two volumes of *A System of Sociology,* I postponed the writing of the third volume in order to study at first hand phenomena typical of the Revolution, and to note them in such form as to make their investigation easier in normal times. With my students and collaborators, and in close co-operation with the academicians, Pavlov and Bekhtereff, I began an investigation of social changes, social groupings, and regroupings in our society. Included was the study of time-budgets of our fellow-men, and the comparative force of different factors in determining human behavior. The behavior of the people around me was stripped of inhibitions which in normal circumstances disguise its mechanism and make difficult its determination. As the principal object of my study, I took the influence of hunger upon human behavior, social life, and social organization. In the study of this problem I had had such personal experience, and the benefit of personal contact in my own environment. The influence of food and acute want of food on human behavior had never before been seriously investigated.

Rich as was the material at hand, I cannot say that my environment was favorable to scientific study, as I was all the time under the necessity of "disappearing" in order to avoid arrest. But as investigation of the phenomena in normal times was out of the question, we decided in one way or another to fit ourselves to the unfavorable environment, and I am glad to say that many of us succeeded in our efforts.

In the autumn of 1921 I, among many other professors, was forbidden by the Soviet Government to teach. Left with no work except researches in the Institute of the Brain and in the Historical and Sociological Institute of the University, I felt myself comparatively free. I had studied city starvation, with myself as one of the subjects, and now I had a very great laboratory in the starving villages of Russia. In the winter of 1921 I started for the famine districts of Samara and Saratov provinces for a scientific investigation of starvation. I will acknowledge at once that in this intention I completely failed. No scientific study was I able to make, but I saw a famine; I know now what it means. What I learned in those awful provinces was far more than any investigation could have given me. My nervous system, accustomed to many horrors in the years of Revolution, broke down com-

pletely before the spectacle of the actual starvation
of millions in my ravaged country. If I came out
less an investigator, I do not think I came out less
a man, less an enemy of any group of men capable
of inflicting such suffering on the human race.

With one of the local teachers, my small group
set out on foot from the last railroad station to visit
the famishing districts of Samara Province. We
entered the village of N. in the afternoon. This
place was as though dead. Houses stood deserted
and roofless, with gaps where windows and doors
had been. The straw thatch of the houses had long
since been torn away and eaten. There were no
animals in the village, of course, no cattle, horses,
sheep, goats, dogs, cats, or even crows. All had
been eaten. Dead silence lay over the snow covered
roads until, with a little creak a sledge came in
sight, a sledge drawn by two men and a woman and
having on it a dead body. After drawing the sledge
a short distance, they stopped and fell exhausted on
the snow. Dully they looked at us as we approached,
and with sick hearts we looked at them. I had seen
starving faces in the cities, but such living skeletons
as these three people I had never seen. In rags,
shaking with cold, they were not white of visage,
but blue, dark blue with yellow spots.

"God help you," we addressed them. Simply
because it was necessary to say something. The lips
of one man and the woman moved but nothing but a
mumbling sound came from them. The third peasant, who seemed a little more alive, said: "God?
We forgot God and He forgot us."

"Where are you taking him?" I asked, pointing to the dead body of the lad lying on the sledge.

"To that corn-loft," answered the peasant, looking towards a low building. "There is plenty of corn there now."

The other man and the woman tried to get up from the snow, but could not do it without our help. We offered to draw the sledge, and with the three peasants went on to the corn-loft, the usual peasant grain receptacle, new and good. The strongest man, it appeared, was constable of the village, and he took out a key and unlocked the loft. There was plenty of corn there now, as he had said. Ten bodies, including three children, lay on the floor.

"Why do you put them here?" we asked.

"The priest is five miles from us. He cannot come every day. We have not any horse to draw the dead to the church or the cemetery, so when the priest comes, once every fortnight, we have the funeral service here and afterwards, if we can, we bury them near our chapel."

We carried the body in and laid it on the floor. The man and woman, parents of the lad, crossed themselves and silently went out. "Soon they will come here also," said the constable.

"How many have you brought here this last fortnight?" we asked.

"About ten or fifteen. Before that more. Some ran away from the village."

"Where did they go to?"

"Where their eyes were looking." Then as he

locked the door he whispered: "It is necessary to lock . . . they steal."

"Steal . . . What?"

"Yes, to eat. That is what we have come to. In the village they guard the cemetery not to let the bodies be taken from the graves."

"Have any murders occurred for such a purpose?" I forced myself to ask.

"Not in our village, but in others, yes. A few days ago in the village of G. a mother killed her child, cut off its legs, cooked and ate them. That is what we have come to."

In the dusk of the early evening we walked to the house of the constable, passing a half-ruined building with the sign "School."

"Closed?" I indicated.

"Who is there to teach now? All the children are dead or dying. New ones are not being born. Besides, the teacher ran away. There was no fuel, no books, no food."

As we neared the house we met a man who looked like a maniac. Without a cap and clad in an old, unbuttoned coat, he shook his long hair and beard frenziedly and waved his arms as he walked. "Ring the bell!" he cried hoarsely. "Ring the bell! They will hear! They will hear!"

"Mad," said the constable laconically. "He is always ringing the bell of the chapel. He thinks the bell will wake up the world and make it come to save us. But nobody will hear," he added gloomily, "not even God."

As he spoke, the clanging of the church bell broke the silence of the dying village. In the darkness of the forlorn and forsaken Russian wild, this appeal to the world of a mad peasant wrung our hearts, reduced us to bitter weeping. Ding-dong! Ding-dong! now quick and alarming like a fire-bell. Ding-dong! Ding-dong! Slow and mournful as a funeral knell. Ding-dong! Ding-dong! For almost an hour it beat on our brains, our hearts. Then dead silence fell again.

This S. O. S. of a mad peasant in the far interior of the land was heard. It crossed the ocean and beat on the hearts of the Great American nation and brought relief that saved from cruel death at least ten million men, women, and children. God will forever remember that deed. God will forever bless that generous people.

We entered the constable's house. It was dark and cold. With flint and steel the man struck fire and lighted the stove. In the faint light we saw a woman lying on the stove. Seeing us, she made an effort to get up, but we begged her to lie still.

"Our son died a month ago," said the peasant simply, "and since we have eaten all, I don't see how we can keep alive much longer."

"Have you sowed your land?"

"A small field only, as much as we could. Excuse us that we have nothing to offer our guests."

We gave a part of our bread to the constable and his wife, and they devoured it, crossing themselves and crying: "Good God! Real bread! Real bread! God bless you for it."

We spent the night in this house and next morning started for the next village. "Be careful," warned our host. "In some of the villages the people have become quite mad and dangerous. Good luck. Thank you for the bread."

Along the road piled with snowdrifts we set off for the church village. We saw no one until we came very near the village, when we met a man with a boy and a girl.

"In the name of God, give us something to eat. We are dying," they cried. We gave them a little bread from our scant supply, and asked where they were going.

"To the railway," they answered vaguely.

"And after that, where?"

"I don't know where," said the man. "Are you not the Commissaries?"

"No, we are not Commissaries. Why?"

"They say the Commissaries have food, and sometimes they take girls. Will you take my children?"

"Unhappily we cannot do that," we said.

"Then if they don't die I must forsake them," said the peasant despairingly. "Perhaps some people will pick them up."

We gave them a little more bread and parted. "They will never reach the railroad," said my companion.

From the very beginning of the famine tens of thousands of people were driven from their homes and went out "where their eyes were looking," with no plans, no definite points of migration, with nothing except an impulse to flee away from death. By thousands they wandered, and finding neither food nor work, they fell down and died.

In the next village and the next we saw the same awful picture. Death from starvation and its companion, typhus. People lying in their wretched houses, patiently waiting the end of suffering. Apathy broken only by delirium, and attempts of some women and girls to sell themselves for a little bread. In some of the villages we saw indisputable proofs of cannibalism. The Revolution promised to save the people from despotism. The Bolsheviki promised to give food to everyone. If they did not keep those vows, at least they gave the people the Communion of human sacrifice, human flesh and blood.

"Cursed shalt thou be in the city, and cursed shalt thou be in the field.

"Cursed shall be the fruit of thy body, and the fruit of thy land, the increase of thy kine, and the flocks of thy sheep.

"The Lord shall send upon thee cursing, vexation, pestilence.

"The Lord shall smite thee with a consumption, and with a fever, and with an inflammation . . . and they shall pursue thee until thou perish.

"Thou shalt betroth a wife, and another man shall lie with her; thou shalt build an house, and thou shalt not dwell therein. Thine ox shall be slain before thine eyes, and thou shalt not eat thereof. Thy sons and thy daughters shall be given unto another people, and thine eyes shall look, and fail with longing for them all the day long. . . . The fruit of thy land and all thy labors shall a nation which thou knowest not eat up; So that thou shalt be mad for the sight of thine eyes which thou shalt see. And thou shalt eat the fruit of thine own body, the flesh of thy sons and of thy daughters.''

This ancient curse filled my mind all during my wanderings and for days after I returned to Petrograd. Not much scientific knowledge did I gain in those twenty days I spent in the famine regions, but the memory of what I saw and heard there made me afterwards absolutely fearless in denouncing the Revolution and the monsters who were devouring Russia. Many and great have been the sins of the Russian people, but in these years of famine, suffering, and death, through all the punishments of God, the nation has expiated, has paid in full for all its offenses.

CHAPTER XXV

NEW PLAYS

"WE have many reasons for being grateful to our Government," said the writer N., in one of his most ironic moods. "We have a kind of happiness here which citizens of capitalistic countries never experience. For instance, when we go to bed at night we are not sure that we shall wake up alive. Then when we do waken and find ourselves alive, what happiness. When we take our places in the queues we are never sure that we shall receive anything. After standing for an hour or more and we receive half a pound of bread, what joy. When we reflect that we have been arrested and may be again, may even be executed, we have only to congratulate ourselves that for the moment, at least, we are free. What citizen of a 'bourgeois' country knows such happiness? Above all, our Government provides us with such constant excitement that we can never feel boredom. No cheap *circenses,* mind you, but thrilling tragedies of real life. Arrests, prisons, executions! Not long ago we witnessed 'The Kronstadt Tragedy.' After that we had 'The Tagantzeff Conspiracy,' then 'The Trial of the Social-Revolutionists,' thrillers, all of them."

One of the greatest tragedies played before our eyes was in the winter of 1921. The Government, having spent all the gold in the treasury, all the private wealth it could seize, still found itself in

need of money. The next resource was the wealth
of the Church. Under pretext of needing money for
famine relief the Government made a demand on the
churches for all the treasures they possessed. The
Church authorities made answer that they were
willing to give their wealth to feed the starving, but
that they wished to distribute the food themselves,
or through the American Relief Administration,
which they thoroughly trusted. The Government,
enraged, because it wished, of course, to seize this
treasure for its own purposes, invented the lie that
the Russian Church authorities and the orthodox
people had refused to give their gold for the relief
of the starving. They then began to take by force
what the Church authorities would not surrender.
The result was a great wave of "Church Disorders"
which swept over the whole country. When the
Chekhists came to a church they found crowds of believers who barred the entrances. In villages and
towns everywhere riotous scenes were enacted, and
many people were killed and wounded, for what
could unarmed people do against machine guns and
cannons? Twice the Chekhist troops attacked Kazansky Cathedral and the Alexandro-Nevsky Church
in Petrograd, and twice unarmed masses drove the
soldiers back. The third time they tried to do it
they were mowed down by machine guns and the
churches were sacked.

Thousands of priests and people were arrested
for this show of "counter-revolution." Most of
them were shot without trial, but some were given
a mockery which was reported throughout the world

as a trial. It was a lovely Summer morning in 1922 when the trial which I shall describe opened in Petrograd. Near the Building of Nobility stood a vast crowd waiting, and guarding them stood regiments of Chekhist soldiers. About ten o'clock three trucks filled with the arrested "counter-revolutionaries," and other trucks with guards and machine guns appeared. In the first truck there were the Metropolitan Benjamin and other priests, Professor Novitsky and other fervent believers. In their worn cassocks, with heads uncovered, their long hair falling around their emaciated faces, the Metropolitan and the priests were like the marytrs of early Christian days. When the people saw them, they fell on their knees and began to sing "Kyrie eleison" and "It is worthy to glorify you," songs with which, in religious services, the bishops are met. The Metropolitan and the priests standing surrounded by armed guards, blessed the people kneeling in the streets, and the songs rose, mingled with sobs and cries. The Chekhists rudely ordered the priests and believers to get down from the trucks, and crazed with the sight, some rushed towards the old Metropolitan. But the soldiers drove them back with guns, and the prisoners entered the building, greeted by shouts and hisses from the Communists, who execrated them as "poisoners of the people's minds."

"Peace be upon you," said the Metropolitan, blessing them. And with those words in their ears the Communists opened their farce of a trial.

In the streets and in the Mikhailovsky Square the crowd continued to sing religious songs. While they were singing, a man in a rich cassock approached. This was Vvedensky, one of the leaders of the Bolshevist "Living Church," and one of the denouncers of the orthodox priests. Immediately the crowd became mad with rage. They shouted every insult they could think of at the man, who to them was Judas reincarnated. As he was about to enter the building an old woman picked up a stone, and threw it with such good aim that it struck Vvedensky in the face, knocking him down. The Chekhists arrested the old woman and began to disperse the crowd. But the people were obstinate. They held their ground, still singing. The Chekhists then opened fire, killing many and arresting all who failed to get away. The street was quiet after that. Blocked by Chekhist troops, none could now enter save Communists, victims, and "witnesses."

For two weeks the trial continued. "For participation in the criminal organization called the Hierarchy of the Orthodox Church," and "For counter-revolutionary resistance to the requisition of Church treasures," the indictments read. Of the first-named crime all the prisoners were unquestionably guilty. For a thousand years the Orthodox Church had existed in Russia, and these priests and believers were members of its "criminal" organization. Of the other charge they were not guilty. They neither instigated nor participated in any physical resistance. They merely insisted upon spending their treasure for starving people rather than for the benefit of the Third International.

These victims all during their trial showed the

strength and calmness of Christian martyrs. Their heroism, their devotion to religion and to the country, their faith in the will of God was so deep and sincere that even some of the Communist judges were moved. Had not the Red god, in the persons of Zinovieff and other leaders, been thirsty for more blood, even this court would never have condemned the Metropolitan and his fellow-prisoners.

Said the Metropolitan in his last speech: "I and only I, as head of the Church, am responsible for the actions which you call criminal, but which I look upon as fulfillment of duty. These priests and believers are but executers of my commands, and they must be acquitted. Judge me as you will, and I shall accept your verdict. If God destines me to live longer and to do His Will, I shall do it. If I am to die, blessed be the will of God." Crossing himself devoutly, he finished: "My Lord and Saviour, forgive them, for they know not what they do. Into Thy hands I commit my spirit."

Followed then ten death sentences, absolutely prearranged, and great applause from the Communist audience, this also prearranged. A few weeks later the Metropolitan Benjamin, his hair shorn and dressed in rags that he might not be recognized even by his executioners, was shot in Moscow. Five others, including Novitsky, professor of the University of Petrograd, had already been murdered.

While this tragedy was going on in Petrograd, another, which we called "The Trial of the Social-Revolutionists," was staged in Moscow. About fifty thousand people marched through the streets carrying banners with the words: "We demand the death sentence for all Social Revolutionaries." In this crowd of marchers I saw many of my friends and acquaintances, many students and workmen, who did not desire the death of Social Revolutionaries, and who I knew hated the Communists with all their hearts. Yet they marched. Why? Because they wished to live. Because they feared, nay, knew that unless they marched they would lose their employment. Some days before the demonstration the authorities announced that any soviet employee who did not participate would be dismissed, and any citizen who refused to march would thereby proclaim himself a counter-revolutionary. In this way a demonstration of fifty thousand people was easily arranged.

About this time Vandervelde, Rosenfeld, and other defenders of the Social Revolutionaries were crossing the frontiers of Russia on their way to Moscow. At each station their train was met by rioters against themselves and the Social Revolutionaries. The riots were arranged in this way. The whole train to which their carriage was attached was filled with Communists, and at each station they got out and with the aid of local Communists staged a demonstration against the foreign visitors.

The writer N. spoke truly. The Soviet Government provided us with a constant series of tragedies, in the witnessing of which young people grew old, the mature grew white-haired, and many spectators died.

CHAPTER XXVI

BANISHMENT

In May, 1922, my book, *The Influence of Hunger on Human Behavior, on Social Life and Social Organization,* began to be printed. Before publication many paragraphs, indeed whole chapters were cut out by the censors. The book as a whole was ruined, but what remained was better than nothing. The Soviet's "War on the Ideological Front" was now being carried on with great energy. The autonomy of the University had been completely annihilated. Rectors, deans, and professors were dismissed, University and Faculty meetings were forbidden. Many non-Communist students were expelled. Only the Communists and youths recommended by the Government were permitted to enter the schools. All non-Communist journals and magazines were suppressed. Co-operative organizations which had grown up in the last months were "governmentalized." We all lived from hand to mouth, expecting every day some new blow.

Nevertheless, we were not entirely without hope. The country was showing unmistakable signs of regeneration. Under the ruins of our civilization, in the depths of the people's hearts and souls, something was stirring, the life and spirit of a new people. Whatever might happen to us, the new birth of Russia was a certainty. Time only was necessary for these new forces to grow strong enough to make themselves felt. We could wait, for the years had trained us in patience.

What were these new creative forces? Let us not speak about them here, for the time has not come to speak without endangering their growth. When the time is ripe, the world will see them.

On August 10, 1922, I left Petrograd for a few days in Moscow. From the station I went directly to the apartment of a friend who had invited me to stay with him. We had breakfast and parted, arranging to meet at five o'clock in his apartment. Having attended to my business and visited friends, I returned to the apartment, but my friend was not at home. At six he had not come and I became a little uneasy. At seven a student came, asking for my friend's wife. I told him that neither she nor her husband were at home, and offered to take any message he cared to leave. The student looked at me fixedly and asked: "Who are you?" I introduced myself, and he said: "Professor, get out of this apartment. Your friend is under arrest and the Chekhists may be here any moment."

I took my bag and left, but I waited near the house until I saw my friend's wife approaching, and having agreed with her about our immediate plans, I went to the apartment of another friend. Alas, he, too, had been arrested. A few hours later we learned that Professors Kizevetter and Frank, Berdyaeff and Yasinsky, Sofronoff and Ozeroff, Myakotin and Peshekhonoff, Osorgin and many others, prominent scientists and scholars, writers and co-operative workers, in all about one hundred and fifty, had in a single day been arrested. Many students also had been taken. A big terror was evidently beginning and might be appearing also in Petrograd. All doubt on this score was removed next day when I read a telegram sent by my wife to a friend in Moscow. This telegram read: "Please detain my son. We have scarlet fever in our house."

We soon learned how timely was this warning for me to remain away from my Petrograd lodgings. In that city were arrested Professors Lossky, Karsavin, Zubasheff, Lutokhin, Lapshin, Odintsoff, Selivanoff, Brutskus, Zanyatin, and others, about one hundred in all, with many students. The Chekhists had gone to my Petrograd address, and there, in Mrs. D's apartment, they found her second daughter, Nadya, dying. Nadya's husband and the physician assured the Chekhists that I was not in the apartment, and they begged the men not to torment the dying woman with futile searching. The Chekhists went through all the rooms, and finding that I was not concealed there, they generously agreed to make no more noise and to leave no guard behind.

I remained in Moscow comparatively safe, for not very many people knew me by sight. I went to concerts and theaters, visited museums and even the library of the Communist Academy. A week passed, and rumors about the arrested scholars and professors began to be circulated. It was said that they were not to be executed but banished. Soon in *Pravda* an article by Trotzky gave official authority to these rumors. "These people," said Trotzky's article, "cannot and will not make peace with Communism. As soon as any new political disturbances begin we are obliged to massacre them as our bitterest enemies. In order to avoid these massacres, let us export these wares abroad. Banishing them, we get rid of our worst foes. Remaining enemies may be bribed and made harmless. Thus we weaken the forces acting against us and reinforce our own bases."

The arrested people began to be released, the authorities warning them that they were to be banished. Each man had to sign two papers, one promising that in ten days he would leave the country, and the other declaring that if they returned to Russia without permission of the Soviet Government they would be executed. If a man protested that he was without money or even without visés to enter a foreign country, the authorities said: "Get visés. If not your banishment will be to the north of Siberia." Therefore the victims got visés, and as it unexpectedly turned out, without much difficulty, the Governments of Czecho-Slovakia, Germany, Latvia and Esthonia granting them at once and without formalities.

As soon as the fate of my arrested colleagues became known, I decided that my own banishment abroad was the best thing that could happen. I could do nothing more for my country, I was living illegally, and sooner or later would certainly be arrested. When arrested I could expect either endless imprisonment or death by starvation and cold in northern Siberia. If I were to live at all I ought to live usefully, and so long had I been cut off from foreign scientific literature that I hardly knew what had been written. All these motives urged me not to miss this favorable moment for banishment, and so I started at once to Petrograd to be arrested.

It was a lovely September morning when I reached Czarskoe Selo. My wife was away from the house, so I began myself to prepare my prison bag, packing it with food and linen, and with two or three books with which to beguile the tedium of prison life. When my wife returned, she tried at once to dissuade me from my purpose, because all those who had been arrested in the kingdom of Grishka the Third were still in prison and no one knew whether or not he would be banished with the people in Moscow. My wife showed me copies of the Petrograd *Pravda* and *The Red Paper,* in which I was furiously assailed and threatened. Still I thought I had better be arrested, and with my prison bag on my back I started for Petrograd, my wife accompanying me. On the way we met friends, who joined with my wife in calling me quite mad to venture into Petrograd. "If Zinovieff and his crew do not shoot you at once," they said, "you will be banished to Siberia, and not to any foreign country."

Finally, I agreed that it might be better for me to be arrested in Moscow, and next morning I went there. With my prison bag I presented myself at the Chekha, and after some time was admitted to

the office of the official in charge of the affair of the
banished scholars and scientists.

"My name is Sorokin," I said to him. "Your
comrades in Petrograd went to arrest me but I was
here in Moscow. I have come to you to know what
you wish to do with me."

The Chekhist, a young man with the white face of
a cocaine addict, waved his hand, saying: "We have
plenty of people in Moscow with whom we don't
know what to do. Go back to Petrograd and let the
Chekha there decide your fate."

"Thank you," I said, "I will not go back to Petrograd. If you want to arrest me, here I am. If not,
as a free citizen I choose to remain in Moscow, or
in any other part of Russia rather than in Petrograd."

"That is an impossible answer," he said, but after
a moment's thought he added: "Well, all arrested
University people are to be banished abroad. Sign
these two papers, and in ten days leave the territory
of the R. S. F. S. R."

Willingly I signed and asked where I was to apply
for my passport. "In the Commissariat of Foreign
Affairs," answered the pale young man, "I am just
going to tell them of you."

"May I leave here?"

"Oh, certainly."

Going out of the Chekha office I sent a telegram
to my wife to sell all our belongings and to join me
in Moscow. There was nothing much except the
remnants of my library to sell, therefore her task
was light. I should have preferred to leave Russia

via Petrograd and Hamburg, but knowing the methods of Zinovieff and the Petrograd Chekha in arresting people without waiting for permission of the central Government, I decided on the route from Moscow to Riga. And I decided to leave quickly.

The process of getting passports and permissions was difficult and irritating. At the Commissariat of Foreign Affairs they told me that it would be five or six days before my passport would be ready.

"But if I am to leave Russia in ten days there will not be time left for me to get my visés and all the permissions of your damned commissariats," I said.

"That is not our affair," they said indifferently.

"It is your affair, since your Government is banishing me in ten days," I insisted.

"Well, you can have your passport in three days then."

"I must have it tomorrow."

"It is impossible."

Determined to make it possible I went to Karakhan, acting Minister of Foreign Affairs in the absence of Chicherin. Karakhan had been a friend of my student days, and I thought it might be amusing to see him now a Bolshevist official. But when I offered my card to his secretary the fellow declared that Karakhan was busy and could not give me an audience. At the moment a man entered the room and greeted me. He was one of my old students in the Psycho-Neurological Institute. "What are you doing here?" I asked.

"Oh, I am head of the information and publicity

department of the Ministry of Foreign Affairs,''
he answered proudly. "Have you read in the newspapers articles by Koltsoff? That is my pen name.''

I said that I had read them and he asked eagerly
what I thought of them. "The same as of your
Government,'' I replied. "Now this fellow here
refuses to send my card in to His Excellency. Please
make him do it.''

They whispered a moment and disappeared. Soon
Karakhan appeared at the door, which was guarded
by three Chekhists. "How do you do, Pitirim Alex-
androvich,'' he said. "I am glad to see you. Come
in.''

The room was comfortably, even luxuriously furnished, and Karakhan, once a lean and spare man,
now looked well fed and fat.

"Your Excellency,'' I said, half-jokingly. "You
know, of course, that I am exiled. Your subordinates
refuse to give me a passport before three days, and
that inconveniences me. Will you be so kind as to
order them to have my passport ready by tomorrow
morning?''

"With great pleasure,'' he answered, and over
the telephone gave the order. "Tomorrow it will
be ready for you,'' he announced, "and it will be
given you free of any charge.''

I thanked him, although it had not been my intention to pay for the passport. Not the next morning
but the next after that did I get the passport. "Ex-
pulsée" was written on it in French. That same
day I got Czecho-Slovakian, German, Lettish, and
Lithuanian visés. Now I had to get many licenses,

and the permission of the Commissariat of Education to take with me some of my manuscripts, one copy each of books, articles, and pamphlets published by me. Then the permission of the Commissariat of Foreign Trade to take with us one old overcoat, two old suits, two towels, two sheets, five shirts, and five trousers. The permission of the Commissariat of Finances was necessary in order to take fifty dollars, one watch and two wedding rings. Three days I spent getting these cursed permits.

All my manuscripts were carefully revised, numbered, and sealed by the censors. A great deal of suspicion was aroused by the botanical materials of my wife. Only by many assurances were they convinced that there was nothing counter-revolutionary or secret in these innocent herbariums and botanical preparations. In the Commissariat of Finances, what was our surprise to be given our permission by one of our own colleagues, a man who, like ourselves, had been sentenced to banishment. At the last minute he was suddenly forbidden to go abroad and was sent back to his old employment. A banished criminal yesterday, today he was a Soviet official granting licenses to his erstwhile fellow-criminals. It was impossible not to laugh at such an absurdity.

About the last visit I paid was to Communist leader Pyatakoff, a man with whom in student days I had been friends. I went to see him in behalf of a former comrade of us both, a man in prison and seriously ill. Pyatakoff promised to do what he could, and after finishing that business, he told me that he was about to write an article on my criticism of Bukharin's work: *The Theory of Marxism.*

I said to him, "Pyatakoff, let me ask you, do you really believe that you are creating a communistic society?"

"Of course not," he replied frankly.

"You admit that your experiment has failed, and that you are building only a primitive bourgeois society. Why then are you banishing us?"

"You do not take into consideration," said the man, "that two processes are going on in Russia. One is the re-creation of a bourgeois society; the other is a process of the adaptation of the Soviet Government to it. The first process is going on faster than the second. This involves a danger to our existence. Our task is to delay the development of that first process, but you and the others who are to be exiled are accelerating it. That is why you are banished. Perhaps after two or three years we will invite you to come back."

"Thank you," I said, "I hope to return to my country—without your invitation."

On a gray afternoon, September 23, 1922, the first group of exiles gathered at the Moscow railway station. The Board of the Agricultural Co-operative Union, and other prominent co-operative workers; Peshskhonoff, a former member of Kerensky's-Ministry, Professor Myakotin, a leader in the People Socialistic Party, their wives and children, my wife and I were in this first group. Into the Lettish diplomatic car, reserved by me, I took our two valises. *"Omnia mea mecum porto"* I could say of myself. In a pair of shoes sent me by a Czech scientist, a suit given by the American Relief Administration, and with fifty dollars in my pocket I left my native land. All my companions were in similar plight, but none of us worried very much. The standard of life on which we had lived for so long we could certainly establish anywhere in the world. In spite of prohibitions of the authorities, many friends and acquaintances came to see us off, with gifts of flowers, handclasps, and tears. Their faces, the disappearing streets of Moscow, the last sight of the Fatherland we devoured with all our eyes. As we traveled on we took from our pockets and read letters sent all of us in secret by peasant co-operative organizations, by students, professors, workers, and other people.

"You are expelled not by the people, but by the internationalist dregs," said these farewell letters. "Russia is with you and you are with Russia. Russia suffers and you suffer. When the day of Russia comes, you will be with us again." Then we destroyed them lest they fall into Chekhist hands at the frontier.

Next day we reached Sebage, the boundary line of Russia. "Our greetings to Moscow," "Greetings to Petrograd," "Greetings to Novgorod," we telegraphed back, while the Chekhists searched our bags. Half an hour later we passed a red flag, and Soviet Russia was behind us. That night, after five years, we lay down to sleep without asking ourselves, "Will they come tonight or not?"

A week later in Berlin I delivered my first lecture

on the present condition in Russia. It became clear that I left none too soon, for the first letters that reached me said that "Our grandmother (the Chekha) is very sorry for having let you go without giving you her last and eternal blessing" (execution). In a Berlin newspaper, *Days,* I read that "At a meeting of the People's Commissaries in Moscow the head of the Chekha, comrade Unshlikht, and commissary of the Foreign Office, Karakhan were censured by the other commissaries for allowing Mrs. Kuskova and Professor Sorokin to go abroad." At the same time my book about Famine was destroyed by the Soviet Government.

Invited by President Masaryk, I went to Prague and had the pleasure of meeting him, as well as other prominent representatives of Czecho-Slovak society. Here I resumed my work and wrote my *Sociology of Revolution.* With many friends, I worked to establish magazines, *The Farm* and *The Peasants' Russia,* and to help the Agricultural Institute, and agricultural and co-operative schools in Czecho-Slovakia for the training of peasant leaders of future Russia. Many thousand students are educating themselves and others for the regeneration of our fatherland. With them I had the joy of entering into communication with people in Soviet Russia. Our new, strong, and creative life has been growing both at home and abroad.

In November, 1923, I came to this great country, on invitation, to lecture before American universities. Here I have written from my journals and from memory, these recollections.

Whatever may happen in the future, I know that I have learned three things which will remain forever convictions of my heart as well as my mind. Life, even the hardest life, is the most beautiful, wonderful and miraculous treasure in the world. Fulfillment of duty is another beautiful thing, making life happy and giving to the soul an inconquerable force to sustain ideals. This is my second conviction, and my third is that cruelty, hatred, and injustice never can and never will be able to create a mental, moral, or material millenium.

PART V
THIRTY YEARS AFTER

CHAPTER XXVII

Some thirty years elapsed after these notes were jotted down. A quarter of a century or so passed after they were published. In the interim, the Revolution has come of age. It has turned out to be a *gigantic success and a colossal failure.*

THE REVOLUTION AS A GIGANTIC SUCCESS

The Revolution's first success has been *its survival amid very difficult conditions and in spite of many powerful enemies.* It triumphed over its internal enemies in the civil war. It withstood the first combined invasion of the Anglo-American-French expeditionary forces in 1918. It coped successfully with subsequent military pressure of foreign powers. It did not suffocate in the noose of the *cordon sanitaire* and did not die of the economic starvation worked for by its enemies. It withstood the terrific onslaught of the Hitlerite and European legions and ground them into the dust. Finally, it still faces — fearless, grim, quiet, and more powerful than ever before — all the forces marshalled against it by the Truman Doctrine, the Marshall Plan, the Atlantic Pact, and the Vatican, not to mention a host of smaller groups, alliances, bands, and persons seeking its defeat.

Its second gigantic success has been its *total, un-*

313

limited character. The Russian Revolution is not
merely political or economic or religious. It is a political *and* economic *and* religious *and* familistic *and*
educational *and* scientific *and* artistic *and* philosophi-
cal revolution. It has attempted to revolutionize all
basic social institutions from the family to business
and the state; all compartments of culture from
science and philosophy to religion, poetry, and music; and the whole mentality and overt conduct of
an individual from his cradle to his grave. In this
sense it is possibly the *most unlimited revolution in
the history of mankind.*

Its third success is *its unprecedented quantitative
scope and world-wide diffusion.* If it were limited to
Russia alone, its scope would be unparalleled in human history. But in spite of all *cordons sanitaires,*
during some thirty years of its career it has been diffused throughout the entire world. With its Chinese
and other allies it has now at least one fourth of humanity as its followers. In any country, including the
most anti-Communistic and anti-Soviet, it has a considerable "fifth column" made up of persons and
groups impressive in their energy, fanaticism, and
animosity. Even intellectually the bulk of these de-
votees is, if anything, above the rank and file of the
"bourgeois population." This unprecedented diffusion has had in the course of these years its ups and
downs; but, all in all, it is still growing.

Its fourth success is that *it has changed even its
implacable enemies into its own image.* Fighting the
Revolution, these enemies introduced into their
group many traits of the Revolution which they are

fighting against. Ferociously fighting the Revolution's totalitarianism, despotism, limitation of the inalienable rights and freedom of the individual, governmental control of business, nationalization and communization of economics, development of spying, and so on, these anti-Soviet and anti-Communist governments and groups have introduced into their countries, under new names and colors, most of these vices and horrors of the Revolution. Fortunately, in these countries and organizations, the revolutionary diseases have not developed yet to the same extent as in Soviet Russia. Nevertheless, these anti-Communist groups are already infected, and the infection seems to be growing rapidly. The techniques and procedures of the committees like that on un-American activities and of the secret political police begin to have unmistakable resemblance to the techniques of the GPU and the NKVD. Growing limitations of the rights and liberties of the Communists, of their "fellow travelers," of all the "subversives," and of all who are opposed to the policies of the powers that be are simply models of the Communist denials of the rights and freedoms of their own opponents. The self-confessions and betrayals of the Budenzes, the Chamberses, the Bentleys and their like are but a replica of the betraying self-confessions of the Communist trials and purges. The Communist revolution can indeed be proud of thus converting even its implacable enemies. What a triumph!

The greatest success the Revolution has achieved, however, is its dual role of grave-digger and worms

*of the disintegrating sensate (capitalist, material-
istic, secular, acquisitive) socio-cultural order of the
West.* This sensate form of Western culture and
society replaced the medieval (ideational and idealistic) forms and has been dominant for the last five
centuries. Having produced many a magnificent
achievement during the period of its domination,
the sensate order has begun to show the unmistakable
signs of decay and decreasing creativity. (For a de-
tailed development and demonstration of this, cf. my
Social and Cultural Dynamics [4 vols.], and my *Crisis of Our Age.*) The First World War was the first
catastrophic shock of this disintegration. The Russian Revolution, a direct child of this war, was the
second. After these two shocks a series of further
and still more catastrophic ones followed: the anti-
Communist revolutions of Fascism and Nazism; the
growing disorganization of capitalist economy; the
cancer of demoralized governments; mental, moral,
and social anarchy; and, finally, the catastrophic
thrombosis of the Second World War, with its subsequent revolutions throughout the world, and preparations for a suicidal Third World War. In these
shocks of the sensate West, the Russian Revolution
has played the decisive rôle. Being a monster-child
of our disintegrating sensate order, the Revolution
seems to have developed the virus of sensate disorganization in the most virulent form. As such, it
has been the main grave-digger and the most voracious worm of the socio-cultural sensate body of the
West — and, eventually, of the Revolution itself. It

successfully devours the dying sensate order and thus also devours itself.

In this way, the Revolution clears the ground from the debris of the dying socio-cultural order and paves the way for a new idealistic or integral order of mankind.

In all these respects the Revolution is indeed a gigantic success, and this success is likely to grow until the dying sensate order is buried and a new creative order is built.

The Revolution as a Colossal Failure

The destructive success of the Revolution is fully countered by its colossal failure as a constructive and creative force.

As a creative "flop," the Revolution has shown itself first of all on *the highest levels of creativity in practically all fields of culture: at these highest levels it has not produced any genius of either first or even second class.* Even more: it has hardly produced any genius that can rival not only the Russian geniuses of the past but even the creative leaders born and trained under the old regime but still living and working in Soviet Russia.) Practically all the banner-names the Soviet parades as its great creators are those of persons who were trained and did much of their creative work under the old regime. Present-day Soviet *musical leaders* — Prokofieff, Miaskovsky, Gliere, Ippolitov-Ivanov, Shostakovitch, Khachiturian, Khreneff, Kabalevsky — all were

born, trained, and launched upon their careers under
the old regime. The thirty-year-old Russian Revolution has not produced a single name that can be put,
even by Soviet propaganda, into this class. Musi-
cally, on this high level the Revolution has been
sterile. Through its regimentation of free creative
genius it has suppressed and suffocated many a creative musical genius. Others like Rachmaninov,
Glazunoff, and Gretchaninov were forced to flee from
Russia. This is true even of musical virtuosos and
conductors like Chaliapin, Koussevitsky, Heifetz,
Horowitz, Piatigorsky, Elmann, Borovsky, and
Brailovsky. Not a single new artist of comparable
stature has been produced. If anything, the Revolution has suppressed the remarkable musical creativity that Russia experienced at the end of the
nineteenth and at the beginning of the twentieth
century: the period of Tchaikovsky, Mussorgsky,
Rimsky-Korsakov, Lliadov, Balakireff, Rubinstein,
Glazunoff, Stravinsky, Prokofieff, and others.

What has been said about musical creativity is
true of all the other fine arts. *In poetry and literature,* the Revolution has not produced any single
name of even remotely great magnitude. Its official
poets — Mayakovsky, Essenin, and so on — produced their greatest works before the Revolution.
Almost all the winners of the Stalin prize in literature, especially those whose novels and plays amount
to anything more than mere propaganda pieces —
Sholokhov, A. Tolstoy, and even Ilya Ehrenburg
and Simonov — were all born and did their creative
work before the Revolution. Even the Soviet star

journalists and publicists, such as Ehrenburg, D. Zaslavsky, and E. Tarlé, did their chief work before the Revolution. In the nineteen-twenties they were all either imprisoned by the Soviet government, or put into concentration camps, or else they fled abroad. In brief, virtually all Soviet stars in literature and poetry were born and trained and did their creative work before the Revolution. It has not been able to produce any eminent literary star of its own.

On the contrary, the Revolution murdered, imprisoned, or banished several eminent poets and writers such as N. Gumileff, E. Zamiatin, B. Pilniak, B. Zaitzeff, Shmeleff, I. Bunin (a Nobel prize winner), Balmont, I. Severianin and others. A still larger number have been muzzled by the government and physically deprived of any creative work (Akhmatova, Pasternack, and so on). As in music, the end of the nineteenth and the beginning of the twentieth century was a period of a remarkable literary renaissance — the period of A. Tchekhov, M. Gorki, L. Andreev, brilliantly continued up to the Soviet Revolution by their contemporaries and the younger generation of the literati. The Revolution smothered this renaissance and ushered in an era of sterility in this field.

The same is true of *plays, the theater, and opera.* Here the standards of the prerevolutionary *opera and ballet* at the Maryinsky and Bolshoi theaters and of *drama and comedy* at the Moscow Art Theater, the Kommissargevsky Theater, and others have been barely maintained and certainly unexcelled. Among the Revolution-nurtured plays and operas not a single significant production has emerged. In the field of the *cinema* a few great films have been produced, but not better than the finest films produced in other countries, and, again, they have been created mostly by persons trained under the old régime, and the government has often hindered the creative activities of some of the artists in this field, like Eisenstein.

Still less may the Revolution brag about its creativity in the fields of *painting, sculpture, and architecture*. Apart from hundreds of thousands of mediocre pictures and sculptures representing Lenin, Stalin, Marx and other "heroes of the Revolution for a short moment" (there remain none of the thousands of similar representations of Trotzky, Zinoviev, Mussolini, Hitler, and so on) and thousands of governmentally ordered pictures and sculptures commemorating this or that governmentally approved event — apart from this sort of painting and sculpture little has been produced by the Revolution. If something better was produced, the artists happened to have been trained under the old régime. But even this best falls far below standards of prerevolutionary creators like Repin, Levitan, Rerich, Vrubel, Kustodieff, Petrov-Vodkin, Serov, and Maliavin. Here again the Revolution destroyed the remarkable creative *élan* of Russian painting characteristic of the end of the nineteenth and the beginning of the twentieth century.

That nothing even remotely eminent has been achieved in *architecture* is well attested by the complaints of the Soviet government itself and by its recrimination of Soviet architects for merely imitating the "bourgeois" styles or the "style of pre-revolutionary Russia." Similar "confessions" on the part of the Soviet leaders of sterility and bourgeois imitativeness in the field of the fine arts are sufficient evidence of the creative failure in question.

Still more deplorable has been the influence of the Revolution in the fields of *religion, philosophy, humanistic and social sciences, ethics, and law.*

In the field of *religious creativity* the Revolution marked itself at its early stage only by drastic persecution, at its later stage by an attempt to use religions for political purposes. Both policies are very old and have been practiced by many moronic governments. The Revolution could not create even an original Communist theology, philosophy, or cult — if we call Communism "religion." Its revolutionary parades and rituals, demonstrations and mass meetings, are just a variety of old political parade or demonstration, of military ritual or old revolutionary cult. The Revolution merely imitated these, instead of creating something new.

Some significant religious creativity has been going on in Russia during these thirty years. But it goes on underground, in spite of the Revolution and its government.

Similar sterility marks *Soviet philosophy*. For thirty years the Revolution has not been able to produce even an original or creative version of dialectical materialism or of Marxist philosophy. What has been produced in the works of Lenin, Bukharin, Deborin, Stalin, not to mention the "petty prophets'' of Communism, is a simplified and vulgarized version of earlier, more thoughtful formulations of dialectical materialism or materialistic philosophy in general. All other kinds of philosophy have been persecuted by the Soviet authorities. The Revolution could not and did not do anything but suffocate the creative efforts of idealistic and other philosophies deviating from the approved brand of Soviet philosophy.

In the field of philosophy also Russia achieved remarkable creativeness at the end of the nineteenth and at the beginning of the twentieth century. V. Solovyev, L. Tolstoi and F. Dostoievsky, N. Fedoroff, S. Trubetkoy, P. Novgorodzeff, V. I. Lapshin, N. Lossky, A. Vvedensky, N. Karpinsky, N. Berdyaeff, S. Frank, S. Bulgakoff and many others were bringing Russian philosophy to its maturity. The Revolution and its satraps suppressed this movement. Instead, we have now a dull and dogmatic reiteration of a mere shibboleth of Marx-Lenin-Stalin "materialistic theology."

Since all *the social sciences and all the brands of law and ethics* except the Marx-Lenin-Stalin "theology" have been persecuted and prohibited, the Revolution naturally could not create anything in these fields. Instead of the brilliant prerevolutionary development of a science of law and ethics led by possibly the greatest scholar of law in the twentieth century, L. Petrajitzky, and by a whole galaxy of eminent scholars in the fields of the general theory of law, the philosophy of law, criminal, civil, international and constitutional law — instead of highly advanced, liberal, and scientifically warranted projects of new codes of law, developed by these eminent scholars — the Revolution executed some of them (Lazarevsky, Kohoshkin, and others), banished or imprisoned many, drove others into exile or to commit suicide (L. Petrajitzky, for instance), and replaced them with such "scholars" as Stuchka and Vyshinsky, who have hardly even smelled the real science of law. Instead of highly advanced moral, social, and scientific codes of law, the Revolution gave the people the butcher's law codes — more bestial and barbarous than any authentic barbarian code. The responsible judges and courts were replaced by judges and "courts" whose main purpose was to murder all whom the government disliked for any reason. And they murdered on a mass scale. While in the years 1880-1904 the average number of capital punishments in Russia fluctuated from 9 to 18 (capital punishment in Russia was already abolished at the middle of the eighteenth century for all crimes except one — an attempt against the life of the Czar or his family), in the years 1918-1922 the Revolution executed at least 150,000 persons a year. And this does not include all the victims of the civil war. Such was the "creativity" of Soviet law and justice during the first period of the Revolution!

Later on, it promulgated the decent-looking constitution of 1936 and decreased the number of crimes punished by death in the Soviet criminal code of 1926. In 1947 capital punishment was abolished altogether.

But the constitution of 1936 has never been realized even partially, and the elimination of capital punishment means a mere replacement of instantaneous death by a firing squad with a slow and agonizing death in inhuman labor and concentration camps and prisons, where from these unfortunate victims, kept under inhuman conditions by "corrective measures," the government squeezes out the last drop of their energy and labor ("for the benefit of mankind and a people's democracy") and slowly but surely kills them. Greater cynicism, greater hypocrisy, or greater cruelty in the guise of "law and corrective ethics" the world has rarely seen. Only Hitler's concentration camps exceeded this for infamy!

Such is the "creativity" of the Revolution in this particular field. The satraps of the Revolution seem firmly to believe that the more human corpses are put into the foundation of the Communist paradise, the more blood spilled as fertilizer, the more tears and sorrow caused, the faster and the more magnificently will the Communist paradise come into being. How far this is from Dostoievsky's challenge, through the voice of Ivan Karamazov: "If for the entrance into the Kingdom of God one tear of an innocent child is necessary, I shall respectfully return to Thee the ticket."

Not much needs to be said of other *social and humanistic disciplines*. Here again — in the philosophy of history, sociology, political science, economics, anthropology, history, and psychology — prerevolutionary Russia, at the turn of the century, experienced a remarkable creative upsurge. N. Danilevsky (predecessor of Spengler and Toynbee in their main conceptual framework), N. Mikhailovsky, P. Kropotkin, P. Lavrov, K. Leontieff, and later on a host of first-class scholars — as eminent as any in the world at that period — were not only bringing Russian social and humanistic disciplines to maturity, but fructifying them and vivifying them for the whole world. The Revolution crushed this movement. Practically all these disciplines were abolished in the universities and colleges. Research and creativity were directly or indirectly prohibited. Many scholars were executed, banished, imprisoned, or subjected to the deadly "corrective measures." The result has been deadly, too. As already mentioned, even in the field of governmentally fostered "Marx-Lenin-Stalin" economics, sociology, anthropology, psychology, political science, or history, the dullest bureaucratic sterility has reigned supreme.

Later on the Soviet government slightly liberalized conditions because they wanted to have something significant created in order to parade it before the world as "the great achievement of Soviet social and humanistic sciences." Alas! Nothing miraculous has come from the muzzled potential creators! In *psychology* the Revolution had to parade my eminent friend, Ivan Pavlov, the great scientist who hated the Revolution and did not hide his hatred. When in the last few years the Soviet government wanted to parade the stars of Soviet history and political science it pulled out of the moth balls my former colleague at the University of St.

Petersburg, Professor E. Tarlé, who wrote all his
main works before the Revolution, who hated it, and
who in the nineteen-twenties was arrested and banished to Soviet Turkestan and who only in the last
decade was restored to Soviet favor. This means
that in all these fields the Revolution could not produce even one star of its own and now is forced to
star the products of the prerevolutionary régime.
And some of these starred Soviet "scholars" are
often not the first-class but the third-class scholars of
the régime. Professor Derjavin is an example: he
was only a petty "privat-dozent" in philology before the Revolution; today the Soviet government
bills him as the great Soviet linguist, philologist,
and master of other sorts of magic.

One need not wonder, therefore, that most of the
achievements of Soviet social and humanistic sciences, extolled by the Soviet government as supreme
works of Soviet genius, such as the Soviet collective
History of Diplomacy or the *Soviet Encyclopedia,*
are, in fact, mediocre performances — dull, just
short of competent, ignorant of many recent achievements outside Soviet Russia, devoid of any true
originality, of any sparks of creativity.

Somewhat better seems to be the situation in the
field of *the natural sciences and technology.* These
have been urgently needed by the Soviet government and therefore have been somewhat fostered,
especially in their applied form. Yet even in these
fields neither a Soviet-nurtured genius nor a particularly important discovery or invention has so far
appeared. When the Soviet government wants to

put its greatest stars here on exhibition, once more they will almost invariably turn out to be my previous colleagues at the University of St. Petersburg or Moscow or, at any rate, eminent prerevolutionary physicists, chemists, mathematicians, biologists, engineers, and inventors. Even the famous — or infamous — Dr. Trofim Lysenko was professor of biology before the Revolution. An overwhelming majority of the members of the Soviet Academy of Sciences in the fields of mathematics, physics, chemistry, biology and engineering are still scientists of the prerevolutionary vintage. In other cases, not being able to grow them at home, the Soviet government had to kidnap or reimport emigrant scientists like Dr. Kapitza from England or to hire the services of foreign scientists.

These facts prove incontrovertibly that the Revolution has failed notably even in this particularly vital field. Murdering, imprisoning, and muzzling the actual and potential creators in these fields, the satraps of the Revolution greatly weakened the creative *élan* even in this "materialistic" area. In spite of an enormous increase in scientific research institutions and research personnel fostered by the Soviet government, contemporary Soviet science and technology hardly exhibit so notable a galaxy of scientists and inventors as Russia had before the Revolution — Favorsky, Konovalov, Chernov, Dokuchaiev, A. S. Popov, Chebyshev, Lyapunov, Fersman, Pryanishnikov, Samoilov, Lebedev, Vernadsky, Markov, Pavlov, and so on. Other creators, such as Dr. V. Ipatieff in chemistry, Dr. I. Sikorsky in aviation, and Dr. W. Zworikin in television, to mention but a few, had either to flee the country or (fortunately for them) were banished, so as to be able to continue their work.

During the thirty years of the Revolution, its satraps, exploiting all the mental and material resources of the Russian nation, have not been able to compete with bourgeois science and technology. In spite of considerable achievements in intra-atomic research, Soviet science lagged in the invention of the atomic bomb. Soviet science discovered nothing so important as the theory of relativity, sulpha drugs, penicillin, new vitamins, and so on. Indeed, most of their gadgets, from automobiles to airplanes and atomic bomb, are but belatedly imitative variations of Western models.

To sum up: the Revolution can hardly brag about its creativity even in these fields; on these high levels of creativity the Revolution has been a fiasco.

Unfortunately, it is a colossal failure not only on these highest levels but *on much lower, more prosaic and extremely vital levels of creativity, whose improvement is the raison d'être, the holy of holies, and the only justification for the Revolution itself.*

It aimed and promised to create a *new communist or socialist form of society incomparably better than the capitalist or any other form of social organization known to history.* Economically, politically, socially, mentally, morally, and even biologically this communist or socialist society of the Revolution was to be a sort of paradise on earth. Everyone would serve according to his capacity and would receive according to his needs. Poverty, inequality, exploitation, and injustice would be abolished. A high material standard of living; freedom for everyone to develop fully his personality; freedom from all forms of exploitation and injustice; freedom from tyrannical government; the government as a wise and true servant of the people, freely elected and voted down; the abolition of the death penalty and other "barbaric" forms of punishment; the blossoming of creativity in all its forms; universal happiness and progress — these are some of the wonders of the new society promised by the Revolution.

After thirty years we find instead a very old and very familiar variety of totalitarian or police state, quite different from the promised utopian society of the Revolution. After thirty years of building, paid for by millions of human lives sacrificed, by the untold suffering of still larger numbers, the Revolution has built merely a variety of the "communist-totalitarian" type of society prevalent in ancient Egypt, especially in the Ptolemaic period; in ancient China, at the beginning of our era and in the eleventh century; in ancient Sparta, Lipara, the Western Roman Empire after 301 A.D., in Byzantium; in ancient Mexico and Peru; and then partly represented by the police states (or *Polizei Staaten*) of the sixteenth, seventeenth, and eighteenth centuries — to mention but a few predecessors of the Soviet type of society. In all these cases most of the instruments and means of production were nationalized; most of the business was run by the government; and the government overwhelmingly controlled most of the actions, relationships, and life of its subjects. It regarded itself as an élite (by the grace of God or by its own effort), which knows best what is good for the people, without asking them or being elected by them.

In brief, the real society created by the Revolution happens to be a variety of the type which in the statements of the Communist government itself was very old, very despotic, very oppressive, very unjust, and very bad, as the Communist leaders characterize all these past totalitarian societies. Some of the naïve Communist ideologists possibly believe that since they themselves are the all-controlling and all-deciding government, their totalitarian variety is quite different from the past varieties. Such naïveté is, however, hardly shared by the majority of the bosses of the Revolution, and still less can it be accepted by history, by the people, and by mankind as a whole.

Tragically failing in this cardinal point, the Revolution failed in all the important properties of society promised or actually built.

A. The Revolution promised to raise enormously the material standard of living of the people. *After thirty years the standard of living of the people is, if anything, still below that of the prerevolutionary period.* The greater part of European Russia still lies in ruins. Reference to the Second World War does not excuse this failure: without the Russian Revolution Nazism and Fascism would hardly have been possible, and without these, there would hardly have been a Second World War. The achievements or failures of any government should be judged according to actual conditions and facts and not according to such an ideal condition as: "*if* we had no opposition, *if* there were no external enemies, *if* the people were wise and would enthusiastically follow any decision of ours, *if* there were an ideal X, Y, and Z." Under such conditions any régime and any moronic government would be successful. The failure of the Soviet regime to raise the standard of living of the Russian people to at least the level of most of the bourgeois countries or somewhat above the prerevolutionary standard in Russia is a real failure, inexcusable and undeniable, especially when one considers all the sacrifices and sufferings of the people entailed by this experiment, and all the cruelties, coercions, and butcheries of the Soviet government in its endeavor to improve the standards.

Nor should the Soviet government or its apologists talk of the vast industrialization and urbanization of the country and the enormous increase of production. The actual data show that before the Revolution the rate of industrial and economic growth of Russia during the period 1890-1914 was as great as the rate during any of the five-year plans of the Soviet regime. If there had been no Revolution and no socialization, the economic and industrial status of Russia would certainly have been higher than the present status. In that case the growth would have been achieved peacefully, bloodlessly, without millions of victims, unspeakable suffering, or unbelievable cruelty and bestiality.

B. The Revolution promised *to abolish political*

autocracy, despotic government, capital punishment and other forms of coercive penalties; and it guaranteed the maximum of freedom of all sorts to the population.

Instead it created as despotic a government as is known in the entire course of human history — certainly incomparably more tryannical than the incapable, impotent, mild, and very human constitutional government of the old régime. The Soviet dictators and the Politbureau are not limited by any law; they are above any law; their fancies are the law. They control, from the cradle to the grave, all their subjects in practically all their important actions and relationships—economic, political, occupational, religious, educational, recreational, medical, and biological. They are an omnipresent, omnipotent, omniscient (through the army of spies) and unmerciful God in relation to their subjects. These have hardly any liberty at all. Their "liberty of speech and the press" is but to listen to, to say, to write, and to read what the government orders, because there are only governmental papers and magazines, radio and television, books and printing houses. Without government approval one cannot print even his visiting card; one cannot even get paper to write on. If one foolishly says something disapproved by the satraps of the Revolution, one finds himself in a prison or concentration camp for "criminally inclined individuals in need of grim educational and corrective measures." And these measures range all the way from execution to a milder form of hard labor.

The subjects do not have the liberty of choosing either in what part of Russia they would like to live, in what town, in what part of the town, in what room or corner of the room: all this depends on the satraps.

The "citizens" do not have much choice in their occupation: they are assigned to it directly or indirectly. The "citizens" have largely to eat, to drink, and to wear what is decided by the government. Indirectly, in a number of cases, the government decides whether or not an individual is to marry, and whom and when.

To sum up: *the satrapian government of the Revolution enjoys unlimited freedom from any limitations imposed upon it by the people; and the people have little, if any, freedom from the government.*

C. The "educational correctives" of the satraps of the Revolution give another measure of the freedom of the Russian people. *During the thirty years of the Revolution, its government has executed at least from 1,000,000 to 1,500,000 of its citizens directly; murdered many more millions indirectly; arrested, imprisoned, or banished them; coercively transferred from one area to another several millions; all in all, not only in absolute numbers but even in the percentage of the total population of Russia, there has hardly ever been in the whole history of Russia a period of thirty years that could rival in this respect the thirty years of the Revolution.* As already mentioned, before the Revolution, in the period 1880-1904, the annual average number of executions fluctuated from 9 to 18. Compare this with the most conservative but apocalyptic figure of 30,000 annual executions during the years 1918-1950. Keep in mind that the total population of prisons, penal camps, and all kinds of places of detention and banishment in the prerevolutionary period amounted to a small fraction of one per cent of the total population. In these revolutionary years it fluctuated somewhere roughly between ten and fifteen per cent. In the initial period of the Revolution, 1918-1922, on an average, one of every five grown-up persons was arrested and imprisoned at least once.

The whole Soviet paradise is, indeed, one gigantic prison in which the Communist "warden" autocratically rules over some 200 million of the inmates. As in any prison, all main resources of this vast house of detention are communized and nationalized; severe discipline is coercively imposed upon the inmates; pitiless hard labor is demanded from them; their remuneration and wages are insignificant; and infraction of any rule of the warden is brutally punished. At the slightest provocation the inmates are executed. This is the picture of the "freedom" that the government has built after thirty years of labor. One can hardly imagine a more tragic bankruptcy!

D. Similarly, *the Revolution did not abolish exploitation.* It only replaced a limited exploitation of the employees by a private employer (of the poor by the rich) with unlimited exploitation of the people by the government and its fellow-travellers. Whereas before the Revolution a citizen could turn to the courts for redress in case of unlawful exploitation, now there is nobody (except God) to appeal to against exploitation by the government.

E. The Revolution *did not abolish social inequality and social ranks and classes.* In terms of *the amount of income or fortune or material standard of living* the Russian population today makes up a tall economic pyramid, with the large stratum of the poor and with many narrower strata of the well-to-do of various ranks, up to the top millionaires, made up mainly of the highest ranks of the Communist officials and their "specialists" (fellow-travellers). In terms of *the amount of rights and privileges* the population of Russia ranges from the "Communist Gods" (the Politbureau and other top ranks), who enjoy unlimited rights of life and death in relation to the rest of the population and its possessions, to the Soviet "outcasts" in the prisons and penal and labor camps, and the outcasts who are out of prisons but may be arrested and deprived of all rights and even life itself at any moment.

Prerevolutionary Russia had some 3 to 4 million members of the Czarist "nobility." Present-day Russia has from 5 to 6 million of Communist "nobility." And this new nobility is much more privileged than the old Czarist nobility. Indeed, it has already become to a large extent a hereditary nobility, with several educational and other privileged institutions open only to its progeny. In hundreds of other forms social inequality and stratified class and semi-caste society have been thriving in Russia during these thirty years of "revolutionary equalization!" *Beati possidentes!* is again a solid reality there.

To sum up: *Whatever creative field one takes, from the highest to the lowest, the creativity of the Revolution is zero or very low or even negative. As a creative force the Revolution and its satraps are a complete failure.*

DIFFUSION OF CULTURAL AGENCIES AND VALUES AS THE MAIN CONSTRUCTIVE WORK OF THE REVOLUTION

Though not truly creative work, the successful diffusion of *literacy, schools, science, technology, medical help, scientific and research institutions, some healthy forms of recreation, and of similar cultural values and agencies has been the main constructive work of the Revolution.* In this work the Revolution has been reasonably successful, so far as it has diffused real values. However, even in this useful work the Revolution's tremendous success — so well propagandized by the Soviet agencies — has been notably less significant than it appears if one compares it with what was peacefully done in this respect in prerevolutionary Russia.

As to *literacy and schools,* through the law passed by the Duma and approved by the Czar, universal literacy was to be realized in 1919. And the greater part of this project was actually realized in 1916. Thus without any revolution the universal diffusion of literacy would have been accomplished earlier and more fully than by the Revolution.

The same is true of *higher education, research institutions, and social service agencies*. They were all developing and spreading very rapidly in prerevolutionary Russia.

As to *nationalized medicine and free medical help,* so much extolled by the apologists of the Revolution, the sober fact is that the free medical service was nationalized in Russia many years before the Revolution; that nationalized medicine was the main form of medicine in Czarist Russia; that this form functioned very well; that qualitatively it was very high and quantitatively was spreading fast before the Revolution. In other words, free medical service and nationalized medicine are not an invention of the Revolution but existed long before it. If there had been no Revolution, its actual diffusion would have been at least as great as under the Revolution, and qualitatively it probably would have been higher than under the Revolution.

The same goes for the *diffusion of "gadget-mindedness," "gadget-inventiveness," mechanization, and industrialization*. As mentioned above, the rate of industrialization and economic development before the Revolution was at least as fast as during the most successful five-year plans. As to "gadget-inventiveness," the number of technological inventions by Russians grew rapidly as we pass from the eighteenth to the nineteenth and then to the twentieth century. The Soviet government itself inadvertently confirms this by claiming a large number of the most important inventions (radio, electricity, telephone, the steam engine, the guided rocket, the submarine, the tank, and many others) to have been made first by the Russians (before the Revolution). It is very probable that if this trend of technological inventions had continued peacefully, without a revolution, Russian inventiveness at the present time would have been greater than it is under the Revolution.

Another limitation of the successful diffusion of values and agencies by the Revolution has been the *diffusion of many doubtful values and the multiplication of doubtful agencies, side by side with the real and truly valuable.* The diffusion of a monopolistic materialist philosophy; of ethics of hate and violence; of hatred for everything "bourgeois" or deviating from the approved Soviet patterns; diffusion of many theories and ideologies that are phantasmagoric scientifically, ugly aesthetically, and demoralizing ethically; diffusion of the silly cults of Marx, Lenin, or Stalin, with the incredibly fatuous glorification of these men, especially of Stalin, as "the genius of all geniuses," "the greatest leader of all the leaders of humanity," "the infallible and superwise," "the unconquerable conqueror of all the enemies of mankind," — similar to the incantation of many illiterate tribes addressed to their gods, kings, and chiefs: unfortunately the Revolution diffused much more of this trash than the genuine values of truth, beauty, and goodness.

Finally, its *work of diffusion has been greatly vitiated through the direct inhibition, prohibition, and suppression of the diffusion of many real values, from the aesthetic to the religious, that were disap-*

proved by the satraps of the Revolution. These facts greatly reduce the magnitude of this constructive work of the Revolution, rendering it less significant quantitatively and qualitatively. However, considerable useful work of this sort has been done by the Revolution and this work should be noted.

The foregoing analysis shows that the Revolution has been most successful as a purely destructive force that eliminates the moribund social and cultural values (which would have died without any revolution). It has been moderately successful in diffusing real and pseudo values. And it has been an abject failure as a creative force.

THE REASONS FOR THE REVOLUTION'S DESTRUCTIVE SUCCESS AND CREATIVE FAILURE

Since the sensate order of the West and, in connection with it, Eastern culture and social institutions are in the process of disintegration, and since the Revolution itself and both World Wars are the most important manifestations of this disintegration, the apparent destructive success of the Revolution is due entirely to this malady of decaying sensate culture, institutions, and personality. Having been produced by this sickness, the Revolution, after its emergence, has become in its turn one of the central foci of "infection" in the Western and Eastern worlds. It has helped to disintegrate what was already falling apart and would have died eventually if there had been no Russian Revolution. In that case there would be other foci of infection, and other "revolts" and "revolutions" and more "anarchy" performing the task of the Russian Revolution. In fact, a multitude of these, beginning with the Fascist and Nazi revolutions and ending with the Chinese, Indonesian, and others, have been doing this very thing.

This general state of disintegration explains the incessant earthquakes, social tremors, and eruptions over the whole planet — in Europe, in Asia, in Africa, and in the Americas. It explains also why the attempts to stop these earthquakes have failed. It is not because the leaders of the anti-Communist or anti-revolutionary movements are more stupid or less skilful than Lenin, Stalin, or Communist and revolutionary leaders in China and Indo-China, but because the anti-Communist and anti-revolutionary leaders are trying to accomplish the impossible — namely, to revive a corpse. In such situations the grave-diggers and worms are always more successful, no matter how mediocre, even stupid, they may be.

It is only the frightened imagination of the Lilliputian politicians that views all these eruptions as the result of the diabolical genius of Stalin or the Politbureau. They inadvertently magnify, glorify, and idolize the power, the genius, and the superman-liness of the revolutionary leaders. Thus these little men contribute a great deal to the success of the Revolution. Decades ago, making a superman out of Lenin, they assured us that nobody could replace him in the revolutionary leadership and that after his death the Revolution would either decline or else radically change its course. Lenin died — and nothing happened. The Revolution continued its course and its leadership fell upon Stalin, who at that time had hardly ever been mentioned as a possible "boss" of the Revolution. Similar assurances by these little members of the various "X-Committees on un-X Activities" or the blatant politicians about the irreplaceability of Stalin are likely to be as wrong as their assurances about Lenin's supergenius. The same is true of their assurances, policies, and expectations in regard to other "leaders" in China or Greece, in Indo-China or India, in the Middle East or the East Indies.

Knowing nothing about the basic process of disintegration of sensate culture or viewing such theories as a purely academic yarn of unrealistic "ivory-tower" dreamers, these little anti-revolutionary and anti-Communist leaders are incapable of fighting the real disease. They fight, instead, a few spots of the red rash covering the social body. No wonder their efforts have been fruitless and the rash and the high temperature have greatly increased during these thirty years!

To sum up: the Revolution is not an isolated, self-sufficient event of human history, but one of four chief manifestations (along with the Nazi-Fascist revolutions and the two World Wars) of the epoch-making disintegration of our sensate Western culture and society that has dominated mankind for the last five centuries.[1] Since this order is crumbling, the destructive work of the Revolution (after its emergence) is easy; like the destruction of the two World Wars, it is actually but a concentrated form of this general crumbling process. Such is the main reason for the destructive success of the Revolution.

The reasons for the Revolution's creative failure are also at hand. *Since the Revolution is one of the main manifestations of the death of the sensate order, such agony, by its very nature, cannot be creative.* For the same reason both World Wars were infinitely more destructive than creative. If any creativity has been displayed by the Revolution and the World Wars, it was a drop in an ocean of destructivity of these Three Musketeers of the Disintegration. Even this "creative drop" has been largely poisonous, like the atomic bomb and other gadgets of destruction.

In a more concrete form this general reason is stated in the last paragraph of the *Leaves*. The Revolution and two wars imply hate and coercion instead of love and freedom; moral cynicism in lieu of the universal and eternal "Don't kill"; destruction of life in place of its affirmation and promotion.

In the *Leaves* these lines were jotted down as a result of a direct experience in, and a close observation of, the First World War and the Revolution. During these thirty years these verities have been

---

[1] For this disintegration, cf. my *Social and Cultural Dynamics*, 4 vols., (New York, American Book Company, 1937); *The Crisis of our Age* (New York, Dutton, 1941); *Society, Culture and Personality* (New York, Harper and Brothers, 1947); and *Reconstruction of Humanity* (Boston, The Beacon Press, 1948).

tested and retested and found to be roughly valid. (See my *Sociology of Revolution, Social and Cultural Dynamics*, vol. 3, *Society, Culture, and Personality*, and *The Reconstruction of Humanity*.)

Hate in various forms and intensities is the prime mover, or the dominant force, of revolutions and wars. Only secondarily are they animated by some modicum of love. But even this love exists only in so far as there is a hated enemy. It is this hatred of the common enemy rather than love that binds temporarily the members of one party or nation into one band and opposes it to the other party. Not a mutual love but a hatred of Hitler and all he stood for bound into one band Stalin, Churchill, and Roosevelt. As soon as this common enemy was disposed of, the previous comrades in arms turned into enemies. Similarly, it is mainly hate against Stalin and Communism that binds together the members of various Atlantic and other anti-Communist pacts. If and when the common enemy is eliminated, these allies are likely to fight one another. Hate does not have any reverence for the hated. It does not recognize any moral restraints. Sadistically, it revels in torturing and even murdering the hated person. "Don't kill!" it replaces with "Kill! The more the better!" It glorifies this wholesale, sadistic butchery. It bestows upon it the titles of "hero" and "savior," honors and ranks, medals and prizes. It even blasphemously invokes the name of the Merciful God of Love for intervention in this hateful business.

Still less are hate-animated wars and revolutions

willing to grant freedom to the enemy. They revel in intimidation and coercion — physical and psychological — of the hated party and of all who are not of their own faction.

Intimidation, terror, compulsion, torture, murder, and blindly furious destruction are the techniques of hate, inherent in its nature. So far as revolution and war are the vastest outbursts of mass hatred, these techniques are also the main operational method of wars and revolutions, inherent in their nature.

Being most effective in destruction, these techniques are entirely unfit for creative construction: the nature, the method, and the techniques of genuine creativity are entirely different from — in fact, opposite to — those of hate, of revolution, of war.

Creativity is the inspired free activity of a genius. It is the highest and purest form of freedom. Creativity is a work of love of the creator for the created. Love is again the highest and purest form of freedom; otherwise it would be coercion. Creativity, freedom, and love are thus in part identical. For this reason each member of this trinity requires the other two members. None of the three can be realized or exist without the other two. Hence the absolute indispensability of freedom and love for creativity; of creativity and love for freedom; of freedom and creativity for love. Love freely creates and recreates. Freedom is always lovable and creative. And creativity is always free and loving.

Especially is this true of *creativity in the field of interpersonal and intergroup relationships.* Any creative transformation of these relationships consists in a replacement of hate by love, of strife by solidarity, of war by peace, of separateness by unity. A series of observátional and experimental data testifies that this objective can be achieved only through the method of love and freedom, and not through the techniques of hate. Whether in interpersonal or intergroup relationships hate, egoism, and aggressiveness in the attitude of one party generate (in 60 to 90 per cent of responses) hate, egoism, and aggressiveness in the other party. Kindness, love, and help in the case of one party engender kindness, love and help in the other (in our experiments in 65 to 97 per cent of cases observed). Therefore, in so far as any revolution or any war seeks as its objective a peaceful, harmonious, unified, solidary, and creative society, the method of hate-destruction-cynicism-compulsion can never achieve this goal. The wars and the hate-inspired revolutions that have employed this method have invariably failed to be truly creative. In spite of being often conceived by idealists, they all are carried on by murderers and profited from mainly by scoundrels. They have all yielded destruction instead of creativity. For the same reason, all those who at present place their hopes in armed coercion, destruction, and hate, and all those who prepare either new wars or violent revolutions — all are doing the work of destruction rather than that of creative construction. No matter what their names, titles, or authorities, they are neither saviors nor creators but destroyers of the creative spirit of truth, beauty, and goodness.

Such, in brief, are the reasons for the creative

failure of the Revolution and of the two World Wars. For all those who are anxious to take part in a genuine reconstruction of humanity, the conclusion is clear. Only in one kind of war or revolution should they participate: in war against the eternal, implacable enemies of mankind — *death, disease, hate, misery, insanity, and uncreativity, whenever and wherever they are found.* The war against these enemies is the only *holy* war. It is the war of humanity against the inimical forces that incessantly attack it and the successful discharge of the creative mission of humanity. These enemies are formidable. Any successful campaign against them demands the complete unification of humanity — of all its parties, nations, creeds, races, and classes. It demands a complete elimination of all internecine wars and revolutions. It requires a radical replacement of the contemporary human war of everybody against everybody by a common cause against the inhuman enemies.

This is the war and revolution in which our participation is not only permissible but obligatory. This means that we must carry on the free work of love for all the fighting factions and for humanity at large. This creative, unselfish work is the key to the reconstruction of the world.